JOHN KNOX

John Knox
From the original in the possession of
Lord Torpichen at Calder House

Eng.ᵈ by S.Freeman

JOHN KNOX

LORD EUSTACE PERCY

Foreword by
THE DUKE OF HAMILTON

JOHN KNOX PRESS
Richmond, Virginia

British edition published by

James Clarke & Co., Ltd., London, England

American edition published by

John Knox Press, Richmond, Virginia

LIBRARY OF CONGRESS CATALOG CARD NUMBER: 65-11937

© THE EXECUTORS OF THE LATE LORD PERCY OF NEWCASTLE

PRINTED IN THE UNITED STATES OF AMERICA

2272

This Book is Dedicated
to My Wife

CONTENTS

7

FOREWORD

"THE GREATEST book about one of the greatest of men" is how I have heard this Biography described. The relationship of a nephew by marriage is, I fear, a very slender qualification for the privilege of writing a Foreword to a work of such scholarship as this life of John Knox. I am, however, grateful to have the opportunity of saying a brief word about so self-effacing an author and to be associated with the re-publication of such a significant and appropriate book to mark the Fourth Centenary of the Scottish Reformation.

Eustace Sutherland Campbell Percy, created Lord Percy of Newcastle in 1953, was born on 21st March 1887, the 7th son of the 7th Duke of Northumberland. His mother, who before her marriage was Lady Edith Campbell, was a daughter of the 8th Duke of Argyll, that great Scottish Churchman by whose gift Iona Cathedral, hitherto part of his family heritage, passed into the possession of the Church of Scotland.

In his book *Some Memories*, published in 1958, Eustace Percy touches only briefly on his childhood as the 12th of 13 children brought up in a household he describes as "a disciplined home of the kind that social historians like to classify as Evangelical". He goes on to tell the story of a pilgrimage via Diplomacy and Politics to the haven of Academic life, which he reached on his appointment in 1937 as Rector of the Newcastle Division of the University of Durham. His Memoirs must surely be unique among autobiographical studies in that, not only will the reader search in vain for any hint of self congratulation or justification, but he will find himself confronted with an author, who seems to be at constant pains to shoulder or share the blame for every mistake or misfortune with which long years devoted to the public service associated him. That he could write so disparagingly about his own utterly disinterested efforts is perhaps in itself the most eloquent testimony of all to the selfless humility of a great man. Early acclaimed a brilliant scholar of prodigious abilities and promise, he was to find the decisions of political life in the tortured period between the wars, an almost intolerable burden on an acutely sensitive conscience. After a distinguished political career in which he held various Ministerial and Cabinet appointments, it was, I think, with a sense of relief that he retired from Politics to take up responsibilities of a more congenial kind in Newcastle. That he there found a spiritual home few could doubt who have heard the tributes of those who cherish happy memories of working with him.

In this life of John Knox the author's own deep religious convictions and sensitive approach to the subject have combined to give us a biography worthy of one of the great giants of history.

As we glance back over the 400 years that separate us from the dynamic figure who dominated the Scottish Reformation, we can almost feel the fresh winds sweeping across Europe, blowing away the staleness and stagnation of mediaeval habits of thought. The seeds they carried fertilized and quickened the minds of men to such potent effect that explosive action was surely inevitable. For us perhaps the most important thing to realize is that it was not the forces thus released that in themselves shattered the Unity of the Church, but the inflexibility of an ecclesiastical system that had grown too rigid to contain them. New wine was being poured into old bottles.

In 1960, we commemorated an event that was paradoxically one of the greatest liberating influences the human spirit has ever encountered and yet one of the two most disastrous schisms in Christian history. If, as Christians, we stand appalled at the shattered unity of the Church, in the East and in the West, we must surely remember, as did the Reformers themselves, that the Birth of Christianity involved an even more radical schism, and that in the first century A.D. the unity of Judaism was destroyed by the same rigid Ecclesiasticism that has been the curse of institutional Religion throughout the Ages.

The role played by John Knox in the tremendous upheaval of the Reformation is surely of prime importance to those who would understand Scottish life or Christian thinking in the world today: for Knox not only restored the Church to a people deprived, but the legacy of his teachings formed the basis of Presbyterian theology as it has developed in Scotland. In his dynamic efforts to translate that theology into Christian practice he established a social philosophy and a theory of general education that has had the most profound and far-reaching influence on Scottish life. To Churchmen in this present age of Ecumenical endeavour, the life and teaching of John Knox have a compelling significance. For his pre-occupation with the 17th Chapter of St. John's Gospel, that final prayer of Our Lord for the Unity of His Church, and his striving to establish the centrality of the Eucharist, the frequent celebration of which he advocated, almost seem to foreshadow the present Ecumenical movement.

How strange it is that this great man of the Scottish Reformation, this utterly devoted and committed, but very human figure, should be so generally misrepresented and misjudged. I hope that this objective and fair-minded book will be widely read and prove a source of enlightenment to many people.

Lennoxlove,   HAMILTON.
Haddington,
East Lothian.

PREFACE

THIS IS not a work of original research; I have therefore omitted footnotes which the scholar will not need and the general reader cannot verify. There are only a few points in the text which may require explanation.

Quotations from Knox's own writings have been printed in italics, except in one or two instances where Knox directly records another's words. In these quotations, and in some others, I have taken the liberty of omitting passages without the customary warning of dots. I know the dangers of condensation, but I think I can assure my readers that my omissions have misrepresented neither sense nor style. Throughout I have modernized spelling and, in a few instances, have substituted modern words for archaisms which could only be rendered intelligible by a glossary.

I have adopted Dr. Hay Fleming's view that Knox was born some time between the end of 1513 and the beginning of 1515. For convenience sake (I put it no higher) I have chosen December 1513 as the date. The traditional date is 1505, but it does not seem to be traditional in any popular sense. It can apparently be traced to a single statement in Spottiswoode's *History of the Church of Scotland*, and more than thirty years ago Dr. Fleming showed reason for believing that this statement originated in a printer's or transcriber's error. On the other hand, there is positive contemporary evidence for the later date. With all respect to Knox's latest biographer, Mr. Edwin Muir, I cannot feel that impressions gathered, at a distance of nearly four hundred years, from Knox's behaviour or from the tone of his correspondence, ought to outweigh this positive evidence.

I have also taken a slightly different view of Knox's first marriage from that implied by his previous biographers. The difficult here is that he and Marjorie Bowes were certainly not living together as man and wife before he left England in January 1554, and they certainly were so living in August 1556; yet, Knox being a priest, they could not apparently have been legally married in England, Scotland or France at any time between those dates. So far as I know, the legality of the marriage was never questioned. It seems to me incredible that Knox should have asked Sir Robert Bowes to sanction a wedding ceremony in November 1553, when Parliament was in the very act of repealing the legalization of clerical marriages. It seems almost equally incredible that he should have been speaking of Marjorie at this time as his wife if there had been nothing more than a betrothal between them. The only, or at least the simplest, explanation of these facts is that the *faithful promise before witness* was a formal contract *de verbo præsenti*, requiring no further ceremony to make it a valid marriage in the eyes of the law, though requiring the blessing of the Church to make it a proper marriage in Knox's eyes. That blessing he could have obtained privately in England at the time of his interview with Sir Robert; he probably did actually obtain it in Scotland in the summer of 1556.

In this, I am assuming that Knox's letter recording his interview with Sir Robert is correctly dated. The dating of his letters at this time is not above suspicion; indeed, the date of one of them is certainly wrong; but any attempt at re-dating would raise more difficulties than it would remove.

On a minor point, I have dated Kirkcaldy's escape from Mont St. Michel a year earlier than the usually accepted date. This is the natural meaning of Knox's account and is, to some extent, confirmed by a Privy Council minute. This evidence seems to me to outweigh Mason's rather vague letter of 1550 which is, so far as I know, the only evidence for the later date.

On the other hand I have preferred Randolph's evidence to Knox's own statement for the date of Knox's second interview with Mary. Unless there were two interviews in 1562, a definite contemporary report must outweigh a much less definite reminiscence, recorded (at least in its present form) four years later. I do not understand Lang's argument that there were no Huguenot disasters for Mary to rejoice over in December 1562. The course of events in France between the capture of Rouen and the battle of Dreux was surely enough to set Knox's nerves on edge.

I hope I have been frank in admitting the dishonesties with which

14

Knox has been charged from 1559 onwards. On the whole, I think I have admitted too much. Obviously, he cannot be acquitted of allowing his prejudices to distort his history, but he can probably pass even that test better than most men of action who have been also historians. Apart from that, the charge that (to quote a recent Scottish historian) Knox "could lie like a Cretan" rests mainly on a curious ground. Among his papers at his death was found an unpublished party pamphlet written in 1559, which suppressed the truth about the "treasonable" correspondence of the Lords of the Congregation, and Knox himself, with the English Government. Among these papers was also found another document detailing that correspondence in full, and it was undoubtedly Knox's intention that the two documents should be published together after his death as successive parts of the same history. Knox is almost the only historical "liar" who has left on record almost all the evidence for his own conviction. Not quite all, it is true. There are minor misrepresentations in the pamphlet of 1559, which Knox did not correct, notably the omission of the pledges given by the Congregation after Cupar Muir. But in these instances it is at least doubtful whether Knox himself knew the truth; it is practically certain that he had never seen the Cupar Muir document.

There is, however, one instance of misrepresentation on which a further word ought, perhaps, to be said: the falsification of the truce of 24th July 1559. Here the charge is that Knox lied, not as an historian, but as a diplomatist. I can only state my personal opinion about this. I think Knox's own confused account of the negotiation on the Links of Leith is near the truth. In the previous talks at Preston the Lords of the Congregation had demanded the withdrawal of the French troops. I think the demand was renewed on this July 23rd, that Chatelherault gave some sort of verbal assurance on the point, and that the Lords did not put much faith in this assurance but took note of it as the basis of a grievance, to be kept in reserve as a pretext for a future renewal of hostilities. When the written terms were presented to them for signature the next day they protested, wrung a further indiscretion from Chatelheraut, and represented this indiscretion to Knox and the other preachers as a definite pledge. Of the form in which Knox passed this misrepresentation on to Croft at

Berwick we have only Croft's own report; in reading that report it is fair to remember that, if Knox wished to convince Croft that the Regent was in the wrong, Croft wished very much to be convinced and to give Cecil information which would convince Elizabeth.

I have expressed in over-positive languge a certain view about Scottish politics in the period 1550–59. This view is, I think, compatible with the evidence, and it seems to me the only one which makes sense of the attitude of men like James Stewart and Cassilis; but I cannot claim that it is more than a reasonable hypothesis.

In my account of the iconoclasm of 1559–60 I have used neutral language, without attempting to discuss how far the reformers in Scotland were responsible for the destruction or decay of ancient buildings. So far as I can judge the evidence, they must, generally speaking, be acquitted of direct damage to Church fabrics; but they cannot be acquitted of indirect damage resulting from the destructive eviction of corporations responsible for the upkeep of those fabrics, however negligent the corporations may have been in discharging their duties.

I must apologize both to theologians and to historians for my use of the word "quietist." That word is properly a term of art for certain definite opinions; I have used it to describe merely a general attitude of contemplative other-worldliness.

I owe so much to Knox's previous biographers—to Dr. M'Crie, Professor Hume Brown and Andrew Lang, as well as to Mr. Muir's recent study—that I am the first to wonder whether an amateur historian is justified in telling the same story again. I cannot plead that I have written a "modern" biography, with new emphasis on "human interest" or on psychology. I have, indeed, made comparatively little of the obvious "human" material: Knox's friendships with women. That a public man should write his most intimate letters to women friends, and that these letters should be preserved while his correspondence with his wife is lost, has seemed to me too commonplace a phenomenon to be lingered over. It is, perhaps, even more commonplace that such a man's intimacies should be rather pathetic and often a little funny. *Joie de rue, douleur de maison,* is a proverb that has many applications. And it seems to me bad psychology, if we are to use that word, to give these friendships any very large place in Knox's life. In this matter he judged himself very accurately. *Churlish* but conscientious, he would not drop his friends but he depended little on them. Moreover, I suspect that the newsletter and business elements in some of this correspondence have been underrated. It is no disparagement of Knox's friendships to observe that Mrs. Barron's husband was James Stewart's banker and that Mrs. Hickman's lent money to Glencairn.

The truth is that the "human" material in such a man's life must be sought in his public work and in his public surroundings. That, I confess, has been my motive in writing this book. It is well that a historian should declare his bias in advance, and I will do so here. Knox lived in desperate times, at the culminating crisis of the fiercest fever that has, perhaps, ever racked the human spirit. For men of English speech he is, so to speak, the typical clinical case of that fever at its acutest, operating upon a mind unfortified against it by training or tradition. It is useless to write of such a man's life in terms of comfortable certainties—to show him off from the standpoint of Presbyterian orthodoxy or to show him up from the standpoint of nineteenth-century liberalism. He and his contemporaries were men in spiritual torture, and it is surely important that we of the twentieth century should try to understand what that torture was.

For, little as we may know it, our own case today shows many of the same symptoms. Today again, for the first time since the Wars of Religion, the civilized world is split, not between competing national ambitions, but between rival international creeds. More and more, every school of political thought amongst us is being caught up into this conflict. Each is engaged in amplifying its policies to catch the ear of a world audience, till even moderate views harden into dogmas, even the preaching of peace rings like a summons to war. The enforcement of absolute truth by political means is becoming the programme, not only of the Fascist and the Communist, but of those who still speak the language of freedom and toleration. True, we do not take God into partnership so explicitly as our forefathers; but there are other ways of breaking the Third Commandment than by direct quotation from Scripture. And in all this, our chief danger is that, unlike our forefathers, we are hardly conscious of our own dilemmas. We have learnt to read and write in the school of "democratic" or "nationalist" respectabilities; we think in phrases which have little relation to the issues in which we are blindly involved.

Our danger is enhanced by our misreading of history. The analogy between our mood and that of the sixteenth century has been blurred to our eyes by a curious misunderstanding. When we see a member of the League of Nations Union passing rapidly from admiration of Article 19 of the Covenant to almost exclusive insistence on Article 10, we are willing to believe that he is being forced to a certain conclusion by the logic of his principles and the compulsion of events. But we allow no such room for development to the men of the Reformation. We assume that they were born violent; when their story begins with the preaching of peace and ends in the taking of the sword, we write off the beginning as, at best, a piece of unconscious hypocrisy. Knox, with his soap-box reputation, has been notably the victim of this assumption; his intellectual discriminations have been dismissed as oratorical inconsistencies; his writings have been often quoted with as little sense of context or chronology as his own citations of Old Testament history. It is by such easy assumptions that we conceal from ourselves the unwilling tragedies of history and prepare to repeat them in our own persons.

That is my confession of bias. Having made it, I must leave my work to speak for itself.

E.P.

I. Prologue in Scotland

CHAPTER I

THE CHURCH AT HADDINGTON
JANUARY 1546

I

IT IS difficult to say of any man when his real life begins. Youth may pack up for many journeys on which it never starts; middle age may walk out of the house one fine morning with no more than a knapsack. Does such a life begin on the high road, or in the lumber-room among the discarded suit-cases?

In such a matter, a man is not always the best judge of himself; but he is entitled to be heard with respect. There is no doubt what John Knox thought of his own life. It began on a frosty afternoon of January 1546—probably the 16th—in the parish church of Haddington town, in Lothian, seventeen miles from Edinburgh. Twenty years later he wrote down his recollections of that afternoon.

He was then probably in his thirty-third year, tutor to "some gentlemen's children" of those parts and living in the household of one of them, Hugh Douglas, laird of Longniddry. To that house, near the shore of Forth, had come, the Sunday evening before Christmas, December 17th, a certain preacher of the reformed religion, George Wishart by name. Knox may have met him in Leith a week earlier; he had certainly heard him preach that Sunday in the church of Inveresk, near Musselburgh; and from the moment of their meeting until this afternoon of the 16th he had been in close attendance on him.

He had never seen his like before, and he was not alone in that opinion. Some months ago, probably in the early spring, Wishart, recently returned to Scotland from a six years' exile in England and the Continent, had left his home town of Montrose, where he had been preaching, and had appeared in Dundee. Expelled from that

21

town, he had passed into Ayrshire; driven out of Ayr itself, he had preached in the village churches and in the fields; he had hastened back to Dundee on hearing that the plague was there; and then, after a sojourn at Montrose, had crossed Forth to Leith. Everywhere he had made an extraordinary impression. In order to understand that impression, we must look back for a moment at the events of the previous thirty years.

2

Scotland had been long astir with a new ferment, but the leaven had been political rather than religious. Many, it is true, had heard of Luther's doctrines; traders had brought news of them to the eastern towns; gentlemen's sons had studied in Paris and had caught the infection. As early as 1525 Parliament had legislated against the reading of heretical books. There had been some local preaching; a few heretics had been burned; a few scholars had fled, Wishart himself among them, accused of heresy for having taught the Greek Testament in the grammar school of Montrose. But in the country generally the infection of discontent came rather from England than from Germany. From England in old days had come the teaching of Wyclif; there was an old root of Lollardy in the west, especially in the district of Kyle in Ayrshire; and Lollardy had spoken a political language not yet forgotten. It had coupled the Pope's name with Antichrist, and had whispered ominously that "the unction of Kings ceased at the coming of Christ". And now England had shown how political power might be used against the claims of the Church. Prelates had been humbled and monasteries were being dissolved; while in Scotland men were still ruled in all their goings out and their comings in by a Church relatively even more wealthy, more politically powerful and more openly corrupt.

The clergy had long been a byword in Scotland, the butt of court satire and of village horseplay. But the raillery had been only half-serious. In a rough country, familiar with violence and coarse morals, the clerk was not expected to be much better than the layman. As were the people, so was the priest; as was the noble, so was the bishop—indeed, what were abbacies and bishoprics but common perquisites for the cadets or bastards of the nobility? And perhaps it paid better to bribe them so; greed and ambition thus satisfied grew fat and sleepy; the Church at least was friendlier than the Castle; it allowed men to laugh in its face, and would even join in the laugh.

But of late these dumb dogs had begun to give themselves airs. The slaughter of Flodden had cut down the strength of the old governing class; the feud between the houses of Douglas and Hamilton during the minority of James V had weakened it still further. The bishops had slipped into the vacant places on the Council, and their advent had been marked by the beginning of persecutions. Patrick Hamilton, the proto-martyr, had been burnt at St. Andrews in 1528. James, his minority ended, had confirmed the churchmen's power by his quarrels with the chief families of the realm. He had driven the Douglases into the arms of the English; he had imprisoned Argyll. Following the traditional policy of Scotland, as his uncle Henry VIII moved further from Rome, he became more militantly orthodox. Three more heretics suffered at Edinburgh in 1534, after judgment by a court at which James himself was present *all clad in red.*

And the bishops who thus increasingly directed national policy were of even less reputable stock than in former days. Never had clerical morals been more loose; never, by the testimony of churchmen themselves, had benefices been distributed so openly "to satisfy the avarice of the world" than in the anarchy which followed Flodden. Simony and lechery ceased to be figures of fun when they set themselves up as governors of the realm and guardians of holy things. Contempt deepened into disgust and disgust into hatred. Scotsmen were not far from believing, in the words of an English ambassador in 1535, that their King was in the hands of "the Pope's pestilent creatures and very limbs of the devil."

This clerical rule had culminated some seven years before Knox's story opens. In those years it had shown itself not only tyrannical but incompetent. It had set itself to play an old game with a new purpose. It was the game of the French alliance which had brought James IV to his death at Flodden; but now, as never before, it was played for European stakes, for Francis I against Charles V, and above all for Rome against Luther.

And, once again, the game had not prospered. The year 1538, the year of Wishart's flight, had seen James V's second marriage to a French princess, this time to Mary of Guise; and with her had come from France the negotiator of the marriage, David Beaton, Abbot of Arbroath and Bishop of Mirepoix in Languedoc, type of Scottish nepotism and product of French education, Primate-designate of St. Andrew in succession to a dying uncle and Cardinal by intercession of the French King. Since then, Scottish policy had slipped more and more into French ways, into heresy-hunting and war with England. Four years of that policy had brought shame, the rout of Solway Moss and the death of James; another sixteen months had ended in disaster, an English fleet in the Forth, Edinburgh burnt, Lothian devastated.

That had been in May 1544. The next year, the year of Wishart's preaching, began better, with a brilliant victory over the English Warden of the Middle Marches at Ancrum Moor near Jedburgh. But it was a barren victory, a prelude to new calamities, as the victory of Haddonrig in 1542 had been the prelude to Solway Moss. In August came a French fleet and, while Wishart was comforting the plague-stricken outside the East Port of Dundee, a joint French and Scottish army set out for England, only to beat an ignominious retreat four days after crossing the Border. That winter, when Wishart was at Longniddry, the country was still full of French stragglers, begging and starving. Next month the English had struck back; five market towns and 243 villages had been destroyed, and all the great abbeys of the Border from Melrose to Coldingham had been sacked.

These outrages bred hatred of England, but what could be said of the ecclesiastical politicians who had brought Scotland to this pass? James had let them have their way in his last years; now they had pushed aside the Queen Mother and brought the Regent Arran to heel, half Protestant though he was. Had James known peace in his last years, since the burning of heretics at Edinburgh and Glasgow in 1539? Had not his French marriage been cursed by the death of both his sons? And had not these new troubles followed closely on the new executions for heresy at Perth in January 1544? What had Scotland to do with this feud between Beaton and Henry VIII, between the priest and the heretic? Well might the women of Edinburgh cry, as they watched their homes go up in flame, "Woe worth the Cardinal."

3

To a people thus emotionally shaken, thus politically pre-occupied, Wishart came like a revelation. There is no need to idealize him. He was no hero but a middle-aged man, as age was reckoned in those days (he was almost exactly Knox's contemporary), for whom the world had hitherto been too strong, a scholar more at home in the classroom than in the pulpit. After his flight from Scotland, he had tried his hand at preaching in the west of England, but, when charged with heresy, he had recanted and "burnt his faggot" at Bristol. After some travel on the Continent he had settled down at Cambridge, where one of his pupils remembered him as "courteous, lowly, lovely, glad to teach, desirous to learn"—a student, in short, of the quiet school of Colet and More, strayed by mischance into these violent forties of the century. Yet he was no mere scholarly recluse. The same pupil said of him that "he taught with great modesty and gravity, so that some of his people thought him severe and would have slain him." And when he wrenched himself back to the Scotland from which he had fled and to the public preaching in which he had failed, there was at least enough of the stern prophet in him to put him in touch with the rough discontents of his hearers.

He had steeled himself to a dangerous adventure, and the iron had entered into his soul. Knox remembered afterwards with relish how he had denounced two friars as *sergeants of Satan*, and with awe how he had foretold God's judgment on the careless people of Haddington. There was something more in such language than moral fervour, such fervour as inspired Latimer's sermons against English landlordism or Colet's against "hunting and hawking" bishops. Wishart was setting a prophetic fashion from which Scotland was to suffer much in years to come. And he also set the fashion of political alliances, from which Scotland was to suffer still more. True, he would have no violence. "It is the word of peace that God sends by me," he told those who would have forced their way into an Ayrshire church which had been closed against him, "the blood of no man shall be shed this day for the preaching of it." But violence was brewing round him, and he was the half-conscious focus of it. As we shall see, he was keeping questionable company and cannot, perhaps, have been wholly ignorant that some of those with whom he sang psalms had their daggers half unsheathed.

But if he set these fashions, he set another in which lay the secret of his power. He was the first to bring to Scotland the word that had already changed Europe. True, he had had forerunners, notably Patrick Hamilton, a gentler and more pastoral spirit, whose little manual of the new faith became a popular textbook of the Reformation in England and Scotland, under the familiar title of *Patrick's Places*. But in Wishart's mouth the word was no longer, as it had been in Hamilton's, an appeal to private devotion; it became a public proclamation.

And it was the proclamation, not of a new theology, but of a new freedom. To him, as to the fathers of the Reformation, the rediscovery of the New Testament had been quite literally a deliverance. "Justification by faith" was an experience before it became a dogma. As the Middle Ages closed, a darkness settled upon Europe; upon the polity of Christendom, the darkness of pestilence internecine war, Asiatic invasion and ecclesiastical schism; upon the soul of the individual Christian the darkness of a sense of guilt and failure. God's judgments were in the earth, and the old Church which had mediated between man's sin and God's wrath had lost its authority. And then, in this darkness, the simplest thing in the world had happened—and the most incredible. Suddenly, the prison door had swung on its hinges. "I felt," said Luther of his own experience, "as if the doors had opened to me and I had entered into Paradise."

This sense of unimagined liberty was soon to fade—that is the tragedy of Knox's own life and the lives of nearly all his contemporaries. But to Wishart it was fresh, fresh as it had been to Colet nearly fifty years before when he lectured at Oxford on the Epistle to the Romans, fresh as to Luther lecturing on the same text twenty years later, fresh as it had still been only five years ago to Calvin himself when he wrote the French version of his *Institutio*. Wishart was rapt by the vision of it, and his hearers felt the spell. Indeed, in these months he was "fey". There was something more about him now than personal charm; there was the "infinite charity" which, in Renan's phrase, is "the fruit of a great tension of soul."

Such freshness could come only from overwhelming personal experience, but the power of Wishart's preaching may have owed something to its form as well as to its content. Patrick Hamilton had learned his message at the university of Marburg from Luther's associates, but Wishart had gone to another school. In his European travels he seems to have visited the Swiss churches and he had translated their first Confession, that of 1536. He was thus the first to bring to Scotland a version of the Reformation which was to appeal more powerfully to the Scottish mind, as indeed to the mind of all western Europe, than either the "low temperatures" of the Lutheran church or the prudent compromises of Anglicanism.

Each of the world's great ages of emancipation has had its own language, and all such language soon grows stale to the taste. It is as difficult for us today to read the sermons of the sixteenth century as to understand why Wordsworth found it "very heaven" to be young in the first years of the French Revolution. Yet even today few of us can read the eighth chapter of the Epistle to the Romans without catching fire, as Colet did, at its "ardour of spirit and grandeur of language." It was on this master-text of the Reformation that Wishart first preached in Dundee; is it difficult to imagine its effect on men, disillusioned with the world and with themselves, who heard it for the first time in their own tongue? Here was no programme of liberation, but the conviction of freedom already won, the glorious liberty of the children of God. This freedom was within the grasp of every Christian. To assert it was not only his right but his duty, for it had been won for him by his Saviour's blood. Who should lay anything to the charge of God's elect? To men thus freely loved, thus imperiously called to a divine communion, what were the anathemas of any cleric, of Beaton and his friars at St. Andrews, smelling out heresy, or of the "petty priest" of the parish, "cursing" for his unpaid tithe? What, indeed, to them was all the sacrificial ceremonial of the Mass, the external ritual of confession and absolution, the promise of pardons in return for money or outward observance? They had no need of such things; for them there could henceforward be no condemnation; they were, as

Calvin boldly proclaimed, "enfranchised and immune from the power of all men.

4

So Wishart preached, and so Ayr and Dundee believed. Yet one has no sooner set these words down than one must qualify them. To write of the Reformation is to oscillate perpetually between climax and anticlimax, to take flight into the blue only to be dragged back to political earth.

So, certainly, many of the common people believed, as they listened to Wishart's preaching; so, too, at least in part, did Knox come to believe as he went about with him in these December and January days. What he had believed before, we do not know. We know only that he was in priest's orders and had been not without favour in the ecclesiastical world, for he had been appointed apostolic notary and had plied that lawyer's trade along with his tutoring. In the legal documents that he attested, he described himself, as late as March 1543, as "a servant of the holy altar," but it seems unlikely that he had ever had a cure of souls; more probably, he served a small chapel at Samuelston, three miles from Haddington, where he had pupils before he went to Longniddry. Neither he nor any of his contemporaries has told us anything of these years, nor in what state of mind Wishart found him. Probably he thought much as others thought in the little circle in which he lived.

But that is to say that he thought, not only as a religious convert, but as a political partisan. For his circle was a queer one. It was a circle of very active politicians. To them, as to the western lairds who had welcomed Wishart to their houses in Ayrshire, the evangelist's presence meant not only a new religious experience, but a new and much-needed political opportunity. And to many of them it was the political opportunity that mattered most. They were all, no doubt, in Knox's own words, *earnest professors of Christ Jesus*; he certainly was so himself; but they were also Scots gentlemen of their time, bred to the partisan traditions of their class. At their best those traditions were a blend of national patriotism with family and feudal loyalties; at their worst they almost deserved the name given to them by a recent Scottish historian, the name of "gangsterism."

To the "labourers to burgh and land"—the artisans and tradesmen of Dundee or the farmers of Ayrshire—the preaching of such men as Wishart might mean a new freedom; but to the great earls and to the "barons" or country gentlemen, too free already from any sense of subjection to authority, it meant a new political purpose in their life of chronic unrest. It gave the "gangsters" a new justification for violence; it gave the "patriots" a new law to take into their own hands.

Eventually, this new political impulse was to create a nation out of an aristocratic anarchy, but at the moment of Wishart's appearance the impulse had gone wrong. The patriots had compromised themselves; the gangsters had been driven underground. In order to understand this, it is necessary to consider a little more closely the events of the preceding three years. In those years the anarchs had begun to group themselves under standards which the modern mind can recognize; but they were, as yet, unused to this new warfare. For the first time Scottish history had begun to grow coherent; in the shifting medley of feud and intrigue we begin to discern a conflict of policies and an alignment of parties; but the new pattern had hardly formed itself before it dissolved.

This crystallization dates from the death of James V on 14th December 1542; its precipitating cause was the project of a marriage between his infant daughter and the heir to the throne of England, the baby Mary Queen of Scots and the future Edward VI. This project seemed, for the moment, to rally round it all sections of lay opinion in Scotland, and it coincided with what bade fair to be a religious revolution. The Earl of Arran, head of the house of Hamilton, cousin of the late King and heir presumptive to the throne, became regent. Cardinal Beaton was first set aside, then arrested. Arran was strongly inclined to the reformed doctrines. Two preachers of those doctrines were his chaplains. In March 1543, Parliament authorized the reading of the Bible in a translation to be approved, but the public did not wait for the appearance of this hypothetical version. *Then*, says Knox, *might have been seen the Bible lying upon almost every gentleman's table. The New Testament was borne about in many hands. Some that, perchance, had never read ten sentences in it had it most common in their hand; they would clap their*

*familiars on the cheek with it and say "this has laid hid under my bed-foot
these ten years."* Possibly Knox's own convictions date from this
time; according to one account, he had his "first taste of the truth"
from one of Arran's chaplains.

But this hey-day of friendship with England and of religious
freedom was to last a bare six months. The dream was shattered,
partly by the anxieties of Henry VIII's position, but mainly by his
tyrant temper. He would not be content with a marriage treaty; the
infant queen must be delivered into his keeping. There was sound
reason for that. Marriage treaties were notoriously made only to be
broken, and this baby was nearly the most dangerous person in
Europe. After Henry's own children—an ailing boy and two
daughters whose legitimacy he himself had done his best to impugn
—she was heir to the throne of England. She could not safely be left
in the hands of a French mother and a wayward aristocracy, to become a pawn in the politics of the Continent.

But Henry must needs go further. He must be recognized as lord
superior of the kingdom of Scotland, the fortresses of the country
must be surrendered to him. To secure these demands he sought to
form an English party out of the Scottish refugees and captives in
London. The Earl of Angus and been long in exile there with his
brother Sir George Douglas; he was Henry's brother-in-law, having
married his sister Margaret, widow of James IV and grandmother
of the infant Queen of Scots. Both brothers had fought on the
English side at Haddonrig only six months before and had narrowly
escaped capture in that disaster. The Earls of Glencairn and Cassilis,
with the Lords Maxwell, Somerville and Oliphant, had just been
taken prisoners at Solway Moss. These men, especially Cassilis and
Glencairn, with Glencairn's heir Kilmaurs, were the natural leaders
of a Protestant party friendly to England. But Henry must needs
bind them, as a condition of their release, to support, not the policy
of an equal union with England, towards which all the best minds in
Scotland had long been moving, but a policy of surrender to
England, repugnant, now as ever, to the national feeling of all
Scotsmen. This was to discredit their party from the outset. Instead
of a national party it became a faction in English pay, "assured
Scots" in the disdainful phrase of English officials.

5

It would be wearisome to recount the moves and countermoves of the next few months; but a short summary may serve to introduce on our stage some of the men who were subsequently to play a leading part in Knox's life.

This English and Protestant party found ranged against it a party which, though for the moment definitely Catholic, contained men who later turned against the Catholic Church and who, even at this time, represented the instinct of national independence rather than any love of Beaton or the French connection. It was a formidable combination: the Earl of Argyll outweighted Cassilis, Glencairn and Maxwell in the west; the Earls of Huntly and Moray dominated the north; the Earl of Bothwell, with the Homes, the Scotts and the Kers, were too strong for the Douglases on the Border. Between these two parties stood the Regent, a weak man of good intentions, and the Queen Mother, at that time a popular figure, with all the prestige of recent widowhood and not yet identified in the public mind with the French policies of the Cardinal.

Gradually Henry VIII's tactics drove these two towards the Catholic party. Beaton regained his liberty and began to resume control. He summoned from France Matthew Stewart, Earl of Lennox, the next heir to the throne after Arran, and a potential rival claimant. His coming reinforced the Catholic party, who proceeded to seize the Queen and Queen Mother at Linlithgow and transport them to Stirling. Arran began to take alarm. At his ear now stood his half-brother, John Hamilton, Abbot of Paisley, also newly returned from France, a man who had been thought to have some leanings towards Church reform, but who shared his family's strange capacity for disappointing the expectations of its friends. Arran was a patriot, but the throne was too great a prize to be ignored, and only a baby's uncertain life stood in his way to it; it would be folly to forfeit it to Lennox by taking sides with a group of English pensioners against priests and nobles who could claim, for the moment at least, to be the guardians both of royalty and of the national interest. And if the Queen of Scots did not marry the heir to the throne of England, why should she not marry the heir to the house of Hamilton?

There followed a *dénouement* characteristic of the quick-change possibilities of Scottish politics. On 1st July 1543, the marriage treaty with England was concluded at Greenwich, without humiliating conditions but not without new secret understandings between Henry and his "assured Scots." On August 25th it was ratified by Arran and a convention of nobles at Holyrood. Yet on September 3rd, Arran was reconciled with Beaton and rode with him to Stirling; there he denounced the treaty and abjured his heresies at the altar of the Franciscan Convent; and on the 9th the baby Queen was crowned. In the following December, Parliament passed a new Act against "damnable opinions contrary to the faith and laws of Holy Kirk," and on 26th January 1544, four men were hanged and a woman drowned as heretics at Perth.

In the twenty-eight months which elapsed between the scene at Stirling and the arrival of Wishart at Longniddry, the English and Protestant party had gradually disintegrated. Lennox, it is true, turned his coat and joined them; but he was merely playing for a crown and was as ready to take Henry for a partner as Beaton. His adherence temporarily added to the party's power but not to its respectability. Even with this reinforcement, its leaders were too weak for an appeal to arms, except as auxiliaries to an invading army from England. Before that army could arrive, the Douglases, Somerville and Maxwell had all been arrested; when it did arrive in May 1544, the expedition degenerated into a mere raid. By the time that Glencairn had gathered five hundred spears in the west, it was already in retreat to Berwick, burning and slaying as it went. Glencairn's small force was easily crushed. After the horrors of that invasion, it became increasingly difficult for any Scotsman to identify himself with England. Glencairn and Cassilis were more or less reconciled to the Regent, though they continued to correspond with the English Court. Lennox alone persisted in open adherence to the cause of England; but he, who had till recently been almost a Frenchman, was henceforward to all intents and purposes an Englishman, newly married to Henry's niece, Lady Margaret Douglas, and about to become the father of that other Henry, Lord Darnley, in whom his designs on the Scottish crown were to be so ironically fulfilled. But this marriage did little to strengthen the ties that bound the Douglases to England. In the winter of 1544-45, Henry succeeded for a time in alienating even his brother-in-law. Seeing his lands ravaged by English raids, Angus called out his forces on the Border and was mainly responsible for inflicting on the English the disaster of Ancrum Moor in February 1545.

After that, some moves were made in the spring and summer of 1545 to reconstitute the old coalition. While Angus's horsemen were riding down the English fugitives at Ancrum, Cassilis went to London and returned in April as Henry's ambassador, with proposals for peace and a renewal of the marriage treaty. When these terms were summarily rejected by a convention of the nobility, there was coming and going between Cassilis and the English authorities at Berwick; correspondence passed; an English agent visited him in June; Cassilis even went so far, in one letter, as to broach the idea of assassinating Beaton. Whether he knew it or not, that was an old story. Such a plot had been hatching for more than a year, as we shall see in a moment. But the negotiations hung fire; mutual distrust kept them vague; the Earls obviously did not feel that the time was ripe.

6

It was at this moment that Wishart appeared in Ayrshire. He probably did not go there uninvited; at any rate he found a strong group of gentlemen ready to receive him: Lockharts of Bar, Campbells of Kinyeancleuch and Chalmers of Gadgirth. John Rough, one of Arran's former chaplains, had already been preaching in the districts of Kyle and Cunningham and had revived their old Lollard traditions. This group had the patronage of the Earls; Glencairn came to Ayr to support Wishart against the Bishop of Glasgow; Cassilis was probably in communication with him.

The balance of political forces being what it was, wise men would not have presumed on this patronage. It was one thing for the Earls to support Wishart in their home country, and quite another to risk an open challenge to the Regent and the Cardinal. Yet this was precisely the risk which these lairds of Kyle were anxious to take. They saw in Wishart an invaluable political card. They proposed to play him, and they chose as their occasion the meeting of a Church Council to be held at Edinburgh on January 13th. After he had left them on his return to Dundee, they sent word to him that they would meet him at the capital and they led him to believe that Cassilis would come with them. It was to keep this tryst that Wishart had crossed Forth; it was for this tryst that he was waiting at the house of Longniddry.

And there he found himself in even more dangerously political company than in Ayrshire. It was a company at least on the border line of gangsterdom. It consisted mainly of three families: Douglas of Longniddry, Cockburn of Ormiston and Crichton of Brunstone. All were of the "English party," anti-clericals, haters of the French, known enemies of Cardinal Beaton. For more than eighteen months Crichton had been deep in a plot, instigated by Henry VIII, for Beaton's murder. How far the others were dipped in the same plot we do not know, but one of Crichton's letters to Henry had been written from Cockburn's house only two months before, and there can be little doubt that Douglas shared the politics of his family. Angus and Sir George Douglas were his cousins; and Sir George, who was in Lothian at this moment and had issued a public defiance to the Cardinal after Wishart's sermon at Inveresk, had been one of the originators of the assassination plot. These men had friends throughout the countryside round Haddington, and Haddington was a key point between Edinburgh and the Border. For months Beaton had seen in Wishart a dangerous firebrand, and here he was smouldering in the heart of the most inflammable material in Scotland. Happily for the Cardinal, the most powerful man in those parts was for the moment his friend—Patrick Hepburn, Earl of Bothwell, father of a more famous son. To him he had sent word to stamp out the fire.

It is no wonder that Wishart's association with such men should have aroused the suspicion of historians. Some have even identified him with a man of the same name, who had acted as a go-between in the assassination plot itself. This identification was never more than a guess, and is now usually discredited. But it is not only modern historians who have disliked his political connections. They were disliked by some of his more sober friends at the time.

There were sober heads even among the Lothian lairds. There was, for instance, David Forres, afterwards General of the Mint, with whom Wishart stayed his first night at Haddington; there was old Sir James Sandilands of Calder, Cockburn's father-in-law. Crichton had mentioned Sandilands, among others, in one of his plotting letters, but had probably taken his name in vain. But the real centre of the reforming movement, as the future was to show, was neither here nor in Ayrshire, but beyond Forth where Wishart began his preaching. In Fife, in Angus and Mearns, and in Perth, there were hot-heads enough among the anti-clerical families, Lesleys, Kirk-caldys and Melvilles, not to mention that dark figure, Patrick Master of Ruthven, one of those ruffians of genius about whom the men of the times whispered strange stories—in Renaissance Italy, tales of poison and nameless immoralities; in Scotland, rumours of wizardry and Satanism. But some of the older men of these families had had distinguished records of public service under James V: Sir James Kirkcaldy of Grange had been High Treasurer, Sir John Melville of Raith, Captain of Dunbar Castle, and the Earl of Rothes, head of the house of Lesley, a Lord of Council. And in the background of the group stood two quite exceptional men: Henry Balnaves of Halhill, a travelled scholar and eminent lawyer, Secretary of State and Commissioner for the peace with England in 1543, now a Senator of the College of Justice; and John Erskine of Dun, the most attractive figure of these dark times, first introducer (it is said) of Greek studies into Scotland and founder of Wishart's school at Montrose, sincere Christian and wise counsellor, *mild and sweet natured*, the only man who could claim, in after years, to have been equally respected both by Knox and by Mary Queen of Scots. And Erskine had strongly dissuaded Wishart from crossing into Lothian. He probably distrusted the men with whom he would consort there; he certainly disapproved the errand which took him thither.

The truth is that, in this January of 1546, the inner group of gentle-men in Lothian to whom Wishart had unwarily committed him-self were the last irreconcilable remnants of their party, quite unable to see how weak their position was. We can judge from Knox's recollections of these years, as they appear in his *History of the Scottish Reformation*, how "die-hard" was the atmosphere in which he then lived. These men had never forgiven Arran's apostasy; they had almost rejoiced in the barbarities of the English invasion, wrought at their very doors; they could see no hope for their country or for their religion save in the English alliance. They alone, or at least one among them, kept the fires of treason and conspiracy burning in the region between Edinburgh and Berwick. Hoping for help from the western Earls, they had seized on the opportunity offered by Wishart's tryst with the Ayrshire gentry. In Wishart's eyes, the purpose of the tryst might be innocent enough. For months he had gone in danger of his life, of assassination or of secret arrest by Beaton's agents; and with his life was bound up the message which he had come to preach. There was only one way to save both: to challenge the bishops to hear him publicly. It would be seen then whether his enemies dared arrest him in the light of day, with his followers round him. Such demonstrations were to become the familiar tactics of the Scottish Reformation, and none was to use them more boldly or more successfully than Knox himself. But it was with very different hopes that the Red Douglases and the plotter at Brunstone looked forward to a sudden gathering of the gentry of both Ayrshire and Lothian at the seat of government.

Their difficulty was that Wishart would not play the waiting game. He would not lie hid. Four miles from Longniddry was the church of Tranent, and there he insisted on preaching. But even that would not content him; he must preach at Haddington itself, *where it was supposed the greatest confluence of people should be, both by reason of the town and of the country adjacent.* Eventually he had his way; and so we come back to the parish church of Haddington on this afternoon of January 16th.

7

As he waited for his congregation that afternoon, Wishart was troubled. It was the second day of his preaching and something was evidently wrong. There had been no *confluence*. Afterwards men thought that the good people of Haddington must have been warned by Bothwell to stay away. In the forenoon of the day before there had been a *reasonable audience, and yet nothing in comparison of that which used to be in that church*; in the afternoon the congregation had been *so slender that many wondered*. The next morning the attendance had been no better; and now, this afternoon, it might well be worse.

At this moment a letter was put into Wishart's hands. The gentle-men of Ayrshire excused themselves; they could not keep the tryst. This was the end; of late he had felt Beaton's toils closing round him and had lived in the shadow of death; now he was left to face his fate alone. He called for Knox, showed him the letter, exclaimed that he wearied of the world, for he saw that men began to weary of God. Knox was unresponsive, almost shocked, *wondering that he desired to keep any purpose before sermon, for that was never his accus-tomed use before*. He remonstrated, would leave the preacher to his meditation, took the letter and withdrew.

But not out of sight. For more than half an hour he watched Wishart pacing up and down behind the high altar. He had never seen him in this mood. True, he had been often melancholy; in all his sermons he had foretold *the shortness of the time he had to travail, and his death, the day whereof he said approached nearer than any would believe*. But it had been the melancholy of resignation. He had already passed through his Gethsemane; those who had been with him beyond Forth had told a strange tale of a night passed in secret agony when he thought none saw him. It was different now. He was thrown off his balance; *his very countenance and visage declared the grief and alteration of his mind*.

At length he came down to the pulpit and saw before him only a few hearers. He forgot the sermon he had announced. Passionately, disconnectedly, for an hour and a half he warned Haddington of the wrath to come; then, with a brief return to the discourse he had in-tended to deliver, he closed the service and went out. The end of the scene must be told in Knox's own words.

Departing from the town of Haddington, he took his good night as it were for ever, of all his acquaintance, especially from Hugh Douglas of Longniddry. John Knox pressing to have gone with the said Master George, he said, "Nay, return to your bairns and God bless you. One is sufficient for one sacrifice." And so he caused a two-handed sword (which commonly was carried with the said Master George) to be taken from the said John Knox, who, albeit unwillingly, obeyed and returned with Hugh Douglas of Longniddry. Master George, having to accompany him the laird of Ormiston, John Sandilands of Calder younger, the laird of Brunston and others, with their servants, passed upon foot (for it was a vehement frost) to Ormiston.

The party was walking into a trap. Within a mile of the house of Ormiston was Elphinstone Tower, and there Beaton himself was staying, with a guard of horse. That night, before midnight, Wishart was arrested by Bothwell in person; an hour or two later the Cardinal's guard surrounded the house and took Cockburn and Sandilands also. Crichton slipped out and escaped. Six weeks later, on March 1st, Wishart was arraigned for heresy at St. Andrews and burnt in the presence of the Cardinal.

He is one of the many figures of history of whom we know too little to write an epitaph. He may have been just a *blessed martyr of God,* or he may have been dipped deep in treason. But is it fanciful to see him as a symbolic figure, moving against the background of European events? In the one year given to him, his preaching had shown Scotland what she had missed, his political entanglements had warned her of what was to come.

It was a year of peace between the nations. In June 1544, the Emperor had made a truce with the Turks; in September the Treaty of Crépy had closed, for the moment, the long war between Hapsburg and Valois, with Tudor England playing a shifting part between them, which had devastated western Europe for a generation. But these rulers had little thought of peace; they were using their breathing space to marshal their forces for a different struggle. Their political rivalries had sheltered the first generation of reformers; now that shelter was to be withdrawn. In April 1545, as Wishart was setting out on his missionary journey, the French soldiery had swept into the villages of the Waldensian heretics along the valley of the Durance, wiping out a whole population with fire and sword. On December 13th, when he was hiding at Leith, the long delayed General Council of the Catholic Church had been opened by the Papal Legates in the little Tyrolean town of Trent. On February

18th, eleven days before his execution, Martin Luther had died at Eisleben, with the tramp of the Emperor's armies in his ears, gathering for war against the Protestant princes of Germany.

The first phase of the Reformation was over, the phase that Scotland had never known, when, in spite of all the childish violence of kings and sectaries, it seemed for a moment that men might turn and listen to a new word from God. The second phase had opened, the phase into which Scotland was to enter unprepared, the years that were to see the nations align themselves and the sects harden as, amid a rising clamour of pulpiteering and persecution, Christendom plunged towards the Wars of Religion.

8

We have dwelt on this episode because it must do duty for those researches into early life and training which are the pre-occupation of most biographers. Of Knox's personal history before he met Wishart we know, apart from the facts already mentioned, literally nothing except that his mother was a Sinclair; that on both his father's and his mother's side his forbears had been tenants of the Bothwells *and some had died under their standards*; that he was born either in or near Haddington, possibly in the parish of Morham, about the year 1513; and that he had studied for some time at one of the universities, probably St. Andrews, but had apparently left it without a Master's degree.

Of his personal appearance we do know something; it was as undistinguished as his station in life or his career. Rather below the middle height; broad shoulders; black hair and beard, the beard at this time short and rather sparse; narrowish forehead; grey-blue eyes deep set beneath ridged brows and above full ruddish cheeks; long nose, long mouth, full lips, the upper somewhat thicker than the lower; a dour countenance, but not unkindly nor untouched by humour—the description might serve for any Lowland farmer. He was a man of the people; among his own people he had lived, preferring to return from the university to the small corner of country where he had been born; among them he was like to die, an obscure dominie, law-trained and legal-minded, clear-sighted and hard-

39

headed within the narrow limits of his vision and his experience, but with little scholarship beyond good grammar-school latinity, uninspired and lacking either talent or inclination to play any public part.

Destiny came to him with Wishart, but still not a manifest destiny. This father of the Scottish Reformation had, in fact, one hidden talent and one obvious qualification for popular leadership. He was a born preacher in days when the pulpit was the main instrument of political as well as religious propaganda; and he was a typical Scot, thinking the thoughts and speaking the language of his countrymen. Yet sixteen months were to pass before he found his vocation; then he was to preach no more than a sermon or two before passing into exile; not until he was forty-one was his voice to be heard again in Scotland, and then only for a few months; not until he was forty-five was he to come home finally to do, in the last thirteen years of his life, the work for which his name is remembered in history.

But to the day of his death he remembered Wishart, certainly as a political warning. He was *a man of such graces as before him were never heard within this realm, yea, and are rare yet to be found in any man; singularly learned, as well in godly knowledge as in all honest humane science.* But he was also a man who had fatally misjudged the ripeness of an opportunity; and Knox, one thinks, never forgot that lesson. He was to use political alliances as Wishart had not dreamed of using them, but he was careful never to trust himself to them until they were strong enough to be effective. When his time came, he showed all Wishart's courage; but he knew how to bide his time, even under the suspicion of faint-heartedness. In this, too, his education began with Wishart; but it was to be finished in the hard school of personal experience. For at his first entrance into public life he was to be involved abruptly in a failure even more spectacular than Wishart's, and a failure due to exactly the same mistake, aggravated by every circumstance of violent folly.

CHAPTER II

THE CASTLE OF ST. ANDREWS
1546–47

I

WE DO not know what happened at the house of Longniddry on the morrow of Wishart's arrest. The "bairns", to whom Wishart had bidden Knox return, were Francis and George Douglas and Alexander Cockburn. Alexander's father, arrested with Wishart, was in the castle at Edinburgh. A little later, he *freed himself by leaping of the wall of the Castle betwixt ten hours and eleven before noon and so breaking ward*. Thereafter he was a fugitive, "summoned to underlie the law at Edinburgh," and his property placed under arrest. Similar proceedings may have been taken at once against Hugh Douglas. In any case, we know that some months later Knox found himself in sole charge of the three boys, *wearied of removing from place to place by reason of the persecution that came upon him*. Whether he went into hiding immediately or was allowed for some time to remain at Longniddry, he was a marked man, waiting anxiously for news, and we know what news reached him.

It was news from St. Andrews, Cardinal Beaton's stronghold— his stronghold in the strict sense. On the rocky point north of the town he had converted the old castle into a place of war. He had stored his treasure in it; he had provisioned and armed it. Never again would he run the same risk as in the winter of 1542–43 when a sudden combination of nobles had thrust him temporarily from power. The Chancellor of Scotland should have his own fortress; the trusted agent of the Pope his bridgehead to Europe. Here, with his back to the sea, he could hold out against any rising until a French fleet came to his relief. And the first news that reached Knox was, no doubt, a word-picture of the burning of Wishart at the west port of the castle, near to the Priory"; the gaunt stake in the bare yard, with the crowds round it, and "over against it" the Cardinal watching from "the castle windows, hung with rich hangings and velvet cushions."

Perhaps that last touch of colour in the scene is only a legend. Knox does not mention it in his *History*. Beaton was one of those figures round whom legends gather. There is about him a flavour of the Italian renaissance tyrant: statesman and inquisitor, sumptuous and ruthless, with his guards and his ladies and his seven bastard children.

But his reign was near its end. Early in June, Scotland was ringing with fresh news from St. Andrews. In the early morning of May 29th, while the masons were still at work on the ramparts of the castle, and the stone-carts were lumbering over the lowered drawbridge, a small party of gentlemen came quietly into the courtyard, enquiring whether my lord was yet awake. Others followed them. The porter, taking alarm, was knocked on the head and thrown into the moat. The workmen were ordered to leave, the servants also, as they arrived on the scene. Of the five ringleaders whose names are known, William Kirkcaldy, heir to the laird of Grange, went to guard the postern gate; Norman Lesley, Lord Rothes's heir, stayed perhaps in the courtyard to complete the evacuation; his uncle, John Lesley, with James Melville and Peter Carmichael of Balmadie, entered the keep. They found the Cardinal in his room with only his *chamber child* with him. John Lesley would have killed him without further ado, but Melville, a personal friend of Wishart, must needs turn the murder into an act of justice. Summoning him to repent, claiming to be God's minister of vengeance upon him for Wishart's death and *because thou has been and remainest an obstinate enemy against Christ Jesus and his holy evangel*, he ran him twice or thrice through the body. The gates were shut; the castle seized.

2

There is no doubt with what feelings Knox heard this news. He had had no hand in the outrage, and he was to find afterwards to his cost that the gangster element, for whom he had no sympathy, had played the chief part in it. But he rejoiced at Beaton's death and, if he felt a need to justify his joy, he would, no doubt, have expressed his sentiments much as Melville did, though it was not till twenty years later that, recording these events, he noted Melville's protestations as a *godly fact*. Beaton had deserved death, and, if the law could not touch this Eglon, a good Christian had every right to play the part of Ehud.

Those who shake their head over such opinions are not thinking as clearly as Knox and his teachers. The old doctors of the mediaeval Church and the new doctors of the Reformation were scrupulous about sanctioning rebellion, but, in so far as they recognized the subject's right in the last resort to overthrow a tyrant, it did not occur to them to question his right to kill him. The actual scriptural example had in fact been quoted by the latest and last of the Scottish schoolmen, John Major, who was even then teaching in the University of St. Andrews. Knox, as we shall see later in his history, was no less scrupulous about the main question. It is an anachronism to attribute to him at this time any doctrinal view about the right of rebellion; he reached his later conclusions on that subject painfully and with much heart-searching. He would have been shocked at the Victorian liberal's levity in encouraging insurrection; but he would have utterly failed to understand why the men who were ready to run guns for Garibaldi should have been horrified by the story that Mazzini had once given money to an assassin. And he would have been at least as right as the Victorian liberal. In this matter of assassination morality draws a different line.

It is always immoral for a lawful ruler to use lawless force, whether his instrument be a hired bravo, or a mob, or an undisciplined soldiery, or an act of attainder, or even a trial by impeachment. That is the standard by which the modern world condemns Machiavelli and the riot of murder and massacre with which his name is popularly associated. But if it is ever right for the subject to take the law into his own hands against a constituted government, it cannot in itself be wrong that he should direct his violence against the individuals in whom the power of government actually resides.

It becomes wrong only if the violence is wanton. The rebel must be judged in all his acts by the old doctrine of the English common law; he must not use more force than is necessary to attain his end.

He must not indulge in the luxury of mere vengeance, however much he may try to clothe his vengeance in the forms of law or cloak it by appeals to abstract justice. And, except in the most primitive society, assassination is hardly ever a necessary act of policy. It is, in fact, almost always a political blunder. No civilized government is really single-headed. That is the truth behind the Victorian liberal's attitude. And by the standard of that truth, the morality of Melville, and of Knox with him, is open to a graver moral criticism than the frank brutality of the Lesleys.

The movement in which Knox was engaged, or was soon to be engaged, was a rebellion; and as a rebellion it must be judged. So judged, the rebel, whether he be assassin or popular executioner or captain of a national guard, is usually to be condemned, not for his acts, but for the name he takes in vain to justify them. The only true justification for rebellion, indeed the only true justification for war, is self-defence; he who kills, except by due process of law, is never entitled to appeal to "justice," still less to claim that he is God's minister. The preachers and scholars, both Protestant and Jesuit, who later, under pressure of the Wars of Religion, devised religious sanctions for rebellion, have wrought more evil in Europe than Machiavelli; Melville's *godly fact* was to do more harm in Scotland than the example of the gangsters who murdered Riccio.

3

But in this moralizing we are imitating Knox's critics; we are running ahead of our story. The Knox who heard the news from St. Andrews in 1546 was not the defeated reformer of 1554, hurling his invectives against Mary Tudor; still less was he the embittered and lonely old man of 1566, writing the first book of his *History* under the shadow, it seemed, of an even worse defeat. He was just a renegade priest, suddenly delivered, as he thought, from imminent danger of death. In all probability his views about tyrannicide at the time were as simple as Mr. Birrell's paraphrase of Dr. Johnson: "If any tyrant prevents your goings out and your comings in, fill your pockets with large stones and kill him as he passes. Then go home and think no more about it."

If he thought thus, he soon found his mistake. The immediate effect of the *putsch* at St. Andrews was to unite all parties in support of the Regent's Government. On June 10th the nobility met at Stirling. There was a mutual renunciation of the "bands" which had bound some to England, some to Arran and some to the Queen Mother. The Queen was to be married neither to Prince Edward nor to Arran's son. The spoils of power were redistributed: the wardenship of the West Marches to Maxwell, the Archbishopric of St. Andrews to John Hamilton, the Chancellorship to Huntly, seats on the Regent's Council to the two Douglases, Ruthven, Argyll, Somerville, Cassilis and Glencairn. After that the news came fast. Summons of treason had been issued against the rebels in the castle of St. Andrews; Parliament had assembled on July 29th and had confirmed the summons; the Regent was mustering his forces; by the end of August the castle was invested.

Then came a lull. The siege dragged on. Scotland's weakness had never been so plain. There was no siege artillery, no heart in the attack. The Queen Mother pleaded for help from France, but none came. That June France had made grudging peace with England, leaving Boulogne in English hands and conceding that Scotland should be included in the peace only if she would reaffirm the broken marriage treaty of 1543. The Valois had, in effect, deserted the Stewarts for the nonce. It seemed more likely that the "Castilians," as they were called, would get help from England. Their sea communications with London could not be cut. William Kirkcaldy had been despatched thither and had returned in an English ship. And in mid-August they received one surprising reinforcement.

After the murder, the families and friends of the assassins had taken refuge with them: William Kirkcaldy's father, brother and three uncles, some of the Melvilles of Raith, Balfour of Mountquhanny and his son, the laird of Pittendriech, and a few others, with their retainers—perhaps a hundred and fifty men in all. John Rough, Arran's late chaplain, had come from Ayrshire and had constituted himself chaplain to the garrison. Except for him and Sir James Kirkcaldy, it was not an impressive company. But now Henry Balnaves, who had attended the meetings of the Lords of Council and Session up to at least the 3rd of the month and had concurred in the summons of treason against the rebels, suddenly joined them in the castle and took command of their diplomacy. In November he went to London and returned with assurances of help. It looked as if the deadlock might end in another English invasion. And the rebels, when they had seized the castle, had captured Arran's son, already held there as a sort of hostage by Beaton. So in December came an armistice. The rebels were to keep the castle until the Regent had secured for them from Rome a dispensation for the murder of the Cardinal.

To both sides, the truce was only an expedient to gain time. Balnaves was off to London again to negotiate for a definite subsidy. Before the negotiations were concluded, Henry VIII died, on 27th January 1547; but the Protector Somerset's Government decided on February 6th to grant £672 a year for the maintenance of eighty men in the castle, £448 for forty horsemen "appointed to keep abroad for the more surety of the said castle," and £1,000 in pensions for seven of the leaders, including Balnaves himself. Balnaves returned at once, with £1,060, representing a half-year's payment as from the previous December 1st; and on February 27th Andrew Dudley was appointed "Admiral of the King's Majesty's fleet addressed into the North Sea, as well for the annoyance of the Scots bruited to prepare to pass towards France, and for the interruption of such munition as is looked to be brought for Scotland out of France, as for the sure conduct of victuallers northward."

It is significant to find, however, that only eleven days later Dudley was instructed to lay up his "great ships," dismiss the soldiers of the fleet, and "reserve for the waftage of the victual two or three ships meet for that purpose." In fact, the new governors of England were in no condition at the moment to risk an invasion of Scotland, occupied as they were in feathering their own private nests and "doubting lest the French King, our new reconciled friend, should make us war for the recovery of Boulogne, or the Emperor, our old imperfect friend, should do the like to set in authority again the Bishop of Rome above our Sovereign the King's Majesty." Their apprehensions were redoubled when, on March 27th, Francis I followed Henry to the grave. They heard that the new "French King's counsel was clean altered"; they received reports from the

Marches "of the Scots' preparation and general assembly of their whole power for some notable exploit intended hitherward." They thought more of defence than of attack, and their fears were not unfounded.

Henry II of France was a very different man from the *vieux galant* his father. He was not only a militant Catholic, with a readier ear for the appeals of a French princess defied by the murderers of a cardinal. He was also, and above all, a practical imperialist, who saw his chance and took it. Not for him his father's knight-errant adventures in Italy; the empire of Britain was a more brilliant prize than the Duchy of Milan. And, in the person of the infant Queen of Scots, it was almost within his grasp. What Henry VIII had feared, but had done so much to make inevitable, was about to happen. Already in April a New French Ambassador was in Scotland, the Sieur d'Oysel. To the Regent and the Council he brought promises of help; with the Queen Mother he spoke of a refuge for her daughter at the Court of France.

Indeed, the Castilians were about to be caught in a movement of which they had not dreamed, the first clash of the Wars of Religion. That April the Emperor was to drive the Protestants of Germany in hopeless rout at the battle of Mühlberg, while Henry prepared his edicts against the Protestants of France. Already in January the Council of Trent had issued the challenge which made schism irrevocable: its report on Justification. Throughout Europe the battle was being set in array round this little band of desperadoes on a remote promontory in the north. But for the moment they ruffled it in the streets of St. Andrews and the "horsemen appointed to keep it abroad" took toll of the country round; while John Rough preached in the parish church and tried conclusions, a little unsuccessfully, with its distinguished canon, one John Annan, the Principal of St. Leonard's College who was *rotten papist* enough to object to the usurpation of his pulpit.

4

Of all this Knox could, of course, have heard only the bare outlines. He had his own troubles, and he was not looking to

St. Andrews for deliverance from them. The new Archbishop, on taking charge of his diocese, had enquired after the whereabouts of its heretical notary. Knox was in hiding and *was determined to have left Scotland and to have visited the schools of Germany.* But this did not suit the anxious fathers who had left their sons in his charge. They got word to him to go to St. Andrews *that himself might have the benefit of the Castle, and their children the benefit of his doctrine.* And at Easter, April 10th, he went there.

It was not, one would suppose, a very desirable atmosphere for children; three months later Knox was telling the castle garrison that *their corrupt life could not escape the punishment of God.* But there were redeeming features; there was apparently no lack of attendance at Rough's preachings; Balnaves' influence was strong; and another unexpected figure had recently appeared in these strange surroundings, no less than old Sir David Lindsay, Lyon King at Arms, James V's friend and Court poet, bitter and boisterous satirist of the Church, who seems to have dropped in after the armistice to watch the explosion that he had been expecting all his life. So Knox proceeded with his tutoring as he could, coaching his pupils in *grammar and other humane authors,* teaching them the Gospel of St. John in the castle chapel and catechizing them publicly in the parish church. He was a great believer in one aspect of education with which the modern world is unacquainted; in the words of his later *Book of Discipline,* he thought that *the exercise of the children in every church should be great instruction to the aged.* It was so in this case; but not in the sense that he intended.

Hearing him in public, Rough and Balnaves and Lindsay put their heads together. Here was a natural preacher and a born controversialist. Rough had reason to know that, for Knox had been lending him a hand in his fight with Annan. He had *fortified the doctrine of the preacher with his pen,* and the pen was a sharp one. If he could talk as he wrote, he was just the bludgeon needed to knock out the opposition, hearten the garrison and win the support of the townspeople. Indeed, his pulpit voice might ring through Scotland. Were not the Castilians, playing for time, in the hope, not only of English succour, but of winning back some of the lost leaders of the Protestant party? Old Glencairn, in particular, was dying, and his far abler son was stepping into the Protestant leadership. So a play was staged. One Sunday in late May or early June, Rough preached on the right of a congregation to elect its ministers and, breaking off his argument, called upon Knox to *take upon you the public office and charge of preaching, even as you look to avoid God's heavy displeasure.* The call was confirmed by the congregation. *Whereat the said John, abashed, burst forth in most abundant tears and withdrew himself to his chamber.*

His reluctance to accept the call was genuine enough. He was running an even greater risk than Wishart. He was too shrewd not to see, even then, how slender were the chances of the rebellion; he knew, from Wishart's example, how little reliance could be placed on this kind of conspirator. This was not the only occasion on which he refused, or tried to refuse, responsible office. Five and six years later he refused successively an English bishopric and a London living, and after the death of Edward VI he wrote quite frankly of his refusals: *What moved me to refuse, and that with displeasure of all men (even of those that best loved me), those high promotions that were offered, by him whom God hath taken from us for our offences? Assuredly, the foresight of trouble to come.* He had the same foresight now; but he had committed himself too far in his controversy with Annan. He had issued a public challenge to him in the hearing of the towns-people, and they would not allow such a challenge to be fought out on paper. *We cannot all read your writings, but we may all hear your preaching.* So a few days later, he found himself in the pulpit for his first sermon, expounding the seventh chapter of the Book of Daniel, the prophecy of the coming of Antichrist.

It was as crude and effective a manifesto as was ever issued by a new revolutionary leader. *The Pope and his kingdom* were the *little horn* of Daniel's vision, *having a mouth speaking great things and blasphemous.* They were St. Paul's *Man of Sin*; they were the *Whore of Babylon* in the Apocalypse, whose *merchandise shall be the bodies and souls of men.* It was not mere invective; on its own plane it was closely enough argued; for it was preached, not to an enthusiastic band of believers, but to a half-hostile, half-frightened, audience of townspeople, with a sprinkling of friars, canons and teachers of the University, among them the great Doctor Major and the Sub-Prior of St. Andrews himself. But it was bludgeon work, the first flourish of what was to be Knox's chosen weapon for the remainder of his life.

The second flourish came only a few days later in a debate staged rather half-heartedly by the Sub-Prior, Dr. Winram, whose sympathies were already half with the party of reform and who, fourteen years later, was to become one of the Superintendents of the new Church of Scotland. We need not linger over this incident. It is significant only for one reason, but that a crucial one to the understanding of Knox. It gave him his first opportunity of laying down the thesis at which he was to hammer for the rest of his life: that all ceremonies devised by man for the worship of God, without express warrant of Scripture, are idolatry. Here again was the bludgeon, swung against one central mark: the sacrifice of the Mass.

5

And yet . . . was this really the weapon of Knox's choice? Was there nothing more in the call given him by his friends, nothing more in his reluctance to accept it? This bludgeon style may have pleased Lindsay, for it was not unlike his own scoldings without their poetry; it may have pleased Rough; but Balnaves had a very different taste. His own treatise on *Justification by Faith*, written in prison a year or so later, moves to a graver measure. He could condemn, but with a judge's dignity; his doctrinal argument is a sustained effort to convince; the whole is keyed to a note of spiritual appeal. Did such a man, politician though he was, pick Knox for his bludgeoning ability, or had he heard him speak in other tones, perhaps in the castle chapel while he read with his pupils *the Evangel of John*.

Knox has always been a puzzle to the historian. It is so difficult to connect the Knox whose work we know and whose writings we can read, either with the religious genius of Scottish legend, or with the blustering fanatic of modern interpretation. We must begin to face this puzzle here, on the threshold of his public life. What manner of man was this unknown preacher, this new hammer of the old Church, over whom the townspeople shook their heads, saying: *others lopped the branches of the Papistry, but he strikes at the root to destroy the whole?* It is tempting to gather a hint here and there and to suggest an answer.

The Gospel of St. John is not as often quoted in Knox's writings as one might expect; there is one chapter of it which (if we may risk a generalization) is quoted only once. Yet that chapter has a curious place in his story. On his deathbed twenty-five years later he made to his wife what must have been a well-understood request: "Go read where I cast my first anchor." She read him "the 17 of John's Evangel": Christ's prayer of intercession before Gethsemane. If that supreme effort of human speech was indeed the private heart of Knox's religion, that fact goes far to explain the influence he exerted and the legend he left behind him. He becomes a much more tragic figure, but also a more intelligible one. Arrested by this first hint, let us pause for a moment to make a tentative sketch for a new portrait.

It is the portrait of a man with two strong sides to his character, but articulate upon only one of them, and that not the one which he himself valued most. On the practical side, he was a shrewd politician and lawyer, with an unerring eye for the essentials of a situation or an argument; he was a vivid hater and an obstinate defender of any position he had once taken up; he had also a strong sense of the picturesque and an even stronger sense of the ludicrous. And on all this side he had great powers of expression; he was not only articulate, he was an artist. He was a trenchant controversialist, both in the formulation of his own principles and in the confutation of his opponents'; a matchless chaplain of an army with its back to the wall; a preacher whose voice could make the eternal war between God and Satan move before men's eyes, as his pen could recreate on paper the tumult of a Border raid or the rough-and-tumble of an Edinburgh riot; a boisterous and (it must be confessed) a heartless caricaturist, who could jeer in retrospect at Beaton's corpse and interrupt his narrative of Wishart's tragedy in order to tell a *merry* tale of a clerical *fracas*.

His other side was a strong spiritual sense, but strong in the direction one would have least expected. He was not an evangelist in the usual meaning of the word. His sense of style and his eye for essentials made him an incomparable summarizer of accepted truth, as he was to show in his drafting of the *Confession of Faith*; but he had very little taste for doctrinal exposition. His one excursion into the field of dogmatic controversy is the most uninspired of all his writings, a dreary treatise on predestination. The only living passage in it is the one where he quotes this chapter of St. John. He failed here, not from inarticulateness, but from sheer lack of interest. Nor was he much of a pastor; the personal care of souls meant little to him, either for himself or as an aim of Church policy. The precedent of the confessional had, no doubt, something to do with this insensitiveness; but it reflected also the national instinct for independence, and even more, perhaps, Knox's consciousness of a certain clumsiness in himself which prevented him from "getting on well" with other people.

No, strangely enough, his real spiritual bent was the mystic's. In the whole sweep of Old Testament and New, what first caught his ear was a voice which almost passes the range of human hearing: neither the word of God to man nor the words of man to God, but a fragment of "the huge soliloquy of God" Himself. Once, and once only, at the close of an evening spent in a new communion, men had been allowed to overhear that voice, as they listened to the Son speaking alone to the Father. On the events of that evening Knox's contemplation was fixed. Here, in the Last Supper, in the teaching that followed it, and above all in the prayer of intercession that followed the teaching, he found the secret of all human worship and of all human hope.

But on this mystical side, he was almost wholly inarticulate, at least in public. When speaking on paper directly to one person, he could, indeed, write of the trials and triumphs of the Christian life with much of Bunyan's understanding. But even then, and still more when he preached on prayer to the soldiers of the Berwick garrison or wrote his *comfortable epistles* to the faithful in Marian England, the trials and triumphs to which his mind turned were rather public vicissitudes than the experiences of the individual soul. His utterance was always reverting to the plane of the Hebrew prophet, the plane of God's strategy, as it were, in the world of politics, rather than of any transcendental scheme of salvation.

Himself, he had found conviction on the heights, but he had no words to convey it from the mountain side; words came to him only when he descended to the dusty levels of the "raving world" about him. He lived by faith and preached the law; the Christ whom he knew as Saviour and Intercessor became on his pulpit lips the Judge of Nations.

And—here is the point—he knew all this. He felt the tragic contrast. To be a preacher was to him the highest office in the Church, but he rated his own preaching low. It was a limited commission, limited both in scope and time. *I am called*, he told Queen Mary, *to a public function within the Church of God, and am appointed by God to rebuke the sins and vices of all. I am not appointed to come to every man to show him his offence.* And, as he said elsewhere, his commission was to his own generation only, *to instruct the ignorant, comfort the sorrowful, confirm the weak and rebuke the proud by tongue and lively voice in these most corrupt days.* He would not record his sermons: *I did ever abstain to commit anything to writ, contented only to have obeyed the charge of Him who commanded me to cry.* To cry—to be, in another of his favourite phrases, a trumpet—that was the limit of his public mandate. And he was painfully conscious that the cry was harsh. That, he knew, was partly his own fault: *My rude vehemency and inconsidered affirmations which may appear rather to proceed from choler than of zeal and reason, I do not excuse.* But it was partly also the necessity of his function, a function in which he took small delight. The trumpet must startle. *Without the preaching place*, he told Queen Mary again, *I think few have occasion to be offended at me; and there I am not master of myself, but most obey him who commands me to speak plain and to flatter no flesh upon the face of the earth.*

6

Such was his judgment on his own public work when that work had reached its climax, when he had found by bitter experience what he could and what he could not do. Did he feel more competent when he was first called to the ministry by men who hardly knew him? No doubt he felt the beginner's zest, but he was beginning late; if experience had not yet taught him his limitations, approaching middle age must have already taught him self-distrust. Indeed, self-distrust was always the dominant feature in his character; the positiveness of his opinions could never conceal his fundamental uneasiness about himself. At this moment he can hardly have been quite unconscious of the choice he was actually making: the choice between public duty and those intimate convictions which every public word he was to utter for the rest of his life would seem to degrade and belie. In any case, it was at this moment that the contrast between public duty and intimate convictions emerged in all its nakedness.

What was the issue with which he found himself confronted in these first days of his preaching? He found himself a leader of revolutionaries who believed that the power of the Church was corrupting the whole social system, that the wealth of the Church was robbery and the authority of the Church a usurpation. And the centre of the Church's social power, the source of its wealth and the seat of its authority was the Mass. To these men, the Mass was what "capitalism" is to the radicals of the twentieth century: the source of all social evil. Against the Mass, therefore, as an institution, he must direct the full force of his attack. And the attack must be delivered in terms that his hearers could understand. Like all revolutionary leaders he must work for quick results, he must mobilize the people against its rulers. The Mass was a fraudulent conversion of spiritual truth to the uses of public power and private profit. As such it must be destroyed; he must expose the swindle and pillory the swindler. He must teach his hearers to hate superstition in others, if haply they might come to be ashamed of it in themselves. Idolatry, idolatry, idolatry, that was the word on which he must harp. "The moving of the body outward, without the inward moving of the heart is naught else but the playing of an ape and not the true serving of God." So George Wishart had spoken at his trial, and the same note was to run through all the early preaching of his disciple.

But though Knox was honest enough in this attack, it represented only the negative side of his positive purpose. The most careless reader of his writings must see that his real aim was not a social revolution. Looking back, nineteen years later, on these first days of his preaching, he summed up their results in these words: *Not only those of the Castle, but also a great number of the town, openly professed by participation of the Lord's Table, in the same purity that it is now ministered in the Churches of Scotland.* That was his real purpose. He hated the Mass, not as a social institution, but as a corruption of the truth. As he bludgeoned its ritual he thought of himself as clearing the ground, not for a new social system, but for the true worship.

Nay more, he surely knew that in Scotland the Mass was no longer a dominant institution; it had fallen into contempt, a contempt which included the truth in it as well as the error. Eleven years later the last martyr of the Scottish Reformation, on his trial at St. Andrews, was to pronounce the final condemnation of the old Church. When his judges asked: "Was not thou a priest, why hast thou left thy Mass?"—he replied: "Because I could not win my meat by it, it was so lightlied." It was, even in 1547, no longer a question of substituting the true for a corrupt worship; it was already a question of teaching men afresh that the sacrifice of Christ was not "a vain thing." It was to this task, and to this task alone, that Knox really felt himself called.

And his attitude towards this task was significantly different from that of almost all his Protestant contemporaries. Nothing is more remarkable in his iconoclasm than his abstention from the "democratic" arguments of other revolutionaries. He referred rarely to the conception so dear to many of his contemporaries and successors, the "priesthood of all believers." In his eyes, the mass-priest had usurped, and discredited, not a function belonging to all Christians, but the function reserved by Christ to Himself alone. And this function was not the government of nations. It was not the "Crown Rights of Christ" that Knox set himself to vindicate; that fatal phrase was invented by his successors. To him Christ was, above all else, the Mediator between God and man, revealing Himself to His disciples on the night of His betrayal. His words to them, as recorded in the thirteenth, fourteenth, fifteenth and sixteenth chapters of St. John's Gospel should, according to Knox's later ordering, be read to the congregation when the Lord's Supper was administered, but not His words to God in the seventeenth. He had taught His disciples to give thanks with Him above the memorials of His sacrifice, but as He turned to intercede for them with His Father He had seemed to draw apart from them, offering a worship in which they could not share. It was the priest's claim to share in this office of intercession that Knox was, therefore, most concerned to deny. More democratic reformers might reject that claim as an impediment to the Christian's right of direct access to God; he rejected it rather as an intrusion into the Most Holy Place where Christ was standing in the presence of God, the only Intercessor, pleading eternally for His own whom the Father had given Him. Let those for whom He thus pleaded give thanks above the bread and wine, His Body and His Blood, in the noblest language that human lips can frame; but let them not break in with petty importunities or childish ritual upon the mysteries of heaven.

But—and here is the tragedy—was it much better to trample round the outskirts of those mysteries with the heavy feet of public debate? That was what Knox must do all his life. He must not only overturn the tables of the money changers, of those who trafficked in the pardon which Christ had freely offered; he must not only cast down the idols of superstition; he must also pour scorn on every symbol that man's love had devised to adorn the worship of God. He must argue harshly about the thing for which he cared most reverently; he must fill with the dust of conflct his own most secret sanctuary.

Yet, in the end, in spite of all his public negations, his private vision saved him. He established more than he destroyed. This, surely, is the key to the Knox legend. In that legend, as it once lived in Scottish hearts, Knox is not the thunderous preacher, but the restorer of the Sacrament. And the legend is true. This is the one thing that he achieved. His pulpit words have faded, as he intended they should; his *blasts of the trumpet* against established governments have been drowned by the fanfares of more convinced revolutionaries. But his conception of the central act of Christian worship set a lasting seal upon the Church of Scotland, differentiating it from all other Protestant communions and making it, in the strict sense of the term, a Eucharistic Church. His political vehemencies, systematized by others to conclusions which his hot-headedness had never drawn, were to torture the body of Scotland for a century, but his vision of this one central truth was to save her soul.

That is our tentative portrait. We shall see how it stands the test of the story we shall have to tell.

7

We have paused to watch Knox entering on his life's work in the brief peace of an armistice. Now comes disaster, swift and overwhelming.

Balnaves had gone back to London in April for the second half-year's subsidy. He had returned in mid-May with more than money—but not much more. The Protector's Council was in one of those moods habitual to English governments in all ages; it was bustling to miss the boat. It was not going to save its friends, but it would spare no effort to encourage them. Balnaves was sent back in company with a master gunner and "Archane de Arrain, one of the King's Majesty's gun-founders." The Master of the Ordnance in the north was instructed to make ready 100 long hand guns and 150 long bows and to send to Holy Island for later shipment "timber and stocks to mount a demi-cannon, 2 demi-culverins, 2 sakers and 6 falcons, and 2 tons of iron and steel." At the same time, all the old business of Border violence and intrigue was set on foot again. A raid was launched across the West Marches, formidable enough to divert Arran's levies southward, but too weak to hold them there. Communications were opened again with the English party among the Scottish nobles, with the usual result: promises of devotion to England from men who, like the English Whigs after 1688, thought it elementary wisdom to have a foot in both camps. Everything was done except the one essential: the organization of a real relief expedition. Not till August 17th did the Protector's Council issue commissions for the levying in all counties of men "able and meet for the wars"; and by then the Castle of St. Andrews had fallen before the guns of a nation better exercised in the art of applying force at the right moment in the right place.

One summer morning the watchers on the castle walls sighted a crowd of French war galleys making into the bay. There were twenty-one of them, with Leo Strozzi, Prior of Capua, in command, the best sea-captain of the day. That was on June 29th; on the 30th

the castle was summoned to surrender. Then followed a two days'
artillery duel, of which the French had a little the worse; they drew
off to Dundee, to await support from the land side. It came within a
fortnight, Arran marching his levies from the Border. Knox was
now sole chaplain of the garrison, Rough having apparently left for
the south. But, if he had entered on his ministry in the town with a
divided heart, it was with even greater misgivings that he entered
the castle. Not yet was he to show his qualities as chaplain of a forlorn hope. The rest of the story cannot be better told than in his own
words; they are an excellent example of his historian's style:

*The siege by land was confirmed about the Castle on the 18th day of
July. The trenches were cast; ordnance was planted upon the Abbey Church
and upon St. Salvator's College, which so annoyed the Castle that neither
could they keep their block-houses, the sea-tower head, nor the west wall;
for in all these places were men slain by great ordnance. Yea, they mounted
the ordnance so high upon the Abbey Church that they might discover the
ground of the court in divers places. Moreover, within the Castle was the
plague, and divers therein died, which more effrayed some that were within
than did the external force without. But John Knox was of another judgment, for he ever said that their corrupt life could not escape punishment of
God, and that was his continual advertisement from the time that he was
called to preach. When they triumphed of their victory (the first twenty days
they had many prosperous chances) he lamented and ever said they saw
not what he saw. When they bragged of the force and thickness of their
walls, he said, they should be but egg shells. When they vaunted England
will rescue us, he said, ye shall not see them; but ye shall be delivered in
your enemies' hands, and shall be carried to a strange country.*

*Upon the penult of July, at night, was the ordnance planted for the
battery. The battery began at four hours in the morning and before ten
hours of the day the whole south quarter, betwixt the fore tower and the
east block-house was made assaultable. The lower transe was condemned,
diverse slain into it, and the east block-house was shut off from the rest of
the place betwixt ten hours and eleven. There fell a shower of rain, that
continued near an hour, the like whereof had seldom been seen. It was so
vehement that no man might abide without a house. The cannons were left
alone. Some within the Castle were of judgment that men should have*

issued and put all in the hands of God. But because that William Kirk-caldy was communing with the Prior of Capua nothing was enterprised. And so was appointment made and the Castle rendered upon Saturday the last of July.

There is dispute as to the terms of the surrender, but one condition is certain: the garrison was to be transported to France. The galleys, with their prisoners, sailed *after certain days* for Fécamp, and thence up the Seine to Rouen. There the *principal gentlemen* were *dispersed and put in sundry prisons*—Norman Lesley, Moneypenny and James Kirkcaldy to Cherbourg; William Kirkcaldy and Carmichael, with Robert and William Lesley, to Mont St. Michel; Balnaves to the Castle of Rouen. The rest, Knox among them, *were left in the galleys and there miserably entreated. The galleys departed to Nantes, in Brittany, where, upon the water of Loire, they lay the whole winter.*

II. The European Scene

Chapter III

THE DILEMMA OF CHRISTENDOM

I

WHEN THE spires of St. Andrews faded behind his galley in August 1547, Knox passed to an exile which was to make a European out of a very parochial Scotsman. It was this Europeanness that gave him much of his subsequent influence. Many of his later associates had studied and travelled abroad, but the Sorbonne and the Louvre, or even the staid pews of a Geneva church, were a poor initiation into the realities of a Europe where peoples were beginning to count for more than statesmen or even preachers. Knox was to learn something of its underworld and of what was moving there. If we are to understand his development, we also must know something of the scene into which he was thus rudely thrust. It is time for us to run our eye over the Europe of the Reformation, and to get into perspective, too, the deep background of historic development against which alone its actors can be clearly seen.

In these nineteen-thirties the Reformation is more out of favour in Protestant countries, except perhaps in Germany, than it ever was in Roman Catholic countries. It is out of favour, not because it is strange, but because it is only too familiar. We look at it with the eyes of Erasmus, the disappointed liberal. Like him, we are weary of the prigs and bullies who today, as four hundred years ago, seem to be tearing the world in pieces between them; we want to assure ourselves that the present turmoil is pure foolishness by demonstrating how silly were the turmoils of an earlier age. The world has gone mad; the scholar can only wait; eventually the world will come back to sanity and *bonae litterae*. Meanwhile, we can take a rueful pleasure in describing just how mad it is. What better way of deriding a modern party dictatorship based on the delusion of racial superiority

63

than by depicting a dictatorship of saints four hundred years ago, based on the doctrine of predestination? The madder we can make the old doctrine look, the madder will its modern counterpart appear.

But, in truth, all this means only that we cannot understand our contemporaries and are therefore determined not to understand our forefathers. Fascism is no sudden madness; neither was Calvinism. Neither the past nor the present can be understood if we isolate it under a glass case in a historical museum. In all ages men have been moved by certain ideas and desires. From time to time those ideas and desires have come to a head in unrest and revolution. At such moments their leaders have sought to formulate their principles and their aims, but the resulting dogmas or programmes are only labels. The men of the sixteenth century did not argue and fight and persecute for Transubstantiation or Predestination or Effectual Grace, any more than a soldier fights for his uniform. The idea is not the dogma, and those who confuse the two make madmen of their fathers and nonsense of history.

An interesting example of this mistake is afforded by one of Knox's biographers, who thinks that he "cast anchor" in the seventeenth chapter of St. John's Gospel because he found in it the doctrine of predestination. But he did not; all that he found there was the idea of election—in his own words, *a plain difference made betwixt one sort of men and another.* That is an idea common to all Christians; but it is quite another question for what purpose the difference is made. In itself, the idea implies special opportunities and special responsibilities, but no more. Many are called, but few chosen; it is hardly an exaggeration to say that there is no more necessary connection between divine election and personal salvation than there is between natural selection and individual expectation of life.

If we want to know what the Reformation was really about, we must go back to fundamental beliefs and motives. Above all, we must realize what the modern world tends to forget, that the men of the sixteenth century were Christians, to whom the truth of the Christian faith and the meaning of the Christian hope mattered, in the last resort, more than anything else in the world. And we must realize, moreover, that they lived in days when the world was very much in need of hope.

2

Ever since Christianity was first preached the Christian citizen has been a puzzle both to himself and to his rulers. By the elementary necessities of his creed he has been a man living in two worlds. In one he has been a member of a national community, in the other of a community "taken out of the nations." In one he has been bound to obey and enforce the laws of his State, in the other to measure his conduct by standards not recognized by those laws and often inconsistent with them. This dualism has been made tolerable only by the prospect of a reconciliation. That prospect is, again, an elementary necessity of the Christian creed. Somehow, somewhere, the conflict of loyalties will end. The kingdoms of this world will pass: the Kingdom of God will be established.

But how and when? There have been three answers to this question. The commonest, the one that has satisfied most Christians at most times, is simply the answer of death. This world is only a place of probation; the Kingdom of God will be, is being, established elsewhere, beyond "the gold bar of heaven." But this answer has appealed mainly to the simple-minded who are not closely concerned in the management of public affairs, and to them mainly in times of comparative tranquillity, when customary conditions of life are at least not visibly changing for the worse. In more threatening times the hope of Paradise has worn thin, for men are not selfish enough to be content with salvation for themselves if they feel that they are leaving their children to face unknown terrors and to undergo a harder probation.

In such times the simple mind has tended to swing back to another answer, to the one given by the earliest Christian teachers. The Kingdom of God is to be established on earth by a divine act as much outside the ordinary course of human experience as Christ's Incarnation and Resurrection. The Kingdom is, in fact, to be established by Christ in person, returning as king and judge. The first symptom of this belief, as it has recurred again and again in history, has been

65

an almost passionate sense of separateness from the world. This separateness by no means necessarily implies superiority; the sentinel is assigned to a special duty, not to a special destiny. But it does imply loneliness. Earthly citizenship matters little; it is even a distracting temptation. The believer, watching for a divine event, must be free to walk apart, following his "inner light". For the event may come at any moment. This has been the first phase of such movements—a quietism in which contemporaries can usually find nothing to admire and posterity nothing to blame.

But it has generally been a passing phase. As troubles thicken, the conviction grows that the divine event cannot be long delayed. Evil is coming to a head; Christ must save His elect before it is too late. There follows a period of strained expectancy—and then, too often, a nervous breakdown. The separated company disintegrates into lawlessness or hardens into arrogance. The inner light becomes a will-o'-the-wisp dancing on all sorts of moral quagmires, or a beacon summoning to war. The Puritan turns into a Ranter; the non-resister snatches at the sword. The elect need wait no longer; they are not the King's attendants, but His forerunners; they already have His commission to clear His path before Him. And, blotted out by the violence of these fanatics, the quiet remnants of the original company fade into oblivion and contempt.

3

So much for the simple-minded; but neither of the two answers which have appealed to them has ever satisfied for long the more sophisticated Christian of the "governing classes" in Church or State. The second answer has, indeed, always been intolerable to him—intolerable in its quietist even more than in its fanatical form. The politician or the ecclesiastic cannot resign himself to the life of the catacombs; he must seek a reconciliation which will give meaning, not merely to his inner life, but to his life's work. But, in his eyes, Christian quietism not only denies the value of his work; it threatens to destroy it. These Faithfuls in Vanity Fair are always condemning his way; what is worse, their beliefs tend to sap patriotism and weaken religious obedience precisely at those moments when the institutions of Church and State stand in the greatest danger. Thus, at the beginning of the Christian era, Christian quietism provoked a tolerant pagan empire to persecution; thus ever since, it has aroused to fury the Christian successors of the Caesars.

These successors have found a third answer to the riddle, one which has, in fact, been the official creed of Christendom for the last sixteen hundred years. The Kingdom of God is to be established on earth by the Christianization of the State. Nay, it has already been so established. The City of God is already among men; it remains only to develop and organize it. Its joint trustees now are the Church and the Christian State, the Pope and the Emperor, the bishop and the king, the synod and the parliament; but eventually, as the Kingdom grows, these two are to become one. This process of fusion may be looked at in two ways: it may be a fusion by conquest or by peaceful penetration. If conquest, it must take the form of an assertion by the Church of dominion over the State; if peaceful penetration, the perfectly Christianized State may itself become the Church. Either way, there will grow up a single centre of authority to which the Christian may pay an undivided allegiance:

All is God's, and yet 'tis true
All we have is Caesar's too.
All is Caesar's—and what odds
So long as Caesar self is God's?

This became the official theory of the Roman Empire in its last decline, both in east and west; this, with even more show of practical wisdom, became the theory of the missionary Church among the barbarian invaders. The State was to use its sword to enforce what an early Father of the Church called "a happy uniformity of doctrine"; the Church was to support with its spiritual authority the policies of the State. But soon the theory of a common purpose began to break down. It was too narrow to cover the facts. It has satisfied men only at rare sunny moments, as in the mid-thirteenth century and in Victorian England, when an ordered security and a civilized culture have seemed to assure them that they are, after all, not far from the Kingdom of God. These moments have passed quickly. Whenever the alliance between Church and State has become close it has soon become intolerable. The two sets of powers, encouraged to their fullest exercise in the same field of individual conscience and community life, are found to be, not complementary, but conflicting. As each institution asserts its authority with the help of the other, each grows uneasy. The mutual help begins to be rendered grudgingly; the alliance becomes a balance of power. Then follows conflict, the conflict which has bickered or blazed in Christendom for at least nine hundred years: the conflict between Papacy and Empire, between the divine commission to Peter and the divine right of kings, between Geneva and the Louvre, between Covenant and Crown, between the Vatican and the Revolution.

4

In this long record of failure, however, there has been something more than a mere cycle of hope and disappointment, authority and revolt, charity and slaughter. There has been one continuous effort, and there have been a few great moments. The effort, usually unconscious, but always discernible, has been to combine the second answer to the riddle with the third: to find in quietism itself the key both to catholic order in the Church and to reconciliation between Church and State.

According to this conception, the "inner light" is something greater than an individual revelation and more normal than an emergency signal. It is the Spirit of God, the corporate possession of the whole company of believers. And it is their possession in the quiet hours when even the wise virgins sleep, no less than in the crisis of a new revelation. For they are, in no mere metaphor but literally, a "new creation," and the light is to this new state of being what the light of reason is to ordinary human life. It is not some flash of intuition, but a faculty to be soberly developed. And it can be developed only with the growth of the new life of which it is a function. For the Christian is committed to a belief which is foolishness by any ordinary rational standard: the belief that his ordinary human nature, not only can be, but is being, changed. He has been made partaker of the divine nature. To the same participation all men are invited and in it is humanity's only hope.

68

But, however universal this hope may be, at any given moment the company thus enlightened must be a separated company. The inner light can burn steadily only before the altar of worship, not in the streets of politics. Yet so long as it burns there, the individual member of the company need not fear to go out into those streets, to submit to the sword of the State or even to carry it himself. His hope is not in the sword, but for that very reason he will bear it better than those who have no other hope. He is the agent of a peaceful penetration of the State by the Church, but his hope is not in that either; the penetration is not a policy but an incident. His life will remain a continual struggle to reconcile two ideals, but the struggle is his own, not the Church's or the State's. Between a Church so dedicated to foolishness and a State intent on the practical duties of government there can be no corporate jealousy, no corporate conflict. Yet in a Church really dedicated to that foolishness, what miracle might not be possible?

A dream, and not a very coherent one at that? Perhaps; yet at rare moments men have seemed to stand on the verge of realizing it, and these have been the great moments of history. They, too, have ended in failure; but, each time, before they passed they generated the forces by which our world is moved. Such a moment was the early sixteenth century; such, perhaps, may be our own day.

The modern world is apt to flatter itself that it has outlived these dilemmas. The Church, we imagine, has grown too weak for either rivalry or partnership with the State; it has sunk to the position of the army chaplain, a useful moral influence at the service of governments. But we deceive ourselves. The old dilemma still persists, the old conflict still rages, wherever, in any political community, the idea of progress has to be reconciled with the idea of stability, the dream of social perfection with the immediate duties of sound government. For progress and perfection are specifically Christian ideas; it was the Christian faith that, once and for all, transferred man's Golden Age from the past to the future. We are, in fact, witnessing the results of the policy of peaceful penetration: a society saturated with the Church's aspirations but unsteadied by its faith. As those aspirations worked of old, so they are working to-day. In some countries the ideas of progress and stability are in precarious balance; in others the State is seeking stability in a rigorous assertion of its authority over men's acts; in at least two, Germany and Russia, dictatorship, not content with such authority, has revived the theocratic claim of Rome and Geneva, to control, not only men's acts, but their beliefs. We shall soon see, indeed we are seeing even now, whether the old balance has become any more secure, the old tyranny or the old theocracy any tamer, because men no longer feel the need to justify their ambitions by an appeal to divine revelation. We shall see, we are seeing even now, whether there is any escape from these dilemmas, save in a return to foolishness.

CHAPTER IV

THE AGONY OF EUROPE

I

ALL THESE trends of Christian belief and aspiration converged to make what we call the Reformation. They converged under the pressure of prolonged suffering, hardly equalled in any other period of human history. The second quarter of the sixteenth century marks the middle point in an era which might well be named the Agony of Europe. It extends from the forties of the fourteenth century to the beginning of the eighteenth—in western Europe (let us say) from the outbreak of the Hundred Years War to the Peace of Utrecht; in eastern Europe from the Battle of Kossovo to the Peace of Carlovitz. One fact sufficiently marks the character of that era. At its beginning the population of Europe was halved by the Black Death; for three hundred years it remained practically stationary.

Just before the beginning of these miseries, the balance of Church and State in Christendom had finally broken down. It had lasted, trembling and swaying, during the two hundred years from the birth of Frederick Barbarossa in 1122 to the death of Dante in 1321. That had been the last age of the *Respublica Christiana*: the age that saw the culmination of the Hohenstaufen Empire, its destruction by the Papacy of Innocent III and his successors, and the fall of that Papacy itself before the new nationalism of France and England. Throughout the fourteenth century the sky had darkened over a Europe disintegrating from within and threatened from without. While the defeated Papacy was in captivity at Avignon, the new secular powers, the French and English monarchies, were at each other's throats. When the first phase of the Hundred Years War was at its hottest, the Agony began. In the course of little more than one decade, Europe was swept by the first epidemic of the Black Death

71

in 1347, saw the first Turk land upon Gallipoli in 1356, and experienced the first of the great peasant risings in the French Jacquerie of 1358. As the century closed, the darkness deepened: from 1378 the Church was split between the Popes and anti-Popes of the Great Schism; in 1389 and 1396 the last armies of eastern Christendom went down before the Turks at Kossovo and Nicopolis.

2

Torn by such disorders and faced by such dangers, Church and State in the first years of the fifteenth century made an effort to regain their balance. Philosophers and statesmen had been groping for a way to express the old balance in new terms, in terms of national sovereignties and a reform of the Church. The *Respublica Christiania* must be re-established, but it must now be a federation in place of an empire, and the relation between Church and State must be different. The State could no longer be *minister ecclesiae*, a lictor discharging the cruder functions of the republic; it must be *defensor pacis*, itself the supreme guardian of public order and public welfare, assisted but not controlled by spiritual coadjutors. Such a reconstitution of the republic was a gigantic task, but the moment for it seemed opportune. In 1402 the Turkish danger seemed to have been removed; the Ottoman army had been annihilated by the Tartars on the plains of Angora; the Sultan was Tamerlane's captive. Twelve years later the new idea of federation was at last embodied in a constituent assembly. Rulers and bishops met in the Council of Constance to put an end to the Schism and to reform the Church.

But, in fact, it was just too late. Next year, 1415, the old feud between France and England was renewed in western Europe; and the Council itself, by an act of blinding folly, threw central Europe into confusion. That July, three months before Agincourt, the Council sent John Hus to the stake. Like Joan of Arc's judges sixteen years later, they thought to burn a heretic, and they set a nation ablaze.

As so often in history, the philosophers did not know what popular forces they had excited. The political thinkers who, throughout the preceding century, had advanced the new conception of *civil dominion* against the claims of the Church, had found two allies stronger than themselves: the mystics and the peasants. Already they were being swept into the headier current of a popular rising. The mystical movement had been growing for close on two hundred years. Béguins and Beghards, Spiritual Francisans, Brethren of the Free Spirit, Brethren of the Common Life—an endless series of fraternities had spread through Europe. Some were orthodox, some heretical. As always, spiritual fervour trembled on the edge of moral anarchy. But all were moved by a passionate sense of separateness from the world, and all looked for some new revelation: the reign of the Holy Spirit or the coming of Antichrist. Of late years economic misery had lent point to these millennial expectations. The peasant, struggling under the pressure of tithe, joined with the mystic to whom a rich priesthood was a blasphemy, and with the political radical who saw national resources drained by Church endowments, in a campaign which went far beyond any programme of Church reform. And this campaign was already being pushed also beyond mere political or economic demands, and beyond mere temperamental vagaries of thought, into the positive formulation of new doctrine. For the Church's power as an institution lay in the doctrine of the Mass, and the attack on the institution became inevitably an attack on the doctrine.

All these tendencies can be seen coming to a head in England in the last six years of Wyclif's life, between 1378 and 1384, except that mysticism had never become a popular movement in that country. Moreover in England the State was already strong enough to repress both Lollardy and peasant risings. It was at the other end of Europe, in Bohemia and Moravia, that the explosion came. There the Turkish danger had loomed larger, mystical fervour had been fanned by the apocalyptic preaching of Milic, and Slav nationalism was boiling up against weak German rule. There, too, had emerged one of the rare spiritual leaders who, for a brief moment, have seemed able to bring catholic order out of mysticism and popular discontent. In 1402, the very year of Tamerlane's victory, John Hus had begun his ministry in the Bethlehem Chapel at Prague. When, thirteen years later, he perished by fire outside the walls of Constance, the "Bohemian Heresy" became a revolution.

73

3

The history of the fifteenth century can be told in few words. It began with an attempt to re-establish a reformed Church in a new League of Nations, a league armed against the Turkish menace. It ended with a Europe split into national dictatorships, each seeking to make its own *concordats* with a restored but unreformed Papacy, while the Turks, barely held upon the line of the Danube, were pushing their raids round the head of the Adriatic and had almost succeeded in establishing a foothold in the heel of Italy. The Papacy, thus isolated among competing sovereignties, was driven to seek a sovereignty of its own. A new Papal State was being carved out among the despotisms of Italy; and Papal diplomacy was learning to speak with the new kings in their own language, not of ecclesiastical jurisdiction or crusades against the infidel, but of alliances and territorial bargains.

In this political scene-shifting the Hussite revolution played a leading part. It devastated central Europe as the Anglo-French-Burgundian feud devastated western Europe—and with a strange coincidence of dates. It raged from 1419 to 1431, when the militant puritans of Bohemia won their fifth and last victory over a "crusading" army—the same twelve years that began in France with the murder of Duke John of Burgundy and ended with the burning of Joan of Arc. It lingered on, after the defeat of the militants at Lipany in 1434, until the final subjection of Tabor, that curious little Mecca of fanaticism, in 1453—as the war in France lingered on after Burgundy had made peace in 1435, until in 1453 the English invasion was finally crushed at the battle of Chatillon. And in that year, too, Constantinople fell. The revolution had done its work. It had not only side-tracked the reforming energies of two Councils, at Constance and Basel; it had diverted against itself the crusaders who might have crushed the Ottoman power in the day of its weakness.

Moreover, the evil it had done lived after it in the feud between Bohemia and Hungary, as the evil of the Hundred Years War lived on in the feud between France and Burgundy. Not till 1477 did Europe seem to be reaching at last a precarious balance of power, when Matthew Corvinus of Hungary registered in the Peace of Olmütz his victory over Bohemia, and Charles the Bold of Burgundy fell at Nancy. And again it seemed that the rulers of Europe had freed their hands too late; for that was also the year when the Turks swept into the territories of Venice, pushing their raid up to the banks of the Piave.

In fact, for south-eastern Europe it was indeed too late. War had ended by consolidating the power of the western kings. Louis XI had created a new France; Ferdinand and Isabella a new Spain; the Hapsburgs, as heirs of Burgundy, were firmly established in the Low Countries; under the first Tudor, England was being reborn. But on the south-eastern frontiers of Europe the balance which had been reached was a balance, not of power, but of exhaustion. Though the death of Mahomet the Conqueror in 1481 gave Christendom an unexpected respite for forty years, her bulwarks could not be repaired. The eight years from August 1521 to September 1529 saw the capture of Belgrade, the capitulation of Rhodes, the extinction of Hungary on the field of Mohacs, and the appearance of the Ottoman armies beneath the walls of Vienna itself. There the tide receded, but Hungary remained submerged for more than a hundred and fifty years. For these ultimate disasters, too, the Hussite revolutionaries must bear their share of blame.

4

But if these were the political effects of the "Bohemian Heresy," it left a much deeper mark upon the mind and memory of Europe. "For God's sake," said Bishop Fisher in the House of Lords, ninety-five years after the battle of Lipany, "see what a realm the Kingdom of Bohemia was; and when the Church went down, then fell the glory of that kingdom." And the Heresy had not only left these general memories behind it. It had loosed three ideas upon the Christian world, each of which was to have a lasting effect.

The first was the idea that the Church itself might become a federation, in a wider sense than that implied by *concordats* between King and Pope. National churches might, perhaps, acquire certain liberties, not only of jurisdiction and patronage, but also of worship

75

and doctrine. The *Compacts* concluded between the Bohemian moderates and the Council of Basel had not, it is true, meant much, even on paper, and they had meant even less in practice; still, they had conceded the use of the Communion cup to the laity. They had thus varied immemorial Catholic usage, if not Catholic doctrine; they had wiped out, for the moment, one irritating symbol of priestly privilege in the very ceremony which was the stronghold of that privilege. Might not concession be carried further? Might it not be carried at least as far as that "free preaching of the word of God" which had been the first of the *Four Articles* originally promulgated by the Hussites?

In the next century this idea, though in bolder form, largely determined the course of the German Reformation. "Not to have rule taken from the bishops"—so the Confession of Augsburg defined the reformers' claims in 1530—"but that they should suffer the Gospel to be purely taught and relax a few observances which cannot be held without sin." When that idea was finally embodied in the Augsburg settlement of 1555, the Pope himself was forced for a time to give it tacit recognition. Lutheranism established by a Lutheran prince in his territories might be a deplorable error, but officially it was not heresy.

And if such liberties could not be wrung from Rome, was separation from Rome so impossible a step, after all? Was institutional unity essential to the Church of Christ; was an episcopally ordained priesthood indispensable to the validity of the Christian sacraments? That was the second idea, and it was a new one. There had been schisms before, between East and West, between Pope and anti-Pope; but never before had schism been contemplated as a principle of action. Yet now, about 1456, when the Hussite wars had died down and Bohemia had been officially reconciled with Rome, there was established among the quieter puritans, who had kept aloof from the fervours of Tabor and had even listened to Peter of Celcic preaching the extreme doctrine of non-resistance, a new Church, the Unity of the Brotherhood, severed from the Roman obedience, with its own self-perpetuating ministry and its own system of government.

In the next century this idea, too, profoundly influenced the course of the Reformation, but its influence was complicated by the third idea which Bohemia stamped into the mind of Europe: the fear of spiritual mob rule. The Bohemian Brethren could not shake off the taint of their early associations. Europe had seen its first war of religion, and the memory was a nightmare. It had seen the seed of the Word of God, freely sown, sprout into sects—Taborites, Orphans, the Brotherhood of Horeb—united only in one thing: their faith in the sword. At first that sword had been used, in the hand of Zizka, to resist invasion; but soon, in the hand of Prokop, it became the instrument of a *jehad*. When Luther was a boy in Mansfeld there must have been old men who could just remember how the Taborite armies had swept through Saxony and Franconia in 1429–30. And when those memories were revived by the Peasants' War of 1525, they drove the Reformation off its course and threw back the sober advocates of Christian liberty into the arms of the State. New ministries they did not shrink from, gospel preaching they were determined to have; but the unit of the new order must be the State—the kingdom, the principality or the self-governing city—and within that unit the interpretation of the gospel must be the same. They dared not follow the Brethren into the venture of a purely sectarian independence, into a breach of State unity as well as a breach with Rome.

5

So, as the fifteenth century closed, a new scene opened; the stage had been cleared for the western kings. What would they make of this old Christendom, with its sense of failure, its spiritual guides discredited, its frontiers open to the infidel, its economic distresses, its disappointed yearnings after the unseen?

Little enough, it seemed at first. Nothing seemed changed; the Hapsburgs inherited the Burgundian feud against France; a Florentine preacher caught up the mantle of the Bohemian prophets. Only, the kings were shifting their battlefield southward. Italy, where the *condottieri* had reduced war to a game of forfeits, was now, in her turn, to be taught the modern lesson that "war is hell"; and, as the French invaders wound down the Mont Genèvre in the September heats of 1494, Savonarola hailed them as the heralds of the wrath to come. The Swiss were to follow them, the Spaniards, the Germans —a new soldiery schooled in the science of organized destruction. For thirty-five years the Hapsburg-Valois feud was to rage from Lombardy to Naples, with the Popes fighting and bargaining for their own hand. Never did it rage more hotly than in its last seven years, when Charles V had united the lordship of the Low Countries with the crowns of Spain and of the Empire—the same years that saw the Turks advance from the lower Danube to Vienna. Before the storm passed northward again, to flicker for another thirty years along the frontiers of France, Rome had been twice sacked, the Italian Renaissance had perished in the ruins, and Italy had entered on her three centuries of subjection to Hapsburg rule. Throughout the whole sixty-five years, up to the Peace of Cateau-Cambresis in 1559, the battle of the kings took an ever wider sweep, as Hapsburg poured the gold of Mexico into the conflict and Valois summoned help from Stamboul; till French pirates were dogging the Spanish treasure-fleets on the Atlantic and, in the winter of 1543, Turkish galley captains were selling Christian slaves in the streets of Toulon. "Terrible news of the Turk," wrote Luther that summer, but could they, after all, rule worse than Christians? . . . "This is the time foretold, that shall follow the fall of Antichrist." Even so had Savonarola spoken; even so Peter of Celcic a century before. Was nothing changed after more than a hundred years of suffering and experience —neither the "childish heart of kings" nor the mystical despair of the prophets? Must even the visions of Renaissance art end in Michelangelo's portrait of Christ the Avenger above the altar of the Sistine Chapel, unveiled to the public gaze on Christmas Day, 1541?

So it might appear, yet in truth, beneath the surface sameness, everything was changed. There were, at least, two new forces in the world. The kings were fighting with a more sober purpose; the mystics had learnt a simpler and more compelling language. The Renaissance was no fairyland of colour and adventure; France, the spendthrift gallant, seeking dragons and princesses in Italy, as England had sought them in France a century before, had broken herself against a new seriousness in the world. In these forties of the century she was at last turning her attention to realities, with all the dangerous zeal of the converted rake; but with those realities Hapsburg and Tudor had been dealing, however clumsily, for years.

6

The new purpose which the kings had set themselves was the reform of the Church. International action had failed; they must shoulder aside the clerical fumblers and take up the task themselves. The Spaniards had already shown the way. In the last twenty years of the fifteenth century they had won from Rome their own Inquisition, their own powers of ecclesiastical patronage and visitation. They had used these new rights energetically, not only to force Jews and Moors into the Church, but to purify the clergy and to revive university learning. Ximenes, from his archbishop's palace at Toledo, had, in fact, begun to do in 1495 what Henry VIII professed to do thirty-five years later; but far more effectively on far less promising ground. And in 1520 Charles V set himself, with real austerity of purpose, to apply the Spanish precedent both to his own patrimony of the Netherlands and to the territories of the Empire.

But this kind of reformation was possible only on one condition: there must be a Papacy in the background, pliant but outwardly independent. The Pope, like the constitutional monarch of nineteenth-century theory, must not govern, but he must reign. His prerogatives must be preserved. Always under the threat of a Council of the Church to keep him in order, always using the national executives as his instrument, he must still be revered as the source of all spiritual authority. But a Pope with his own territorial ambitions, gambling at the new game of kings with Paris and London, could not play this part. In 1513, the orators of the Lateran Council had hailed Leo X, the Italian prince, as the saviour who should rescue the suffering spouse of Christ: "shepherd, physician, governor, the counterpart of God on earth"; ten years later Adrian VI, the Dutch scholar, could only confess that from this "summit of Mount Zion" had flowed all the corruptions of the Church. Charles, if he were to carry out his national reformations, must be able to deal with the Pope on a more than national basis. He must revive the old universal empire of the Middle Ages—not, perhaps, as a permanent institution, but as an instrument of reform. Thus, for the nonce at least, he must rule Italy, as well as Germany. And Italy must come first. The Papacy must be shaken loose from its petty statecraft, its bureaucracy reformed, its crowds of sinecurists dispersed. Then he could turn his attention to Germany, summon a Council to restate essential doctrine and revise the practices of the Church, and force the Lutheran princes to accept the comprehensive programme of reform thus promulgated.

It was a perfectly sound scheme, and it very nearly succeeded. True, its execution took far too long, and the kings would not wait. Not till 1544 was Charles really free to insist on the summoning of a Church council, and by that time England, the Scandinavian countries, the Lutheran states of Germany, and the Protestant cantons and cities of Switzerland had already broken with Rome and had completed or were carrying out their own schismatic reformations. Still, it was not necessarily too late. In the next few years England actually returned to the Roman fold and the Lutheran princes were forced at least half-way thither. There was as yet hardly a single organized Calvinist congregation in France; the future leaders of revolt in the Netherlands were still Catholics. It looked for a moment as if Protestant Switzerland might be isolated, as Bohemia a century ago, in the midst of a reunited Christendom.

It was into this crisis of contending forces that John Knox took his first trembling steps in 1545–47, and he was to live in doubt of the issue all his days. His public life began at the very hour when the Council of Trent opened its sessions; he died in the year of St. Bartholomew.

But the issue of the contest was to be decided by other forces than the policies of kings. Charles's grand scheme implied a change which he could not himself engineer. For its success it was not enough that the Papacy, the fount of religious honour, should be institutionally efficient and morally clean; it must also be spiritually rich. For fifty years there had been a new movement of spiritual discovery; that was the second change which this world of the sixteenth century had undergone. How had the new riches been distributed among the loyalists and the schismatics?

CHAPTER V

FROM LUTHER TO CALVIN

I

AT THE end of the fifteenth century the future of Christian civilization depended mainly on the answer to one question: could popular mysticism be absorbed into the life and worship of the Church? Mysticism had passed the stage of cliques and confederacies; it had become, under the pressure of suffering, the general climate of simple religious opinion. It had brought sober citizens together in guilds of Praying Brethren, and had set excited crowds, even of children, moving on all the roads of Europe in vague pilgrimages to distant shrines. Here was revival, but also revolt—revolt from silent pulpits, from altars where "monks say Mass as a cobbler mends a shoe," and from a parish priesthood ignorant, neglected and despised. Was there any voice left in the Church to which such men would listen?

The answer came in a strangely learned form. In the universities of Italy, Greek became the fashionable study; Plato was rediscovered; men began to read the New Testament in the original. Reading it, their mind changed. The Platonic background no doubt meant much, but the book itself was a revelation. For a while its discoverers were content to bask in the new light; but that could not last. In a world so corrupt and so miserable a scholarly piety could not be enough. If these were the words of Christ and His apostles, of what spirit were the Popes of Rome and the prince-bishops of Germany? The spirit of folly, said Brandt and Erasmus and their fellow-wits; but it was worse than that. In 1517 Luther began, like the kings, to speak with a new seriousness, and in the language, not of scholars, but of the people. Learning was never so suddenly transmuted into prophecy.

What that prophecy was like on the lips of men like Wishart we have already tried to suggest; but in these early days it had precisely the same ring on the lips of *erasmista* scholars in Spain and reforming ecclesiastics in Italy. The Church had recovered a common language. It was the language of the *Oratory of Divine Love*, formed by Italian prelates in a little church in the Trastevere at Rome, as much as of the "praying circles" at Basel and Mainz, where anabaptists "broke bread with one another in sign of unity and love." Gaetano da Thiene, saint of the Roman Church, labouring to reform the parish clergy and to revive among the laity the practice of frequent communion, was no less convinced than Luther, insurgent and condemned heretic, that the humblest Christian believer was "most free lord of all," freely pardoned and free of his Father's house. Luther's first challenge to the Papacy, his attack on the traffic in indulgences, found as warm an adherent in Cardinal Contarini as in any German radical. "Justification by faith" was common doctrine among all but professional controversialists; even later, in 1541, when those controversialists had done their worst and Contarini met Lutherans and Swiss at Regensburg in a last effort at free conciliation, Calvin was astonished at the extent of their agreement. Twenty years before, agreement had seemed not only possible but inevitable. The Pope might anathematise, but even Spanish ecclesiastics were ready to applaud Luther's *Liberty of a Christian Man* and tolerate his *Address to the Nobility of the German Nation*; they baulked only at his *Babylonish Captivity*. The streams of German and Latin renaissance were flowing together, and Reginald Pole, walking in the garden of San Giorgio Maggiore at Venice with Contarini and Ghiberti, was planning a more fundamental reformation than the King of England who had cast him out.

2

But if popular mysticism was to listen to the new message, two things were necessary: energetic action in Italy, infinite patience in Germany. Luther's preaching had rallied many of the seekers, but many more were drifting into a more extreme puritanism, and were coalescing in new confederacies. Already in 1521, when Luther was

in hiding at the Wartburg, his own Wittenburg seemed to be dis-
solving into anarchy. His return restored order, but could his voice
carry to all the other centres where quietism threatened to disintegrate into violence?

This "left wing" movement puzzled contemporary opinion and
has been misunderstood by historians. Its shifting groups have been
lumped together under the title of "anabaptists," and anabaptism
itself has been identified with the vagaries of those madder sectaries
who, fleeing from persecution in 1533, established a polygamous
Kingdom of God in the city of Münster. In fact, anabaptism, if we
must keep that name, was not a creed but a temper, the familiar
temper of "separateness". Even its distinctive doctrine of adult baptism was not held by all its members, and in those who did hold it
the doctrine was little more than a simple-minded effort of reverence. So awful a conception as membership of the Body of Christ
must involve, not only dedication in infancy, but rededication in
manhood. Tens of thousands who did not hold that doctrine shared
that mood. Among the persecuted, there was little difference between the anabaptist peasants of Tyrol and Salzburg, the Waldenses
of southern France and the early "Lutheran" conventicles of the
Low Countries. Among the fanatics, there was as little difference
between the future Calvinists who placarded Paris with blasphemies
in 1534 and the anabaptist insurrectionaries at Leyden in the following year. The movement was the parent of the later Baptist Church,
but that Church was only one among its many spiritual children. In
the seventeenth century it was to reappear in England and Scotland
in many of the groups which historians are often content to label
"puritan" or "covenanter"; indeed the character of modern
England has been largely determined by the fact that, almost alone of
European countries she offered some sort of refuge to its eccen-
tricities and its simple pieties.

The question, in these fifteen-twenties, was whether Rome and
Germany could find a refuge for them. If not, the Reformation
would lose—the phrase is no exaggeration—its most vivid spiritual
force. These pietists would never be lured back to the gothic
splendours and grinning gargoyles of the mediaeval Church; Contarini and his friends of the *Oratory* must construct a simpler building

for the old household of faith, and that quickly. But even so they could only be won back gradually. Luther must hold them from violence, must teach them patiently the full implications of the liberty he had already asserted for them. *Tu ne Me chercherais pas si tu ne Me possédais; ne t'inquiète donc pas*—Pascal's eternal reply to the restless mystic must be driven home to them.

Of course this picture of a partnership between Luther and Contarini must not be taken literally. Nothing was further from Luther's mind than any such partnership. And there was, in fact, one profound difference between them: this same difference of the *Babylonish Captivity*. To Contarini, as to Thomas More, Papal supremacy was essential to Christian order; but to Luther the Pope was Antichrist, and who could hope for Antichrist's conversion? We shall never understand the Reformation if we suppose that this talk of Antichrist was the sort of invective into which fanatics drift in the heat of battle. It was, on the contrary, the original *casus belli* of the whole conflict. Non-Italian Christians, listening to what Acton calls "the extremity of adulation," which became the fashion at the Roman court towards the end of the fifteenth century, could form only one conclusion. These Italian princes, addressed as *deus alter in terra*, could be none other than the Man of Sin, for in actual fact they sat in the seat of God, claiming to be God. Hence the bitterness of the conflict.

All the same, the picture of a partnership does represent a reality. Convergence was a fact; reconciliation was a possibility. Luther's attitude towards the Papacy was hardly more hostile than the Emperor's; events were to prove that the reformation of the Roman Curia was a practical aim. And however involuntary the partnership may have been, at least on Luther's side, the Italian and the German each seemed, at the moment, eminently fitted to play their respective parts in it; Contarini, Senator of Venice, the part of practical reform, Luther the part of the missionary. With all his vehemencies, no man was ever less a schismatic than Luther, none ever preached non-resistance with simpler conviction. The action that he urged was always action within the framework of existing order. He loathed, as Calvin did later, the violence of the image-breaker; but he loathed hardly less conferences and formulae and nicely drafted confessions. It was not for him to set up a new Church by making deals with Zwinglians or Waldenses. Why should the Bohemian Brethren split hairs about the Sacrament?— it was all one whether the worshipper adored Christ on the altar or adored Him not; *Glauben und Liebe*, faith and love, were the only things that mattered. Even his Elector must learn to sit still: "God cannot away with our scheming and meddling." Let the Word of God be preached, and God would look after His Church.

3

Yet reform in Italy was delayed and, at the critical moment, Luther lost his nerve. Nothing could be done at Rome till Clement VII died; and even when Paul III, last Pope of the Renaissance, succeeded in 1534, the united efforts of "select cardinals and other prelates," met for the "reformation of the Holy Roman Church," stuck in the ruts of the Papal bureaucracy. Reports were written, but no action taken; a Council was summoned, but Charles, at war with France again, was not ready, And meanwhile, Luther had made his irreparable mistake. In 1525 the Peasants' War had thrown him off his balance, and in that single moment of catastrophe Lutheranism ceased to be a mission and became a sect.

Luther's collapse is one of the great tragedies of history, not the less tragic for being so natural. We, who have seen, in our own day, the terror of communism wrench the mind of Germany from its moorings, ought to understand it. With the memory of the Taborites behind him, he had had to struggle against the imputation of Hussism from the first moment that he had broken with Rome. Hussism was the "pestilence"; once let his opponents fix that name on him, and he was out of court. And here, sure enough, were "robbers and murderers" taking the name of Christian liberty in vain. Here were the old furies rising on the very same ground—Münzer and the Evangelical Brotherhood inciting the peasants and miners of his homeland to "fight the battle of the Lord." "Whoever has seen Münzer may say that he has seen the devil himself, alive and raging." Nor was he alone in these alarms; on the contrary, it is the worst of the tragedy that the greatest popular leader in Europe was dragged along in a general panic. The new reformers joined the old rulers in a ruthless campaign against all followers of the "inner light." The indiscriminate slaughter that marked the suppression of the peasants' rising marked also the beginning of the age of persecution.

Hitherto, save for a burning or two in France, executions for heresy had almost been confined to the Netherlands, where Charles had established the Inquisition in 1522 and the first Lutheran martyrs had suffered in 1523. Now, within two years of the Peasants' War, in the fatal year 1527, the year of the Sack of Rome, the Archduke of Austria issued his imperial mandate against the anabaptists and Zwingli at Zürich set an example to Protestant persecutors by drowning Felix Manz for "rebellion." The hunt was up, and the hounds, once given blood, cared less and less to distinguish one quarry from another, anabaptist from "sacramentary," Zwinglian from Calvinist. Luther himself had foreseen the end. "I can never approve the death penalty for teachers of error," he wrote in 1528. Let men be warned by the papists and the Jews. They undertook to kill the false prophet and the heretic, and they found themselves before long invoking their laws to justify the murder of the prophets of God. "The same, I fear, will happen to us." That prophecy came true, and Lutheranism, pioneer of emancipation, took refuge from the hunt by turning domestic chaplain to the princes of Germany. That act of abdication had its fine side. It is to Luther's honour that, in those days of anticlimax, he stuck to his dislike of Protestant confederacies, and refused to convert a national secession into universal schism. But it was abdication; by the end of Luther's life Lutheranism had ceased to be a spiritual force outside the frontiers of Germany.

By then, too, Roman liberalism had played out its hand and had lost. In 1541 came the Conference at Regensburg: Contarini for Rome, Melancthon for Germany, Bullinger, Bucer and the rest for Switzerland and Strasburg. Negotiations broke down, and the breakdown marked the failure of the *Oratory of Divine Love*. Contarini had staked his reputation on the possibility of reconciliation and he survived his failure only a year. He had done his work when, in his last open letter to the Pope, he endorsed the central thesis which Luther had laid down more than twenty years before. "The

granter of indulgences cannot sell what is not his but the Lord's. The express command of Christ is: 'freely ye have received, freely give.' "
That ground had been made good; in future the struggle was to centre in other issues, and the initiative in the work of reformation passed to other hands.

4

It would, perhaps, be more true to say that in future the struggle was to centre in the old crucial issue which had been obscured by the subsidiary doctrinal controversies of the last twenty-five years. It was the same issue that had wrecked the last chance of agreement between Luther and Charles V, the issue raised by Luther's assertion that even General Councils of the Church had erred. The issue was simply the authority of the Church. Now, at the Regensburg Conference, the face of the battle was made finally plain. The negotiators had reached agreement on the doctrines of original sin, free will and justification by faith. Then came the split. *Ventum est deinde ad ecclesiam*, wrote Calvin; *in definitione congruebant sententiae; in potestate dissidere coeperunt.* That has remained the issue between Catholic and Protestant ever since; it is the one real issue that distinguishes Catholic education from Protestant and gives its charter to every modern Catholic school.

The issue must not, of course, be over-simplified. It is not even today, still less was it in 1541, a clear issue between liberty and authority; when, in any civilized community, has the face of the battle ever been as plain as that? But even then it was plain enough. Both sides believed that the Church must be a body of men united by a common faith in certain essential truths; both agreed that such a Church, through its constitutional organs, had both the power and the duty to maintain outward conformity by spiritual censures; both, in varying degrees, held that the State, in its own interests if not in the interests of the Church, might properly enforce such conformity by law and physical punishment. But what was the standard of faith? Or, perhaps more accurately, what was its mode? Was the Christian to believe what he was authoritatively taught by those to whom the Holy Spirit had been given for that purpose? Or was he to believe what the Holy Spirit, given to *him* for that purpose, led him to believe through his own study of God's published revelation? That published revelation was, it is true, not merely the Bible as it might be read by any Christian; it was the Bible preached by an authorized ministry. But the preaching must be "from faith to faith." Faith was personal conviction, not passive acceptance. "The theologians of the Sorbonne err grievously when they think that faith is a simple assent to the word of God, made by the intellect. For if the word of God only hovers in the brain, it has not yet been received by faith. It is only truly received when it has taken root in the depths of the heart."

These are the words of the 1541 translation of the *Institutio*, the words of Calvin the intellectual. If, then, the issue was not one between authority and liberty, it was in a very real sense one between obedience and persuasion. And, as such, it was an issue that Protestants might raise, not only against the old Church, but also against the new reforming State. "It is first of all necessary," wrote Bucer of Strasburg to Edward VI in 1550, "to explain to men the mysteries of the Kingdom and by holy persuasion to exhort them to take up the yoke of Christ. Those are not to be listened to who will that the religion of Christ be thrust upon men only by proclamations and by laws."

And, of course, the issue went even deeper. Both sides agreed that the Christian Church was not merely a school of belief but a mode of life. It was union with God; a partaking of the Divine nature. Only by such union could a man escape damnation. But how was such union to be achieved? Was it a personal relationship between God and the individual believer which the believer could maintain and strengthen by his own repentance, his own faith, his own active participation in the common worship of the Church? Or did it depend on the action of some earthly intermediary, on intercessory acts performed by a priesthood whose members alone had direct access to the divine?

But though this was the real issue, it was too abstract a one for party slogans or party programmes. As always in the great controversies that have determined human history, the issue had to be made concrete. And its concrete symbol was, on the one side, the Mass, and, on the other, the Communion. The Conference at

Regensburg merely stuck in its discussion of Church authority; passing to a consideration of the Sacrament, it broke down. *Illic fuit insuperabilis scopulus*. And, as on the question of Church authority, the insurmountable stumbling-block did not lie in matters of doctrinal definition. On those matters Protestants were deeply at issue among themselves; Luther, Bullinger, Calvin, Cranmer, all had their own definitions. What divided Protestant from Catholic was the recognition of a simple fact. It was impossible to question the supreme authority of a priesthood whose peculiar function it was to make "the sacrifice and oblation of Christ for the salvation of the quick and the dead." Such a priesthood must not only know the truth; it must be able to control the flow of that divine life without which no man could be saved. Its teaching could not be impugned by mere men to whom no such power had been entrusted its right to offer this sacrifice for some and not for others, its right to impose conditions for that purpose, could not be challenged. The Calvinist minister, no less than the Roman priest, might excommunicate the unfaithful member of his flock, but he did not claim to hold the keys of heaven. His sentence might be a social tyranny, but his very insistence on the irrevocability of God's election robbed it of its spiritual terrors. In the hands of the old Church, on the other hand, excommunication was not an act of institutional discipline, but a sentence of spiritual death.

5

But, if these were the issues and this the concrete symbol of them, which side was likely to win? On "form," the advantage, in these early fifteen-forties, did not seem to lie with the Protestants. Their fighting case was based largely on the abuses of the old Church: private masses sold for money, Papal indulgences hawked in the market-place, a clergy too ignorant to teach, "bishops distributing benefices to their babes" while they collected fines from poor priests for the women in their houses. Twenty years later, the ablest of Knox's Catholic opponents in Scotland himself summed up the Protestants' indictment: "Was not the sacraments of Jesus Christ profaned by ignorant and wicked persons, neither able to persuade to godliness by learning nor by living?" But these abuses were already in course of reform; none now attacked them more strenuously than Catholics; a revolutionary party which could only harp upon them might well find itself stranded without a programme of its own.

The misuse in Protestant countries of the word *Reformation* has led to the writing of much bad history. Protestantism was not a reform; it was a revolution. Even in its mildest shape, it was a revolution in the sense of the English revolution of 1688. It was a shifting of the seat of authority. It was, in fact, the first phase of that social and political revolution which has been the central theme of all European history for the last three hundred years. It was the first campaign in that long struggle for individual and social liberty, and the countries where that campaign was won have been to a large extent immune from later campaigns, from French and Russian revolutions and from wars of Italian liberation. As against this revolution, the Reformation, in the proper sense of that term, took place, not in Protestant, but in Catholic countries; and, disastrously as it had been delayed, no renovation of an old institution, once begun, has ever been more thorough or, indeed, more rapid.

So reformed, the old Church was becoming in many respects more attractive than the new sects. The freedom desired by the ordinary man is freedom of action rather than of thought; and the old Church, claiming obedience in belief, interfered comparatively little in men's lives. The assertion of the new sects, on the other hand, that a man's salvation depended on his own faith, was a hard saying for the worldling, and even harder for the over-conscientious. Paradoxically, but inevitably, it led often to a stricter moral censorship than that of the confessional; for it is natural to require a higher standard of works when works are the attestation of a saving faith than when they are regarded as in themselves a means of salvation. Moreover, the new emphasis on faith was apt even to raise a fiercer hunt for heresies; for there will always be a hundred propagandists capable of shaking their neighbours' faith for every one who has the power to subvert their obedience.

It was not these attractions, however, that gave the old Church its advantage at this time. Greater than these was the attraction of a vivid spiritual life, all the more striking because it was so new and so unexpected.

No one can understand Knox or his contemporaries who does not realize that, in these early fifteen-forties, the advantage of spiritual "drive" lay with Rome. And, at Rome, it lay no longer with moderates and conciliators, but with the out-and-out loyalists. Lutheranism had spent its force; Calvin, lately returned to Geneva in 1541 after his initial failure, was still no more than the struggling patriarch of a small city. Every effort at real union between Swiss and Lutherans had broken down, while the Roman Church was making imposing proof of its unity by its preparations for the approaching Council of Trent. And Protestantism, thus brought to a standstill, had to confess that it had wrought no moral deliverance in the earth. Erasmus had asked bitterly whether these evangelical preachers had ever made one man better; Luther confessed that his followers were greedier and more heartless than the children of the old Church. "Our evangelical rascaldom," wrote a Nürnberg reformer in 1532, "makes the Roman rascaldom of monks and priestlings look pious"; and, six years before, Dürer had bequeathed his *Four Apostles* to the Nürnberg city fathers as a warning in parable against the misusers of Christian liberty. Against all this moral looseness, Rome was setting a new standard of spiritual discipline. The dominant force in Europe was Ignatius Loyola and his Society of Jesus, just recognized by Paul III in 1540. Cardinal Caraffa, who was to inaugurate in 1555 a new line of militant Popes, had found in this middle-aged Spaniard the driving power that he had sought in vain in his old associates of the *Oratory of Divine Love.*

The outstanding fact of these middle years of the sixteenth century is the immense popular appeal of this new Jesuit Order. Its leaders were not only learned theologians, who directed the Council of Trent in the new ordering of Church doctrine and administration. They were also enthusiastic popular educators, wiser and more thorough than any Protestant. Above all, they taught their disciples to meet popular mysticism on its own ground. Loyola's *Spiritual Exercises* might be dangerous training for the adept; but at least he learnt from them the language of intimate devotion. The mere truth is that the Jesuit missionaries won back the Austrian peasants and craftsmen to the Church when rulers and reformers alike had abandoned them to the sword.

6

Against all this—against the Jesuit missionaries, against the Church Fathers at Trent, against the secular rulers of all western Europe save a few small German States, the Protestants could, at this moment, put only one thing: a book. Calvin had written his *Institution of the Christian Religion* in 1536; he had published its French translation in 1541. It was only a book; but it was one of the few books that, when sown, have really "sprung up men."

The modern world, having heard that the *Institutio* contains the doctrine of predestination, does not trouble to read it; but, as then published, it did not, in fact, contain that doctrine in any form which can offend the modern mind. Calvin, at least at this time, allowed as wide a scope to man's free will as Mr. Bertrand Russell. If there is anything in it that offends, it is not any new interpretation that Calvin put upon the Christian faith, but his acceptance of an old and universal misinterpretation of that faith.

In truth, when the modern mind thinks that it is rejecting Calvinism, it is really rejecting an older doctrine which limits, not man's freedom, but God's. It is easy to believe that God, if He exists, must be an "absolute sovereign," disposing the lives of men. What is inconceivable is that His dispositions, the whole sweep of human history, the whole range of His dealings with the individual soul, should be directed to no end but a kind of Old Bailey verdict of acquittal or condemnation. But this narrowing of human destiny to a bare choice between heaven and hell, a stark contrast between the "elect" and the "reprobate," was not, of course, peculiar to Calvinism. It had been the universal assumption of the Church for at least a thousand years, ever since the early Christian's hope of Christ's second coming was blotted out by the terrors of the Day of Judgment. True, Protestantism emphasized the starkness of the contrast by rejecting the softening compromise of purgatory; but Calvin at least provided another way of escape for the anxious soul, in his doctrine of the "invisible Church known only to God." And he did much more. He could not paint the ultimate destinies of man in milder colours than his contemporaries, but he directed men's eyes to more immediate issues, and gave them, in practice, a nobler incentive to action than the hope of heaven or the fear of hell.

That is the real significance of the *Institutio*. When it was first published, it contained something much more explosive than the dogma of predestination; it contained a philosophy of history, a statement of the Christian faith in terms of divine purpose. That was new, how new it is difficult to realize today. The mediaeval conception of Church and State, with all its grandeur, had been a static one: Church and State were but the set scene where God dealt with the individual soul. And in this Luther had been as mediaeval as any schoolman. He aimed only at clearing from the scene its clutter of superfluous stage properties and traditional "business," that the individual soul might be left face to face with God. His appeal to Scripture was largely negative: an appeal, as it were, to the simplicity of the Author's original stage directions. But to Calvin the set scene was vaster; it was the universe itself; and on that scene Church and State were themselves the actors, agents of a majestic "scheme of salvation." His appeal to Scripture was an appeal, as it were, to the earlier acts of the play, as indicating the Author's technique in working out the plot.

That technique, the method of God's purpose, was clear. God worked always from the few to the many, from the "elect" to the nations—not only from Jew to Gentile and from Church to world, but also, within the Jewish State or the Christian Church, from His chosen messengers at any given moment to the general company of His children. The living God did not stand still, and He was never with the big battalions. To be called to deliver a new message was the natural expectation of the faithful; to be few and weak was to be the more assured that the call was genuine. Only let the called realize that, however few, they are always an organic and an organized communion. Sharing a common life, they must have a corporate discipline. Not suddenly, not by sporadic enthusiasms, will God work out His purpose. His, too, are the settled disciplines of the world. *Omnis potestas a Deo*, the secular powers are also ordained by

Him; and His new revelations tend always to a new order, not less settled and effective than the old.

7

It is a wise child that knows its own father, but surely the modern liberal's dislike for Calvin is the oddest example of filial disrespect. For this philosophy was the parent of the liberal movements of three hundred years, at least in Britain, Holland and North America, and it continued to dominate those movements until, in the nineteenth century, Marx invented his counter-philosophy of materialism.

Like liberalism, it retained its living force as a philosophy even after it had become discredited as a system of government. Like the Englsh liberals of the nineteenth century, Calvin himself, and still more his uninspired lieutenants and successors, de Bèze and the rest, allowed themselves later to be forced, under pressure of controversy, into a sort of defiant legalism. Could it be freedom to allow child labour in the mines? Yes, the economists had proved it. Could God really desire a man's damnation? Yes, search the Scriptures and see. But while such have been the dingy camp colours of liberalis.n and Calvinism in times of peace, they have continued to display very different banners in the day of battle. And when the *Institutio* was first launched in these early days, prefaced by Calvin's flaming letter to the King of France, it rallied all the insurgent remnants, both radicals and moderates, who had been scattered by Luther's fall. It defied the royal persecutors in the name of the true faith; it justified the millennial hopes of the mystic where Luther and Loyola could only appeal to his sense of private devotion; it held out to the sober-minded a prospect of ordered liberty. Like the English Labour Movement in the latter years of the nineteenth century, its appeal was none the less effective because it called on men, not to overthrow an old order, but to capture it.

Nevertheless, this rallying cry might well have fallen on deaf ears if the Jesuit missionaries and the Fathers of Trent had been left to meet religious liberalism on its own ground. When it first sounded, the rulers had not yet finally declared war on the liberals. Henry

VIII, indeed, had reversed the engines in England in 1539 by the Act of the Six Articles; in France the Edict of Fontainebleau in the following year seemed to mark the adoption of persecution as a definite State policy, But though the faggots had been heaped, the fires were hardly lighted. Only when the torch was applied did Geneva begin to take its place in Europe as a city of refuge and the headquarters of a revolt.

The war was first declared at Rome in 1542 when the Bill *Licet ab initio* established the Roman Inquisition under Caraffa. Hostilities did not really open until the years 1546-47, after Charles V had made peace with France and had concluded his armistice with the Turks. Those two years saw a new edict in the Netherlands, the violent extinction of the first reformed congregation in France at Meaux, the burning of the first Protestant martyr at Rome, and the establishment by Henry II of the French version of the Inquisition, the *Chambre Ardente* at Paris. Henry's decree was dated 8th October 1547; and it was just at that moment that John Knox, chained to his galley-bench, rowed round the coast from Seine to Loire and settled down to his first winter of captivity at Nantes.

CHAPTER VI

THE EVE OF WAR

THIS SURVEY of the European scene must close with two words by way of postscript. The history we have sketched had left two marks on Europe, and those were to be the distinguishing marks of the approaching Wars of Religion.

In the stresses and disappointments of the years 1525–47 Europe, Catholic and Protestant, had lost something which she was not to recapture for two centuries. She had lost faith in benevolence. The anabaptists, with all their virtues, had depreciated the currency of humanitarian thought, much as the indiscriminate devotees of social democracy have depreciated it in our own day. The debased coinage passed out of circulation; to tender it in the commerce of ideas became almost equivalent to a confession of fraud. *Whatsoever ye speak of charity and love, and howsoever ye seem to be zealous over the truth, yet shall you in the end produce no other fruit than your fathers have done before you;* so Knox wrote of the anabaptists in 1559. *The Church of God may look for no other thing at your hand but for the confusion of all God's ordinances and for more cruel persecution than ever yet it did sustain since the days of the Apostles.* Those words were no expression of personal opinion; they represented the common judgment of Europe. It was in that panic spirit that Geneva burnt Servetus, in that spirit that Italy and Switzerland alike hounded Bernardino Ochino to his death.

And the terrible thing is that the judgment was not wholly wrong. The Europe of the sixteenth century was no settled civilization. Outside the frame of customary village moralities and the personal relationship of master and servant, men had no sure loyalties, no instinctive code of conduct. City life was disorderly, scarcely controlled by the minute censorship of morals exercised, long before the Reformation, by municipal councils. The soldier, enlisting against the Turk, became the terror of his own countryside. In such a society, ideas of freedom and love led all too easily to strange conclusions. England, a century later, was to have plenty of experience of those conclusions. She was to see their political application by an army of Independents and Fifth Monarchy men; she was to see their moral application by Ranters "pretending that they only had attained to perfection that could do what they would and not sin." Knox was not so far wrong after all when he warned *as well the people as the princes* to beware of *those that hate and detest all lawful powers.*

Yet no generation can unlearn the common language of humanity without paying heavily for it. This second generation of reformers was to pay very heavily indeed; how heavily Knox's life will show.

That was one of the marks of the coming age. The other was that, by an irony often repeated in the history of Christendom, Calvin the apostle of order had borrowed the fundamental error of the militant anabaptists. Revolted, as they had been revolted, as the humanitarian reformer is revolted today, by the unchristian character of contemporary civilization, not of a reformed Church, but of a new social order.

That was the secret flaw in Calvin's conception of the Purpose of God. It was a Jewish conception. It traced the development of the Purpose, not in terms of a "new creation," but in terms of human history. God raised up His ministers, age after age, not to re-initiate men into a life-giving communion with Him, but to re-establish a godly polity. They must not themselves use violence to that end, but they could be sure that God would always find violent executors of His judgments outside the number of His elect. Even so had the anabaptists spoken, until, losing their foothold on this narrow distinction, Melchior's militant disciples began to teach that, once God's judgments had been made plain, the faithful must assist in their execution. We shall see Knox stumbling on the same brink and sliding into the same fall. That, indeed, is the whole plot of the story that we shall have to tell, and it explains the new, though uncertain, alliance between orthodoxy and anabaptism which was so largely to determine the course of rebellion and revolution in Scotland and England in the seventeenth century.

Those whom this cap fits in our own day may well try it on for their instruction. There is no nobler instinct than that which revolts against a civilization calling itself Christian but denying Christ in all its acts. None nobler, but none more dangerous, for it does not pause to ask in what sense a civilization can be Christian, or how far law can be the agent of life. It assumes, however unconsciously, that the new creation can never be more than a patch of enlightened teaching on the old garment of the State, that it can never be woven on the hidden looms of life into a new garment for mankind. Seeing, therefore, no alternative save between hypocritical inaction and forceful application, it sharpens the needles of new law and chooses the strongest thread; it strains and coarsens the patch, only to find that the tougher the stitches, the worse the rent. The compulsion towards such efforts is strong upon us today; how can we leave the poor to suffer daily injustice or the war-mongers to plunge our world into new slaughter? Even so the men of the sixteenth century asked how they could leave the faithful to suffer persecution or the new kings of the west to drive their trade of power politics. They had as much reason to see in the Mass the source of all these evils, as we have to see it in capitalism or the banking system; their insecurity was greater than ours and their principles certainly no less exalted. A few years ago we may have flattered ourselves on the contrast between our humanitarianism and their insensitiveness to human suffering but we can hardly do so today; we have learnt afresh how ruthless the religion of humanity can be. Of all the teachings of history the clearest is this: that those who seek to realize ideal aims by force of law are always unscrupulous and always cruel.

III. England, Dieppe and Frankfurt
The Making of a Revolutionary

CHAPTER VII

FROM NANTES TO BERWICK
1547–49

I

KNOX'S NINETEEN months in the French galleys are his biographer's most difficult problem. The bare facts are pretty clear. Until April 1548 he lay at Nantes, pestered to *give reverence to the Mass*, as it was periodically celebrated on board or on shore, and to kiss Our Lady's image when the Salve Regina was sung on Saturday evenings. In May, his galley joined a great fleet assembled at Brest. Then *the galleys, being twenty-two in number,* with *three-score great ships, besides victuallers, took the plain seas* for the north. It was the convoy of an army. "Passing by the narrow seas of Calais and Dover, with good luck they land in the river of Forth; and in Leith shore the 16th June, they had landed five thousand old men of war well practised in the field, with great cannons and field pieces." But if they had eluded the English fleet, an English army was waiting for them; and the first sight that met them, as they crept up the coast, was Dunbar town in flames—"burning handsomely," as the English commander reported.

From June to September the bulk of the navy remained on the east coast of Scotland, between Forth and Tay. Knox may have been in a brush or two with English ships. Certainly his health broke down; at one moment he was *so extremely sick that few hoped his life.* In September most of the galleys returned to France. There are indications that Knox's galley was among the few left behind to winter in Scottish waters. If so, he must have been transferred to another, perhaps as unfit for further service. That winter he seems to have spent at Rouen, still *lying in irons, and sore troubled by corporal infirmity, in a galley called Notre Dame,* but able to correspond both with Balnaves in the castle there and with the prisoners at Mont St. Michel. In February or March 1549, he was released and went to England. On April 7th the Privy Council directed the sum of five pounds to be paid "to John Knock, preacher, by way of reward," and soon after he was appointed minister at Berwick.

2

But what did these months mean to him? Obviously a sedentary dominie does not find himself dumped on a rowing bench in rough company without suffering accutely. In after years he never forgot those days, but he seldom referred to them. He was modest about *the torment I sustained in the galleys*. To his companions of the Castle of St. Andrews he spoke of himself at the time only as *your brother in affliction which partly hath experience what Satan's wrath may do*. His real feelings he set on paper only once, to point the moral of a discourse on prayer. *I know how hard the battle is betwixt the spirit and the flesh, under the heavy cross of affliction, where no worldly defence but present death does appear. I know the grudging and murmuring complaints of the flesh; I know the anger, wrath and indignation which it conceiveth against God, calling all his promises in doubt and being ready every hour utterly to fall from God.* In short, his life was ruined, and the cause for which he had allowed himself to be dragged from comfortable obscurity had hopelessly collapsed.

Perhaps it is best to leave it at that, without attempting to draw pictures of the galley-master's lash, the squalor of life among ruffianly convicts, the permanent undermining of the captive's health. For the rest of his life Knox suffered intermittently from stone, but that was the common complaint of the age; he died in his fifty-ninth year, but Calvin in his fifty-fifth. The galleys were not then, perhaps, the hell that they later became. Knox had many of his own countrymen with him, no doubt the roughest of the castle company, but still kindly Scots. They might be *threatened with torments* for heretical behaviour, but they were apparently allowed with impunity to toss Our Lady into the Loire—*she is light enough, let her learn to swim*. It was not the policy of the French King to drive these Scots too hard. All but the *common servants* had been released from the galleys before Knox; the *principal gentlemen* were kept in honourable confinement for another eighteen months only because their earlier return to Scotland might have been too dangerous. Balnaves continued to receive his pension from England without hindrance. This leniency had a purpose. Henry II of France was playing for nothing less than a kingdom. These men were, he hoped, his future subjects, and he might need their support. As enemies of the Hamiltons he might have the more use for them in the future.

If we are to speculate, it is more interesting to wonder how much Knox knew or guessed of Henry's game in this summer of 1548. He had a shrewder political judgment than most Scotsmen, even if he had little political aptitude. He had put no faith in promises of English help when he was besieged at St. Andrews, and he "prophesied" accordingly. Now, as he afterwards was proud to remember, he prophesied deliverance for all his companions; and he was right again. But did he realize that the fulfilment of his prophecy depended on the collapse of the cause with which he and his companions identified themselves? They would be delivered when, and only when, Henry was sure that the game was in his hands. And did Knox guess how completely, in spite of appearances, England was on the defensive, how completely the initiative had passed to France?

3

In spite of appearances—for at first sight England seemed as strong and as ruthless as ever. Knox, of course, knew what had happened in Scotland within six weeks of the fall of the Castle of St. Andrews. Edward Seymour, Duke of Somerset and Protector of England, had reappeared, apparently unchanged, in the countryside where in 1544, as Earl of Hertford, he had so well carried out Henry VIII's instructions to "put all to fire and sword, burn Edinburgh town and raze and deface it." On 7th September 1547, his army had camped round the old house at Longniddry. An English fleet was in the Forth. Three days later the greatest muster that Scotland had seen since Flodden had been routed and destroyed at Pinkie Cleugh. Simultaneously five thousand men had broken across the West Marches. True, once again, the invasion had seemed to end in the futility of mere frightfulness: the burning of Leith in the east and Annan in the west, then immediate retreat to Berwick and Carlisle. But this time, Somerset left a post of observation behind him, as a warning of his return—the garrison of Broughty Castle on the Tay, seized by his fleet in the general panic after Pinkie; and next spring, sure enough, his lieutenants were back again. They seized Haddington in April, fortified it, and devastated all the country round till "in the neighbourhood of Edinburgh there is not a mill or even a blade of grass."

But behind this show of strength there was a new moderation. On Somerset's part it was genuine statesmanship, but it was none the less an admission of weakness. Before Pinkie and after, he had offered the mildest terms: only let the marriage contract of Edward and Mary be renewed and the Scots might keep their Queen and their full independence. But the offer came too late. After Henry VIII's hectoring, it would be years before any Scotsman would trust an Englishman; after Pinkie the one thought in Scottish minds was whether the King of France would "undertake the protection of the Scottish kingdom." That was how the scared nobility of Scotland were talking at Stirling in October. At once the Queen Mother and d'Oysel pounced on their opportunity, "to perform that intention which long in heart and mind they had." Yes, the Regent and Council might safely leave them to handle Henry of France—and what more precious possession could Scotsmen "commit to his faith and credit" than their five-year-old Queen? And so word was sent to Paris and was confirmed by a more formal resolution of the nobility at Stirling on 8th February 1548. Whereat Henry "lap for blitheness and was so blithe that it is uncredible." He was at peace with England; not for another eighteen months did he think it wise to declare war; but he could always lend the Scots a fleet and an army.

That was why Knox found himself rowing up Forth in June 1548; that was also why the English occupied Haddington in April. Somerset had heard of that agitated convention at Stirling; among his informants were Glencairn and Hugh Douglas of Longniddry. He knew from Wooton, his agent in France, how large an armament France was preparing. But it is clear from the records that, by the

seizure of Haddington, he hoped, at best, to prevent a French invasion of Northumberland. It was his "policy to hold off the French,
hoping that they would be broken by long sojourn in a country so
barbarous as Scotland," He was on the defensive. Not so his opponent. Henry had two objects. His fleet was to bring the little Queen
to France, and an English army at Haddington could not prevent
that. His army was to exhaust the military resources of England, in
order that he might, in his own time, drive the English garrisons
from the county of Boulogne; and what more exhausting enterprise
could England undertake than to hold this salient in Lothian?

4

So it proved. Haddington was invested and on July 17th the
Scottish parliament met in the abbey outside the walls "to put," as
the Queen Mother wrote to France, "all things in the hands of the
King." The marriage treaty was concluded. A few days later Knox
may have seen "some ships and four galleys" slipping out of Leith
as if bound for France. When out of sight of land they turned north
and, rounding Scotland, put in to Dumbarton. There they took
aboard Mary Stewart with Lords Erskine and Livingstone, her
governors, and "four young virgins of the special nobility, Livingstone, Fleming, Seton and Beaton." With them, too, was a grave
youth of sixteen, James Stewart, Mary's half-brother, destined by
their father for the usual ecclesiastical career of a royal bastard and
already, since the age of five, Prior of St. Andrews. History has
seldom staged the first act of one of her tragedies with such regard
for the dramatic unities. If she had only detailed Knox's galley for
the escort, the scene would have been perfect.

And Henry's other object was not less fully secured. We need not
follow in detail the fortunes of the French and English armies in
Lothian and on the Border, but we may complete here the history of
Henry's triumph. For nearly a year after Mary Stewart had arrived
at his Court of St. Germains, he waited his opportunity. Haddington held out, but it became England's running sore. Then on 8th
August 1549, France declared war; the French armies marched into
the Boulonnais; in a few days the English had been driven behind the

walls of Boulogne itself. On September 19th they evacuated Haddington; on 21st February 1550, they surrendered Broughty Castle. In March came peace; France won Boulogne, "the Englishmen were clean dung out of Scotland." That summer all the prisoners of St. Andrews were released, save only the godly Melville who had died in his prison at Brest. Three months before, in a public proclamation, Henry had already been speaking of "maintaining the kingdom of Scotland in the obedience of our son the Dauphin." Now he thought that England, too, was in his grasp. A little longer, and he would be Emperor of Britain. If his emissaries in Ireland did their work, that island would fall to him too.

A knowledge of these facts is necessary if we are to understand the feelings with which Knox took refuge in England in the spring of 1549. Outside Switzerland, England was the only remaining citadel of Protestantism. As Charles V, exploiting his victory of Mühlberg, sought to enforce upon Germany the shadowy compromise known as the *Augsburg Interim* of 1548, the centres of Protestantism in the Empire had gone down one after the other. In 1547–49, Strasburg, Constance and Augsburg had fallen; Peter Martyr and Ochino had fled to London, Bucer and Fagius to Cambridge; a crowd of refugees followed them. Strasburg weavers formed a "church of strangers" at Glastonbury; John Laski, Polish noble and ex-bishop, was allowed to establish a presbyterian congregation in the Church of the Augustinian Friars in London. But the citadel was almost ludicrously weak. England was becoming a mere cipher in Europe, disunited, poor in material resources, lacking a settled system of government.

One memory of his galley days Knox cherished ever after. *Lying betwixt Dundee and St. Andrews*, sick almost to death, one of his companions *willed him to look to the land and asked if he knew it. Who answered: "Yes, I know it well, for I see the steeple of the place where God first in public opened my mouth to His glory, and I am fully persuaded, how weak that ever I now appear, that I shall not depart this life till that my tongue shall glorify His godly name in the same place."* If, a year later when he took up his ministry at Berwick, he had any eye for the signs of the times, the fulfilment of that prophecy must have seemed remote indeed.

Chapter VIII

A TASTE OF FREEDOM

1549-50

I

Yet, in his first two years in England, Knox was, perhaps, hardly troubled by such thoughts. He spent those years at Berwick, where he found precisely the kind of task to call forth all his best powers. It was a garrison town, a base of operations; and it suffered from more than all the necessary evils of warfare in that age. In addition to the English levies, it was crowded with foreign mercenaries: Albanians and Germans, Italians and Spaniards, the Scottish companies in English pay. There was "better order among the Tartars" than among this pentecostal crew. Pay was chronically in arrears; prices were high; "no man can have anything unstolen"; lodgings were monopolized by the Scots; the sick evacuated from Haddington died in the streets. In all the country round, the foreigners were at daggers drawn with the native English and Scots.

For the success of Knox's mission we have only his own testimony twelve years later: *God so blessed my weak labours that in Berwick, (where commonly before there used to be slaughter by reason of quarrels that used to arise amongst soldiers), there was as great quietness all the time that I remained there as there is this day in Edinburgh.*" Exaggeration? Perhaps; peace came before he had been there a full year, and quieter times followed naturally upon disbandment. Yet the Berwick garrison was maintained at two or three hundred men above peace strength; and there were similar reinforcements at the subsidiary fortresses of Norham, Wark, and Holy Island. And Knox, though he picqued himself on his powers of prophecy, was not apt to over-value his practical achievements; he was "set in his opinions" but was otherwise prone to regard himself as a failure. That he liked to look back on his days at Berwick is therefore not bad evidence.

His memories were pleasant. He had built up a strong congregation to whom he could write afterwards with confident affection. He had spoken to them sometimes *with rude boldness*, but he had given himself no airs. He had *accompanied* with them as their *common brother, like the common sort of God's elect children.* He had *never pretended, by policy or craft,* to any other mission than that of preacher. And he could praise them for their *Christian charity and brotherly love* and for their *godly care over the poor.* Above all, he and they had established and observed together the true *practise of the Lord's Supper, prepared, used and ministered in all simplicity, not as man had devised, neither as the King's proceedings did allow, but as Christ Jesus did institute and it is evident that St. Paul did practise.* At that Supper *minister and congregation sat both at one table, no difference betwixt them in preeminence nor habit.* It was of Berwick chiefly that he was thinking when he wrote in January 1554, on the eve of his flight to the Continent: *Sometime I have thought that impossible it had been so to have removed my affection from the realm of Scotland that any realm or nation could have been equally dear to me. But God I take to record in my conscience that the troubles in the realm of England are double more dolorous unto my heart than ever were the troubles of Scotland.*

Indeed, the period of close on five years that he spent in England must have been the happiest in his life. Only in the last year or so did troubles begin to close in on him. Until then, he showed little of the stridency and self-assertiveness which were to take possession of him later. His biographers have usually assumed that he looked on Geneva as his spiritual home, but England has really a better claim to that title. He called Geneva *a perfect school of Christ*; but a school is not a permanent habitation. Nine turbulent years after he had left that school, he wrote wistfully of *the quietness of conscience and contentment of heart* which he had known there; but it was not to that city that he wished to return, but to the *dispersed little flock* of the English congregation there, now once more at home in England. Amongst them *I would be content to end my days, if so it might stand with God's good pleasure. I can give no reason that I should so desire, other than that my heart so thirsteth.*

In identifying his name with Geneva the world forgets that he was never much more than a bird of passage there. Of his sixty-three months of wandering between 1554 and 1559, he spent barely half in Geneva, and his longest period of continuous residence lasted little more than a year. In England he had struck far deeper roots; it was there that he found a spiritual climate really congenial to him.

2

And that is curious, for the English climate of 1549 was the mildest in Europe—Poland perhaps excepted. It is often said that religious toleration was inconceivable in the sixteenth century; but the Protector Somerset conceived it, and he was the only statesman whom Knox ever really admired. He thought him *simple*, too honest for his time; he deplored his carelessness about attending sermons; but that was the extent of his criticism. Somerset was, in fact, one of the oddest anachronisms of history. He shared the two main vices of his contemporaries: he waged war without mercy and enriched himself without scruple. But in policy he was a Tory democrat born out of due time. He dreamed all the right dreams, and pulled all the wrong strings. He would have solved the Scottish problem in 1548, as the young men of the Round Table would have solved the Irish problem in 1912, by establishing a federal Empire of Britain. He was for the peasant against the enclosing landlord, and his attempted reforms encouraged the agrarian risings of Knox's first summer in England.

Above all, he dreamed of solving the religious problem by free discussion. All the laws against heresy were to be repealed, and most of the laws against treason. Even the Royal Supremacy might be freely impugned by word of mouth, though not in writing. Only, the extremists were to be restrained from words or acts which might cause a breach of the peace. Priests must not be mobbed in the streets by prentices; the Sacrament must not be unreverently spoken of; there must be no unauthorized breaking down of images or removal of altars. Beneficed clergy must preach at least once a quarter, but not outside their cures, except by special license; and unlicensed preaching by others must be forbidden. But these restrictions on free speech were honoured more in the breach than the observance, and neither Somerset nor Cranmer thought the breaches dangerous. Some conformity there must be, but it should be conformity, not of doctrine, but of worship. There should be a Book of Common Prayer which the clergy, but not the laity, should be bound under penalties to observe; but the penalties should not be too severe and should be only laxly and gradually enforced.

This was, in fact, the state of English law and administration when Knox settled down at Berwick. And he liked it. It gave him complete freedom of speech; it gave him, in practice if not in theory, wide freedom of action. He was not the only minister, by any means, who in those days consistently violated the first Act of Uniformity which had come into force just at the moment of his arrival in England. On all sides that Act was regarded as provisional and tentative. Some common order there must eventually be, but faith could not be "co-acted"; this first Book of Common Prayer seemed rather to invite discussion of what the common order should be than to establish it. And there is no evidence that at this time Knox denied to others the freedom he assumed for himself. On the contrary, there is some indication that he deliberately refused, both at this time and later, to make himself the leader of a faction in the Church. Over all the land, from pulpit and printing house, rose a bable of voices. The foreign Protestants mourned the "recantation" of Cranmer and his "foolish bishops"; Cranmer and Gardner argued the merits of Low Church and High; the puritan Hooper clamoured for "a perfect and apostolical reformation." In this babel Knox joined, as we shall see, and his preaching attracted increasing attention in the north. It *wrought in the hearts of many such favour unto me as displeased some men.* But he seems to have been content with such preaching as, in his judgment, was necessary for the instruction of his own congregation, and he reproached himself later because *I for man's pleasure so long resisted the godly and just request of such as sought my company.* He had, for the first time in his life, a cure of souls, and that was enough for him.

3

But among the subjects of instruction necessary to his congregation the foremost was, of course, his old enemy the Mass. On that he could not keep silence. Why, indeed, should he? In preaching his favourite doctrine he was, no doubt, on the edge of law-breaking, but nothing he said went further than Cranmer's own words a few months later: "What availeth it to take away beads, pardons, pilgrimages and such-like popery so long as the two chief roots remain unpulled up? The roots of the weeds are the popish doctrine of transubstantiation and of the sacrifice and oblation made by the priest for the salvation of the quick and the dead; which roots, if they be suffered to grow in the Lord's vineyard, they will overspread all the ground again with the old errors and superstitions."

Such views, however, as we shall see later, were less welcome in the north than in London; and Cuthbert Tunstall, Bishop of Durham, felt bound to take notice of them. But his position was delicate. Berwick was in his diocese but outside the jurisdiction of the King's Council in the North of which (until February 1550) he was Lord President. The secular authority was the Warden of the East Marches, and the acting Warden was Sir Robert Bowes. That old official of the Council, legal member since its foundation twenty years before, lawyer by profession but soldier by necessity of the times, though no friend to new-fangled doctrines, probably cared more for the garrison chaplain's efficiency than for his opinions. So all that happened was a summons to Knox to appear at Newcastle and *give a reason why so constantly I do affirm the Mass to be, and at all times to have been, idolatry and abomination before God."*

Accordingly he delivered a discourse in St. Nicholas's Church on 4th April 1550, before what was probably a rather informal gathering. He represented himself as speaking *in presence of the Council and Congregation, amongst whom was also present the Bishop of Durham and his doctors*; but it appears that the Council in the North did not, at that time, hold any sessions outside Yorkshire. Peace had just been made; commissioners were being appointed to discuss the settlement of the Border country. There would be no lack of royal officials at Newcastle that Easter.

With one exception fifteen years later, this sermon is the only direct record that we possess of Knox's preaching style. Since it was by preaching and almost only by preaching that he did his work and won his fame, his style is worth a moment's consideration at this point.

Knox, to put it brutally, is commonly thought of today as a tub-thumper. This view is based almost entirely on a famous description of his sermons at the very end of his life, when he was too infirm to mount the pulpit steps unaided and yet, when fairly started, "was so active and vigorous that he was like to ding the pulpit in blads and fly out of it." But this is surely a picture of an orator in decay, when over-emphasis of gesture is used to eke out failing powers. Though we have so few records of his actual preaching in his prime, we have other indications of what it was like, for he was one of those men who obviously write as they speak. Both his pamphlets and his letters are rhetorical, dashed off, one would judge, with a flowing pen. Indeed, he had but the one style for all purposes, even for serious conversation; it was perhaps in these Berwick days that Sir Robert Bowes took a dislike to Knox's habit of addressing him as if he were a public meeting.

And this rhetoric was a sort which it is difficult to connect with shouting and fist-banging. It is mainly remarkable for its power of handling long sentences. The oratory that depends upon the rhythm of sustained periods may be accompanied by a wealth of gesture, but it is incompatible with staccato outbursts. The flow may indeed be interrupted from time to time by parentheses of sarcasm or adjuration, when we can imagine some extravagance of voice or attitude; but even here passion is hardly the dominant note.

This particular sermon of April 4th was a debating speech, and it is therefore more broken and pointed than usual. The argument is simple, consisting of two scholastic syllogisms. The first was the same that he had propounded in his disputation at St. Andrews: *That all worshipping, honouring or service of God invented by the brain of man in the religion of God, without His own express commandment, is idolatry. The Mass is invented by the brain of man without any commandment of God. Therefore it is idolatry.* This first part of the argument need not detain us, for it was only a preparation for the second part which contained the real attack. *But what if,* so Knox passed to this attack, *I shall admit to the Papists that the whole action of the Mass were the institution and very ordinance of God, and never one jot of man's invention therein—if I admit it to be the ordinance of God (as it is not), yet will I prove it abomination before God.*

The second syllogism was this: *All honouring or service of God, whereunto is added a wicked opinion, is abomination. Unto the Mass is added a wicked opinion. Therefore it is abomination.* The *wicked opinion* was, of course, the doctrine round which as we have seen, the battle was being set in array throughout Europe in this second phase of the Reformation. *It plainly hath been taught, by law it is decreed, and in the words of the Mass it is expressed, that the Mass is a sacrifice and oblation for the sins of the quick and the dead.* And the next sentence drives the point home in language that needs some slight modernization to sharpen it: *So the remission of sins undoubtedly was believed to be effected by that same action and work presently done by the Priest.*

The modern mind is not used to sermons, but as this was, after all, the central theme of Knox's life—since it was by his manner of handling it that he made a revolution and originated a tradition—we must needs sit down, for once, in his congregation and listen to his voice. But as the voice is unfamiliar, we may be allowed a few words of running commentary.

4

It begins soberly enough: the preacher will not be content with a mere assertion of the doctrine of justification by faith.

Sufficient it were for me, by the plain words of the foresaid prophets, herefor to conclude it abomination, seeing they plainly show that remission of sins cometh only of the mere mercy of God, without all deserving of us or of our work proceeding of ourselves; as Isaiah writeth saying: "I am He which removeth thine inquity, and that for My own sake." But if I shall prove this foresaid opinion which hath been holden of the Mass to be false, deceivable and vain, and that it is no sacrifice for sin—shall then either consuetude, long process of time or multitude of Papistical patrons defend that it is not abomination and idolatry?

Then comes the first step in the argument. Assuming the need for some sacrificial rite, what is the nature of the sacrifice? It cannot be any actual sacrifice, in the ordinary sense.

And first I ask, who offereth this sacrifice, and what is offered? The

Priest (sayeth the Papists) offereth Jesus Christ unto the Father. Then demand I if a man can offer unto God a more precious thing than himself. And it appeareth that not, for Paul commandeth that "we offer unto God a holy, lively and reasonable sacrifice," which he calleth our own bodies. And Jesus Christ, having nothing more precious than Himself, did offer up Himself. Paul sayeth, "by one oblation hath He made perfect for ever them which are sanctified"; and also "remission of sins once gotten, there resteth no more sacrifice." And thereto testifieth Jesus Christ Himself upon the cross, saying "consummatum est"; that is, whatever is required for pacifying My Father's wrath justly moved against sin, whatever is necessary for the reconciliation of mankind to the favour of My eternal Father, and whatever the purgation of the sins of the whole world required, is now complete and ended, so that no further sacrifice resteth for sin.

Hear, ye Papists! Two witness speak against you. How can ye deny the opinion of your Mass to be false and vain? Ye say it is a sacrifice for sin, but Jesus Christ and Paul say the only death of Christ was sufficient for sin, and after it resteth none other sacrifice. Speak! Or else ye are like to be condemned.

Follows the second step: if not a sacrifice in the plain sense, can the name be justified by any other interpretation? Can it, for instance, be in some sense a commemorative sacrifice?

Ye will say it is a memorial sacrifice, under the which Jesus Christ is offered unto the presence of God the Father by the Church, under the appearance of bread and wine, for remission of sins. I answer with Paul, "He appeareth now in the presence of God for us." So that it is not requisite that any man offer or represent Him to the Father, for that He doth Himself, making continual intercession for us.

But let us consider this doctrine more deeply. The Church, say they, offered Jesus Christ unto God the Father for a memorial sacrifice, or in a memorial sacrifice. Is there any oblivion or forgetfulness fallen on God the Father? Hath he forgotten the death and passion of Jesus Christ so that He need to be brought in memory thereof by any mortal man? Advert, Papists, and consider how Satan hath blinded you; ye do manifestly lie, and do not espy the same. Ye do blaspheme God at every word, and can ye not repent?

This is, theoretically, the weakest passage in the argument. Those who, like Knox, regard the Sacrament as a service of thanksgiving to God for His act of redemption, are skating on the thin ice of verbal distinctions when they deny that it may be both a commemoration before God and a sacrifice to Him. But Knox was speaking in terms of current practice, not of doctrinal theory. For that practice, talk of a memorial sacrifice was only a cloak. Now comes the real attack.

They say it is "sacrificium applicatorium," a sacrifice whereby they do and may apply the merits of Christ's passion unto sinners. They will be layers to of plasters! But I fear the wound be not well probed, and therefore that the plasters be unprofitable. Ye say ye may apply the merits of Christ's passion to whom ye list. This is proudly spoken. Then may ye make peace with God at your pleasure. But God sayeth that, as none may move His wrath against His chosen (and hereof ought ye to rejoice, brethren: the Pope, nor his Priests, nor Bishops whosoever, may not cause God to be angry against you, albeit they curse you with cross, bell and candle), so may no man compel Him to love or receive in favour but whom it pleaseth His infinite goodness.

I desire to be certified where God made His promise unto you, Papist Priests, that ye should have power to apply (as ye speak) the merits of Christ's passion to all and sundry who told or numbered money to you for that purpose. Taketh God any part of the profit that ye receive? Alas, I have compassion upon your vanity, but more upon the simple people that have been deceived by you and your false doctrine. Are ye better heard with God than Samuel was? He prayed for King Saul, and that most fervently, and yet obtained not his petition, nor might not apply any merits or holiness unto him. And it is said to Jeremiah, "Pray thou not for this people, for my heart is not towards it, for they love to go wrong and do not abstain from iniquity."

What say ye to these words, Papists? The prophet is forbidden to pray, for God sayeth He neither will hear him nor yet the people; He will accept none of their sacrifices, and that because the people manifestly rebelled against God, rejoiced in inquity, committed idolatry and abomination. And He manifestly showeth that nothing may appease Him but true repentance and conversion again unto God. O Priests! Hath there not as great iniquity abounded in your days as ever did from the beginning? Have ye not been enticers and leaders of the people to all idolatry? Yea, hath not the mischievous example of your abominable lives provoked thousands unto iniquity? And yet do ye say that ye may apply the merits of Christ's passion to whom ye list! Hear ye not that God never will accept prayers nor sacrifice till true repentance were found? Of that ye were dumb and always kept silence. Your clamour and crying was, "Come, come to the Mass; buy with money, substance and possessions, remission of your sins. We have the merits of Christ's passion. We may offer Jesus Christ unto the Father, whom He must needs receive for an acceptable sacrifice and satisfaction of all your sins."

5

The argument goes on, but we need not follow it further. In order, however, to round off our illustration of Knox's style, we must quote again from his conclusion: that contrast between the Mass and the Lord's Supper which was the centre of his thinking and the motive of his life. Here we come from the negative to the positive.

Let no man intend to excuse the Mass with the pretext of the Lord's Supper. For now will I prove that therewith it hath no congruence, but is express contrary to it, and hath taken the remembrance of the same out of mind. And, farther, it is blasphemous to the death of Jesus Christ. First they are contrary in institution, for the Lord's Supper was instituted to be a perpetual memory of those benefits which we have received by Jesus Christ and by His death. And first we should call to mind in what estate we stood in the loins of Adam, when that we all blasphemed in the majesty of God in His face. Secondly, that His own incomprehensible goodness moved Him to love us, most wretched and miserable, yea most wicked and blasphemous, and love most perfect compelled Him to show mercy. And mercy pronounced the sentence which was that His only Son should pay the price of our redemption. Which thing, being rightly called to memory in the present action of the Supper, could not but move us to unfeigned thanksgiving unto God the Father, and to His only Son Jesus, who hath restored us again to liberty and life, and this is it which Paul commandeth, saying, "As oft as ye shall eat of this bread and drink of this cup, ye shall declare the Lord's death till He come." That is, ye shall laud, magnify and extol the liberal kindness of God the Father and the infinite benefits which ye have received by Christ's death.

But the Mass is instituted, as the plain words thereof and their own laws do witness, to be a sacrifice for the sins of the quick and the dead; for doing of the which sacrifice God is bound not only to remit our sins but also to give us whatever we will ask. And that shall testify divers Masses celebrated for divers causes: some for peace in times of war; some for rain; some for fair weather; yea, and (alas, my heart abhorreth such abomination) some for sickness of bestial. They will say they severally take prayers for obtaining such things, and that is all which I desire they say; to the obtaining of such vain trifles direct they their whole purpose, and so profane the sacrament of Christ's body and blood which should never be used but in memory of Christ's death. Then should it not be used to pray that the tooth-ache be taken away from us, that our oxen should not take the lowing ill, our horse the spavin or farcy, and so of all manner of diseases for our cattle. Yea, what was it wherefor ye would not say Mass, perverted Priests?

In the Supper of the Lord all were equally participant, the bread being broke and the cup being distributed amongst all according to His holy commandment. In the Papistical Mass the congregation getteth nothing except the beholding of your duckings, noddings, crossings, turning, uplifting, which all are nothing, but a diabolical profanation of Christ's Supper. Now, duck, cross and nod as ye list, they are but your own inventions. And finally, brethren, ye gat nothing, but gazed and beheld while that one did eat and drink all.

It shall not excuse you to say the congregation is participant spiritually. O wicked Antichrists! Sayeth not Jesus Christ, "Eat of this and drink of this, all do this in remembrance of Me"? Christ commandeth not that we should gaze upon it, bow, duck and beck thereto, but that we should eat and drink thereof ourselves, and not that we should behold others do the same, unless that we would confess the death of Jesus Christ to appertain nothing to us. For when I eat and drink at that table I openly confess the fruit and virtue of Christ's body, of His blood and passion, to appertain to myself, and that I am a member of His mystical body, and that God the Father is appeased with me, notwithstanding my first corruption and present infirmities. Judge, brethren, what comfort have these men taken from us which will that the sight thereof shall be sufficient.

So the sermon draws to its peroration, but from that we need not quote. It has, however, also a postscript, and that is essential to the balance of the whole.

I will ye observe that, where I say there resteth no sacrifice nor yet is there any priests, I mean any priests having power to offer such oblations. Otherwise I do know that all true Christians are kings and priests, and do daily offer unto God a sacrifice most acceptable: the mortification of their affections, as Paul commanded the Romans. But hereof may I not remain to speak presently.

6

Such was the voice of Knox when he joined in the strife of tongues that raged through England in these days. And the possessor of that voice was not likely to be allowed to remain a garrison chaplain. He might be content with Berwick, especially in that summer of 1550, the first summer of peace, when men might pass at ease up the Tweed and down the coast. In such a time, the Liberty of Norhamshire would be a pleasant country, with a growing field of work. Soldiers, villagers and fishermen, from the depot at Holy Island to Norham and the valley of the Till, relieved from fears and alarms, might turn a new ear to the Scots preacher from the central garrison. But Knox was soon to be called from these pleasures and this work. The political and religious climate of England was changing, and his work was to change with it.

It was probably this summer that he met a lady who was to play some part in his life and an even larger part in the world's gossip about him. Sir Robert Bowes came of an old Durham family, the Bowes of Streatlam, and his younger brother, Richard, had married the co-heiress of as old a Yorkshire family, Elizabeth Aske of Aske in Richmondshire. Their son was to inherit Streatlam and his descendants were to live there for two hundred years, till another Bowes heiress married John Lyon, Earl of Strathmore, and united her name with his. Richard Bowes had followed his brother to the Border as early as the beginning of the Scots war. Together in 1542 they had led the raid into Scotland which ended in the disaster of

Haddonrig, and had shared captivity as prisoners of war. For the last two years Sir Richard had been Captain of Norham Castle. His eldest son, some twenty-two years old, was commanding a troop of horse, and his wife, with at least one of his daughters, Marjorie, had come from Aske to keep him company. The brothers were Catholically inclined, and it is perhaps not fanciful to say that Elizabeth Bowes had some reason, on her side of the family, to hold the same opinions. A younger branch of the Askes had served the Earls of Northumberland and had given a leader to the Pilgrimage of Grace only fourteen years before. But at Berwick she (presumably) heard Knox preach and is generally supposed to have incontinently cast her troubled soul at his feet. In fact, however, we know nothing of their friendship until more than two years later. It belongs to Knox's days of trouble, not to his days of peace.

CHAPTER IX

THE PREACHER AND THE POLITICIANS
1551–54

I

WHEN KNOX preached at Newcastle in April 1550 the government of England had already passed into new hands. In the previous October Somerset had fallen. That was inevitable: his foreign policy had ended in disaster both in Scotland and in France; his home policy had been discredited by the Catholic rising in Cornwall and by Ket's agrarian rebellion in the eastern counties. But his supplanter, John Dudley, Earl of Warwick, was a poor substitute in all but political astuteness. Abroad, he accepted disaster; not content with concluding a defeatist treaty with France, he diverted England into the French orbit. "Now that you have eaten the cabbages," he told the French ambassador in the autumn of 1550, "I suppose you want the garden." And he left the garden gate open. At home, if Somerset was the first Tory democrat, Dudley was the first Whig. He did not invent landlordism and political bribery, far from it; but he made them a system. For the first time enclosures were legalized and Parliaments packed. Henry VIII had used the doctrine of treason to fortify his personal government against his new nobility; Dudley revived the laws repealed by Somerset in order to erect that nobility into an oligarchy. Henry had crushed the northern rebels in 1537 with every circumstance of perfidy and brutality, but he had used his victory to redress the balance between landlord and tenant; Dudley saw to it that the destruction of Ket's levies on Mousehold Heath in August 1549 should be a landlord's victory.

His religious policy was partly determined, no doubt, by the motive of spoliation, but there was shrewder calculation in it than that. If he was to establish his power, he must win public opinion, and popular propaganda was, in those days, in the hands of the Church. Clerics alone could mediate between the political gentry and the common people. And though England was not Protestant, it was anticlerical. Even the northern rebels in 1536, Catholic though they were, had declared that "there is no manner of estate within this realm that hath more need of reformation nor to be put under good government than the spiritual men." The old clerics were too discredited and too slack for Dudley's purpose; he must turn to the new preachers. So, though he had overthrown Somerset by a Protestant-Catholic coalition, in February 1550 he threw over his Catholic allies. From that time on Somerset's policy of toleration was reversed. Persecution was never serious; the only persons who suffered death for their faith were one Englishman and one Dutchman, both for heretical opinions about the Person of Christ. But the enforcement of uniformity became the Government's aim—and uniformity on a much "lower" level than the First Book of Common Prayer. It was a queer foreshadowing of that later alliance between Low Church and Whig which seemed so natural to the historians of the nineteenth century and seems so questionable today.

This change of political climate brought Knox out of his seclusion at Berwick. Towards the end of 1550 he was appointed preacher in Newcastle and held forth in the pulpit of St. Nicholas's Church. How far he had the official cure of souls there seems uncertain; a certain William Purye appears to have been vicar in 1551–53. A year later he was appointed one of the six royal chaplains, two of whom were to preach in the north. Knox was one of these and Newcastle remained his headquarters until September 1552, when he took his turn to preach before the Court in London.

Of his first year in Newcastle we have no record. He no doubt encountered a good deal of opposition. The north clung more or less to the old Church; the Pilgrimage of Grace was still a fairly recent memory. Sir Robert Brandling, Mayor of Newcastle, was probably a Catholic; so was Shrewsbury, whom Dudley had appointed Lord President of the Council in the North in February 1550. This appointment, made at the very moment when the new dictator was ousting the Catholics from the Council in London, was a significant concession to northern prejudice. But Knox was not the man for such concessions, and Newcastle probably grew not a little restive under his preaching. He had a faithful congregation there, but there were too many immigrant Scots in it for the taste of the local residents. Still, we have no reason to suppose that in this first year he had much cause to regret his transfer from Berwick. And his appointment as royal chaplain is at least an indication that his preaching had proved reasonably successful.

2

This appointment was the more remarkable for being made at a moment when the new chaplain had just startled Newcastle by a sudden incursion into politics. On 16th October 1551, Dudley executed his long-planned *coup d'état*. Somerset, who had been re-admitted to the Council eighteen months before, within six months of his fall, was arrested and sent to the Tower. Dudley and his friends appeared in new trappings. Dorset, son-in-law of Henry VIII's younger sister and father of Lady Jane Grey, was created Duke of Suffolk; Paulet, Marquess of Winchester; Dudley himself, Duke of Northumberland. And forthwith on All Saints' Day Knox burst out in the pulpit of St. Nicholas with a sweeping condemnation of this palace revolution. He declared that *the devil and his ministers intended only the subversion of God's true religion by that mortal hatred among those which ought to have been most assuredly knit together by Christian charity and by benefits received.* The vineyard of the Lord *would bring forth no good fruit*, and so its *hedges, ditches, towers and wine-press* were being broken down. And apparently in this tragedy the new Duke of Northumberland was cast for the role neither of hero nor of villain, but of puppet. It was *the wicked and envious Papists* who had brought about this *ungodly breach of charity.* Having used Northumberland, they would throw him aside, for they *diligently minded the overthrow of him that to his own destruction procured the death of his innocent friend.*

Does this outburst mark the beginning of the prophetic mania which later took possession of Knox's mind? In a sense, yes, but then, in a sense too, it was no mania at all. There was shrewdness as well as naïvety in Knox's interpretation. Taking a long view, it was, perhaps, more shrewd than Dudley's own calculations. Puzzled by the twists and turns of the political adventurer, he fell into the usual error of making wild guesses at a "hidden hand"; but in essence he was right. Just then England was, in fact, the puppet of Europe. Henry II of France had had a finger in the plots and risings of 1549. He was Somerset's enemy and he thought that he had Dudley in his pocket. He thought, too, that Charles V was intriguing with Somerset, and he may have been right. And who were Henry and Charles to pull the strings of Protestant England—Charles who, the year before, had issued the consolidated edict which was to be the charter of persecution in the Netherlands, Henry, who, this same summer of 1551, had followed suit with the Edict of Châteaubriand?

Moreover, how could such suspicions as Knox's fail to be confirmed by the fact that Somerset was sent to the scaffold alone in the following January, while all his supposed accomplices got off scot-free or were even advanced in office—all except poor Tunstall on whose diocese Dudley had his own designs? Henry Neville, Earl of Westmorland, for instance, who had tried to plot a rising in the north in 1550, got Somerset's Garter and was made Hereditary Sheriff in Durham; while Shrewsbury was made Keeper of all the Royal Castles in Yorkshire and Nottingham. Brilliantly successful though Dudley's tactics might appear, he knew himself that the public opinion of the country was against him. He had not dared to summon a Parliament for two years; the one which met after Somerset's execution was restive in spite of his attempts to manipulate the elections; not till March 1553 did he dare to risk another, and then he was careful to pack it thoroughly. Knox was representing the sound instinct of the nation when he judged that Somerset's *away-taking* had fatally weakened both the Protestant cause and the government of England on which that cause depended.

And he went on saying so, the stronger Dudley's power in the north became. The north had always been one of the new Duke's main cares. He had taken the Wardenship of the East and Middle Marches soon after Somerset's original fall, intending to proceed there himself; later, abandoning this intention, he had made Sir Robert Bowes his Deputy Warden, but had entrenched his power in Northumberland by obtaining a grant from the Crown of the

Percy manors there. While he was preparing his plot against Somerset in 1551 he had sent his close friend, Dorset, to Berwick as Warden-General of all the Marches. Bowes had been transferred to London, sworn of the Privy Council in September 1551, and made Master of the Rolls in the following year. Now Dudley took the Warden-Generalship himself and came north in June 1552.

Crossing the Tyne, he found Knox in full blast. He had to listen to his preaching *in the town of Newcastle and in other places more*. He seems to have listened to him with mixed feelings. This was not the sort of fire-brand that could safely be left burning in his new bailiwick. He was Lord Justice and Lord Lieutenant in Northumberland, Cumberland, Newcastle and Berwick; he was garrisoning Alnwick and Tynemouth with his own men. What sort of storms might not this prophet of calamity raise there? Already he was claiming confirmation of his predictions in the epidemic of sweating sickness which was running through the north; this, he was saying, was the first of God's judgments—with perhaps a side-glance at the fact that Dudley's own daughter had just died of the fever. The influx of Scots into Newcastle, too, was a danger. Scotland, after all, was "in the possession" of the French King, and the Council had been anxiously surveying the fortifications at Berwick and Norham. They were irked by continual demands from Scotland and France for transit passports; some sort of *cordon sanitaire* must be maintained on the Border. Moreover, how would this purist regard that ingenious piece of graft that Dudley was contemplating in Durham: a division of the diocese by which the King might appropriate—and later grant to his faithful Warden-General—"£2,000 a year of the best lands within the north parts of his realm"? On the other hand, a first-rate preacher was not an asset to throw away. He was coming south that autumn to preach before the Court and that would be the time to find other work for him.

3

So Knox came to London, perhaps in the Duke's own retinue. Dudley, having appointed Lord Wharton as his deputy on the Marches, joined the Council at Salisbury towards the end of

August 1552, and six weeks later a foreign observer assumed that Knox was his chaplain. What followed confirmed his resolve that Knox should not return.

In the previous spring, Parliament had passed a new Act of Uniformity, and the new Book of Common Prayer was now ready. In September copies were actually coming from the press. Knox doubtless saw a copy on his arrival, and one thing in it touched him nearly. The first Book had contained no specific direction that the laity at the Lord's Supper should communicate kneeling. It had been taken for granted but not stated, and Knox had been within his technical rights in carrying out his own ideas at Berwick and New-castle. Other ministers had done the same. But the new Book con-tained a rubric which prescribed kneeling; and it was to be enforced from All Saints' Day next. Knox was due to preach at Windsor hardly a month before that date. He appeared in the pulpit of the Royal Chapel in the last week of September primed to the lips with this grievance.

"He inveighed with great freedom" and he made something of a sensation. It was not the first protest that the Council had received; Hooper, now Bishop of Gloucester, had urged the same point eighteen months before. Now, however, on September 27th, the Council instructed the King's printers "to stay in any wise the utter-ing of the books of the new service," and Cranmer was called upon to defend the rubric. He found little difficulty in doing so. The argument from Scripture, he wrote on October 7th, was absurd: no doubt Christ and his disciples did not kneel at the Last Supper, but neither did they sit; "if we will follow the plain words of Scripture, we shall rather receive it lying down on the ground, as the custom of the world at that time was almost everywhere, and as the Tartars and Turks use yet at this day."

The point was disputed between the bishops and debated at the Council table, but it was not settled before Knox had intervened again. On October 20th, the royal chaplains were asked to report on the new draft Articles of Religion, and Knox seized on this tactical advantage. The 38th Article affirmed, not only that the new Book was "godly in respect of doctrinal truth," but also that "the charac-ter of its ceremonies" was "in no wise repugnant to the wholesome liberty of the Gospel." No, said the chaplains, *kneeling in the action of the Lord's Table has sprung from a false opinion, and feedeth the same in the hearts of men, and permitteth the idolater to continue in his idolatry.*

The result was a compromise. On October 27th, the Council decided to retain the practice of kneeling but to explain it by the famous "Black Rubric," which declares that by kneeling "no adoration is intended or ought to be done." Knox accepted the compromise and recommended it to his friends at Berwick. He regretted it, but he would *neither gainstand godly magistrates, neither break common order, nor yet contend with his superiors or fellow preachers*; his old flock might conform with a quiet conscience to this *especial commandment of the upper powers.* A little later Article 38 was slightly remodelled so as to omit mention of "ceremonies." Such are the last-minute shifts by which Englishmen are wont to settle, not only their political programmes, but their formularies of faith and worship.

But, indeed, Knox's mind was not on formularies. This short October episode was to him only an episode. He had not sought to lay down the law; he had pleaded only for liberty, and he was puzzled and hurt at the storm he had raised. Cranmer, the moderate, whom he admired as he never admired the fervent Hooper, had called him, by implication at least, a "glorious and unquiet spirit." Smaller men were no doubt using even harder words. Dr. Richard Cox, Canon of Windsor and Vice-Chancellor of Oxford, Cranmer's favourite assistant in liturgiology, never forgave this "runagate Scot" for meddling in matters too high for him. It was this charge of presumption that Knox was most concerned to refute when he wrote to his Berwick congregation. Let them not think that *some spirit of pride* had crept in upon him; still less let them *suspect craft or deceit* in him. His quarrel was not with *my fathers whom I fear and honour and my brethren in labours and profession, whom I unfeignedly love.* His quarrel was with the politicians and it was to very different issues that he now addressed himself in the pulpit, first at Hampton Court, whither the King had moved at the end of September, and later probably at Westminster.

4

Knox was making his first direct acquaintance with politicians and he sickened at them. Like all the reformers of Christendoms save Luther in his early years, he had put his trust in princes. Above all he had trusted them in England. In these dark years they were the last hope of Protestantism in Europe. And now, what did he find in them? In the words of Ridley, Bishop of London: "insatiable covetousness, filthy carnality and voluptuousness, intolerable ambition and pride, ungodly loathesomeness to hear poor men's causes and to hear God's words." The King was all that Knox had expected: *of so godly disposition towards virtue and the truth of God that to my knowledge none of his years did ever match him in that behalf, if he might have been lord of his own will.* But his life evidently hung upon a thread; since his illness in the previous spring men had talked freely of his death. And he was pathetically alone. Round him was a *multitude of wicked men placed in authority,* guilty of *crimes so manifest and heinous that the earth could not hide the innocent blood, neither yet could the heavens behold without shame the craft, the deceit, the violence and oppression that universally were wrought.*

Fanatical rhetoric? Hardly, for the judgment of historians has been no milder; and the government of England smelt badly even in the not too delicate nostrils of the sixteenth century. Dr. Cox, no squeamish respecter of pious foundations, had been protesting against their spoliation by the politicians; two years earlier the heart of the English ambassador in France had been "made to bleed by hearing the base sort of the French Court talk of the buying and selling of offices in England, the decaying of grammar schools and the universities, with many other enormities." At any rate, not only Knox but all his fellow-chaplains were in full cry against these scandals. Their denunciations grew hotter in the following Lent but they were already hot enough.

It was not only in the pulpit that Knox vented his disgust. He had made friends with two London families, the Lockes and Hickmans, both merchants of the City. Mrs. Anne Locke became his intimate friend, and to her and Mrs. Hickman he unbosomed himself. Though no man might believe it, the whole fabric of the English reformation was cracking; they might find themselves driven out of England as he, Knox, had been driven from Scotland. Later, he was to remind them of his foresight.

It has been said that, during these years in England, Knox hardened with success and with the triumph of his cause. Surely it was a curious hardening, On the only evidence we have, he hardened, not against his religious opponents, but against the secular leaders of his own party. From the outset, so far as we know, he never shared his party's admiration for Dudley. He never thought him, as Hooper did, a "most faithful and intrepid soldier of Jesus Christ." He had no love for Cuthbert Tunstall, *dreaming Durham* as he called him later; but he gave Dudley no thanks for sending the old man to the Tower, the 11th of this October, on a trumped-up charge. In sober fact, Knox was up against the worst government that England has ever known. He was often wild in his attacks on its members, he tended to see Papists behind every bush, but if public petulance in such circumstances is to be described as spiritual hardness it is a sort of hardness very familiar today among the mildest and most respectable politicians.

It was at this moment that Dudley sent for him and offered him the bishopric of Rochester. The offer, as the Duke explained to Secretary Cecil on October 27th, with amiable frankness, was designed to kill three birds with one stone. Knox would be "a whetstone to quicken and sharp the Bishop of Canterbury, whereof he hath need," and "he would be a great confounder of the anabaptists lately sprung up in Kent." The humour of this proposal lay in the fact that, three weeks before, Cranmer had pointed out to the Council that Knox's desire to exclude from Church worship all ceremonies not expressly prescribed by Scripture must lead straight to anabaptism. The second bird was an even funnier fowl. If Knox were moved to Kent he would not be a disturbing influence in the north when it came to enforcing the new Prayer Book there. He might, by inference, disturb Kent as much as he liked; Cranmer would be none the worse for being pinned to his diocese by home worries. And lastly, if he were transferred, "the family of Scots now inhabiting Newcastle, chiefly for his fellowship, would not continue there, wherein many resort to them out of Scotland, which is not requisite." This last bird was probably Dudley's real quarry, for, a month later, when nothing had happened, he urged again "that some order be taken for Knox, otherwise you shall not avoid the Scots from out of Newcastle." This second letter produced its effect. The scheme was approved and the offer was made.

Unfortunately Knox refused it point blank and on December 7th was sent down to Chelsea to explain himself to the Duke. He came at a bad moment. The Duke's pet scheme for dividing and milking the diocese of Durham had turned on the willingness of the Dean to take over Tunstall's crozier and surrender the Bishop's "stately houses" to the Crown. But the Dean, wonderful to relate, had declined "under the colour of a false conscience." He had done more. He had actually indicated that he did not know whether the good Duke were "a dissembler in religion or not." Really these clerics were intolerable; why should they "prettily malign and judge of others against good charity upon a froward judgment"? And now Knox had upset the other scheme. He had shown himself "neither grateful nor pleasable." So the Duke would "have no more to do with him but to wish him well."

5

With such ambiguous good wishes Knox started for Newcastle again on December 9th. He did not go in disgrace. A letter from the Council went with him, praising his services and commending him to Wharton. But he went in weariness and disgust. *This day I am more vile and of low reputation in my own eyes than I was either that day that my feet was chained in the prison of dolour (the galleys I mean) or yet that day that I was delivered by God's only providence from the same.* He was ill too; his letters in the following months complain constantly of his *old malady*. His nerves were on edge, and within a month he was the centre of a worse storm in Newcastle than he had ever been in London.

He signalized his return to the pulpit of St. Nicholas by a Christmas sermon in which he hit out more wildly than usual. Those who in secret opposed the religious changes of the day were *secret traitors to the Crown and Commonwealth of England. They thirsted nothing more than the King's death which their iniquity would procure.* Newcastle was up in arms at once. Brandling laid an information against him and within a week Wharton was writing to Dudley for instructions, being "not altogether without suspicion how Knox's doings hath been taken" in London. Knox wrote, too, and Dudley sent his letter to Cecil in order that he might "perceive what perplexity the poor soul remaineth in at this present." It may have been at this time that the Sheriff in Durham, too, intervened in the quarrel, on the strength of some sermon in his county. *My Lord of Westmorland has written unto me this Wednesday at six of the clock at night, immediately thereafter to repair unto him, as I will answer at my peril. I could not obtain license to remain the time of the sermon upon the morrow.* At any rate he was formally arraigned before some authority: *against me were written articles and I compelled to answer, as unto an action of treason.*

The storm blew over. Knox was supported from London. Dudley "would not wish his abode should be of great continuance in those parts"; he had better be used as a travelling preacher; but it would never do to let him be hounded out of the north. The Mayor of Newcastle had a "malicious stomach towards the King's proceedings" and was trying to score a tactical victory. Wharton and Brandling should be told that "his Highness hath the poor man and his doings in gracious favour." Let it be made clear that "no man shall be so hardy to vex him or trouble him for setting forth the King's Majesty's most godly proceedings." And let Brandling especially be rebuked "for his greedy accusation of the poor man." All the same if Knox was to be a travelling preacher it would be no bad thing to give him a base of operations in London rather than in Newcastle. So on February 2nd the Council asked Cranmer to present him to the vicarage of All Hallows, Bread Street.

Knox remained in the north for barely two months, in ill health, full of *great labours* and brooding over the certainty of disaster. *The pain of my head and stomach troubles me greatly; daily I find my body decay. Unless my pain shall cease, I will altogether become unprofitable. Your messenger found me in bed, after a sore troubled and most dolorous night.* Yet he must preach, not only in Newcastle but elsewhere. On the days *of study and prayer unto God* which he tried to keep, he must needs scribble his forebodings on his Bible margins—for instance:

130

tribulation commonly followeth that Church where Christ Jesus is most truly preached. Such jottings became his sermon-texts and the note of prophecy in them grew: *The last trumpet is blowing within the realm of England and therefore ought everyone to prepare himself for battle. For if the trumpet should altogether be put to silence, then shall it never blow again with the like force within the said realm till the coming of the Lord Jesus.*

6

By March 1st he was in London again, to be offered All Hallows —and to refuse. Apparently also he had to answer before the Council some *heinous delations* brought against him. His answer was satisfactory; *this assault of Satan has been to his confusion.*

If we are to accept the dating of his letters in the transcribed copies, he stayed only a few days, long enough to hear the Lent preachings before the Court. His own sermons paled before the outpourings of these chaplains—and they were not all of Knox's school. Grindal, future Archbishop of Canterbury, *plainly spake the death of the King's Majesty, complaining on his household servants and officers.* Haddon, one of the greatest Latinists of the day, *learnedly opened the causes of the bypast plagues, affirming that worse were to follow unless repentance should shortly be found.* Bradford, who was to die at the stake two years later, *spared not the proudest.* The politicians were furious; Dudley insulted Cranmer openly in the House of Lords; and Knox betook himself again to Newcastle intending to stay there at least till Easter.

But early in April he was back once more, to take his turn in the Court pulpit. One Sunday, before April 12th, he preached his last sermon before the King at Westminster. If his own later report of it is not exaggerated, his sermon outdid all the efforts of his colleagues. *Entreating this place of Scripture—He that eateth bread with me hath lifted up his heel against me—I made this affirmation: That commonly it was seen that the most godly princes had officers and chief councillors most ungodly, conjured enemies to God's true religion and traitors to their princes. And for proof I recited the histories of Achitophel, Shebna and Judas. If David and Hezekiah were deceived by traitorous counsellors, how much more a young and innocent King? I am greatly afraid that Achitophel be counsellor, that Judas bear the purse and that Shebna be scribe, controller and treasurer.*

The sermon is famous, with its implied portrait of Dudley as Achitophel and of Paulet as Shebna—Shebna the *crafty fox*, the Lord Treasurer who *could show such a fair countenance to the King*. But there is a touch in the portrait of Achitophel which is usually missed. *Of Achitophel it is written that his counsel in those days was like the oracle of God*. Knox could attack in the grand manner, with a salute to his opponent's greatness.

But this sermon was a little too much. On April 14th Knox was summoned before the Council at Greenwich. Why had he refused All Hallows? The old question of kneeling at Communion came up again, but after *great contention* he was *dismissed with some gentle speeches*. He was, however, kept in London. On March 18th the Council had written to Wharton again "for the avoiding of the Scots that dwell in Newcastle"; they should not have their preacher back, especially in his present frame of mind.

So in June Knox was sent to preach in Buckinghamshire and remained there, with flying visits to London, for some two months. He was there when the King died on July 6th; on the 16th he was pouring forth an incoherent lamentation in the pulpit of Amersham; on the 19th he was in London, growling over the *fires of joy and riotous banqueting at the proclamation of Mary*. Dudley's twelve-day *coup d'état* was over; but Knox was not one of his accomplices. At Amersham, where Sir Edward Hastings and the gentry were raising the county for Mary, he had inveighed against the idea of *marriage, confederacy or league* with the Empire or with any Catholic power; he had denounced the Emperor as Nero; but his subsequent judgment on Dudley was no less severe: *Our King is taken away from us, and the devil enflameth the heart of that wretched and unhappy man (whom I judge more to be lamented than hated) to covet the Imperial Crown of England to be established to his posterity.*

London was no place for Knox after Mary had entered it in triumph, but the fever of activity was still on him. He must preach where he could. In July he was at Carlisle, but when, on August 16th, Mary issued her proclamation of temporary toleration, he came south again. Perhaps he was in London when Dudley went to the scaffold on the 22nd, asserting that he died, as he had really lived, in the Catholic faith. From London Knox went to Kent. He was full of labours and anxious to attest his loyalty to the Queen. He prayed for her, but he prayed also that papistry might not be suffered to prevail in the realm. It was prevailing; England was no longer a place for foreign Protestants. On September 15th Laski, with 175 of his congregation, set sail from Gravesend; perhaps Knox saw them off and thought of accompanying them. He was in London on September 20th and again on November 6th; but in mid-December he set off for the north, *with less money than ten* groats and *not in good case to have travelled* being *soure troubled in the gravel.* On the 22nd he was in Newcastle *with troubled heart and weak body.* Parliament had met in October and in November had passed the Act forbidding, as from December 20th, any "form of service but what had been used in the last year of Henry VIII." He thought of going to Berwick, but his friends persuaded him *partly by admonition, partly by tears* to flee the country. By the end of January he was in Dieppe.

7

The pace at which Knox lived during these months was quickened by private worries. He had become engaged to Marjorie Bowes and her mother was anxious that the two should marry. His friendship with the mother has been the occasion of much facetious comment, but the known facts about it are ordinary enough.

In 1553 it was a friendship between a woman of, perhaps, fifty-five and a rather awkward bachelor of thirty-nine. The tradition is that it had begun at Berwick three years before, and that, soon after, Knox had betrothed himself to the daughter out of affection for the mother. But there is little evidence for that tradition. The earliest of Knox's dated letters belong to 1553, and a rather different interpretation can easily be put upon them. For all they contain, Knox may have been drawn to the mother partly because he had fallen in love with the daughter, and an ordinary acquaintance between pastor and parishioner may have quite recently grown into friendship. On the whole, something like this is the more probable interpretation.

In his last months at Berwick, and at intervals since, Knox had been indebted to Mrs. Bowes for many kindnesses of the sort that a gentlewoman in her own country may show to a stranger not too popular with other local magnates. In return, he spent hours in reading the Bible with her and found her appetite for instruction stimulating, if a little exacting. She had long been a victim of religious melancholia and when she proceeded from doctrinal enquiries to intimate confessions, he winced and became dour, for he had a troublesome conscience of his own and her naïvetés pricked him unpleasantly.

So it went on until, perhaps, the summer of 1552 when Knox betrothed himself to the daughter. The betrothal probably took place before witnesses and was, therefore, a legal marriage; but at the moment neither party thought of claiming it as such. Then followed Knox's four months absence in London from August to December. Left alone with her conscience, Mrs. Bowes fell back into fundamental doubts. Salvation was by faith alone, but had she faith? Was she saved after all? Knox was always declaiming against idolaters, but, on his own showing, had she not been the worst of idolaters? And so on. Tens of thousands were asking the same sort of questions all over Europe; what became cant in a later generation was grim earnest in these days. "I hear the wicked enemy assaults you with heavy thoughts," wrote Luther to Elsa von Kanitz in 1527, offering comfort in almost the same words as Knox. A civilization does not pull down its house in search of hidden treasure without learning that "truth is agony and bloody sweat." And Knox, as we have seen, was very near despair himself. So, on his return to Newcastle, the two began to exchange the very intimacies from which Knox used to *start back. Dolour complained to dolour*, and Knox got rather the worse of the exchange. He must always be comforting, while she was always touching him on the raw. *My daily labours must now increase and therefore spare me as much as ye may.* Yet on the whole it helped him. Though she intruded on him even in his days *of study and prayer to God*, and though in his chronic illness *nothing is more contrarious to my health than writing*, he was able to answer his own doubts in answering hers. Those whose trade is talking are seldom happy unless they can do their thinking aloud.

A nation pays dearly for its humourists: no Englishman can see this sort of friendship without thinking of the *Pickwick Papers*. And, indeed, some moments of this correspondence are pure Dickens, as when Mrs. Bowes accuses herself of all the sins of Sodom and Gomorrah and Knox's duty compels him to point out that she does not know what those sins were. There is, too, the vignette of Knox just arrived in London on 28th February 1553, talking of Mrs. Bowes to *three honest poor women* who *were come to me complaining of their great infirmities and showing unto me the great assaults of the enemy. And I was opining the cause and commodities thereof, whereby all our eyes wept at once for the space of two hours.* In the middle of these lamentations one of Mrs. Bowes's weariful letters was put into his hands *whereof a part I read unto them and one of them said —O, would to God I might speak to that person, for I perceive that there be some more troubled than I.* Reading that, it is difficult not to think of another lady in the Fleet snuggery who "arrived at a very pathetic and decent pitch of misery."

But humour has one compensating advantage: it is at least anti-septic. Having laughed at Stiggins and Mrs. Weller we do not sus-pect them of impropriety. Knox's contemporaries were not so charitable. In his old age the slanders of his opponents forced him to a public refutation; and there was plenty of tittle-tattle in Northum-berland at the time. *Very shame has holden me from your company when I was most surely persuaded that God had appointed me to comfort your afflicted soul. More ought I to regard the affliction ye sustain than any slander of such as knoweth not the necessity of them that labour under the cross.* Knox was in a false position, but it was one which few minis-ters of religion can wholly escape. The relations between a spiritual director and his lady penitents are apt to be uneasy, even when priesthood sets him on a pedestal; the Protestant pastor, descending from that pedestal, necessarily runs a greater risk. Yet, to some tastes at least, Knox's letters ring more true than Fénélon's; and, to those who know Fénélon's correspondence, Mrs. Bowes's conscience is a pleasanter study than Madame de Montbéron's.

8

Indeed, Knox's tone in this correspondence is entitled at least to our respect. His rolling style always verges on pomposity, but on the whole he keeps a high level of dignity. Though sentimental, he is seldom sloppy. Quotation would be wearisome; two sentences sufficiently show the tenor of the whole: *And so, sister, ye are sick but shall not die. Your faith is weak and sore troubled, but ye are not unfaithful, nor yet shall not your infirmity be imputed unto you.* And Mrs. Bowes herself should not be too rashly written down a fool. Knox's own description of her many years after in reply to scandal-mongers has done her some disservice. She was the worst case of a troubled conscience that he had ever known; he had *seen her not for a start but in long continuance pour forth tears and send to God dolorous complaints oftener than ever I heard man or woman in my life.* But melancholy is not hysteria and we do, after all, know something else about Mrs. Bowes. A woman has some claim to be judged by her sons, especially when she has had the chief part in their upbringing. Two of Mrs. Bowes's sons are known to history: one was not more than fourteen and the other only six when their father was taken prisoner at Haddonrig. One of these, on his death in 1580, was described, in a letter to Cecil himself, as "the surest pillar" of Elizabeth's government in the north. Both were among the most valued and respected servants of that government and kept the Queen's flag flying in Durham during the rising of 1569. It is at least possible to imagine a picture of their mother very different from the "weariful woman" even of R. L. Stevenson's sympathetic study.

As to Marjorie, the view that Knox's betrothal was a tepid affair rests solely on the fact that his first (and only surviving) letter to her is undated and refers to her mother's spiritual troubles. It is an argument from silence. Again, the assumption that Mrs. Bowes's family disliked both the friendship and the marriage rests on the same slender foundation. Certainly in September 1553 when Knox was in London, George Bowes, the eldest son, acted as intermediary for his mother's letters to him, and when Knox went north in December Marjorie's elder sister met him with family messages. It is at least possible that the children shared even then their mother's religious opinions and took her side.

It is not even certain that their father was unalterably opposed to the marriage. All we know is that in September 1553 Mrs. Bowes had recently asked his consent, and on the 20th of that month Knox in London told her that he had written to Sir Richard and that he would charge himself with the negotiation, whatever it might cost. *It becomes me now to jeopard my life for the comfort and deliverance of my own flesh, as that I will do by God's own grace.* Six weeks later he broached the subject to Marjorie's uncle, Sir Robert. His request must apparently have been that, in view of the then pending repeal of the law permitting clerical marriages, the legal validity of his contract with Marjorie should be recognized by the family.

The request was natural, but it was also delicate and the occasion was hardly well chosen. For one thing Sir Robert had his own difficulties. As a member of the Council he had implicated himself in Dudley's conspiracy. Like other civil servants in the same position his offence had been overlooked, but he had not been readmitted to the Council and had resigned the Mastership of the Rolls. For another thing, he was just starting on an official mission to the Border. At any rate, he would not even give Knox a hearing. Knox wrote of this rebuff in tones of profound dejection. He had meant to speak *in most simple manner*, but Sir Robert, one fears from old experience, forestalled him: "Away with your rhetorical reasons for I will not be persuaded with them." All seemed over. He would be driven to leave England, *for I cannot abide the disdainful hatred* of those on whose kindness he thought he could rely. *Such things as I have desired and ye and others have long desired are never like to come to pass.*

This interview may indeed have had a good deal to do with Knox's flight. Sir Robert may well have given the Government a hint that he should be watched. Anyway, a messenger carrying his letters to Mrs. Bowes was arrested, and, though the letters were innocuous, he felt that he must find out how things were going at Berwick. He hoped *to have spoken with my wife* but his arrival in the north *was so soon noised abroad that with great difficulty could I be convoyed from one place to another.* Though he did not think himself in as much danger as his friends suspected, he decided on flight. *And so can I not espy how that either of you both I can speak at this time.* A few days later he sent his farewell in the form of an exposition of the sixth Psalm: *I cannot express the pain which I think I might suffer to have the presence of you and of others that be like troubled but a few days. But God shall gather us at His good pleasure, if not in this wretched and miserable life, yet in that estate where death may not dissever us.*

Chapter X

THE PAMPHLETEER

1554

I

KNOX STAYED one month at Dieppe, and then set out for Switzerland. His flight was the turning point of his life. But it was much more: it was a turning point in the history of Europe. Something new was about to happen, and this Hejira marks the beginning of it.

The flight itself was the most natural thing in the world, as natural as it had been for Bucer and the rest to leave the cities of Germany in 1547. The evangelical preacher of that day belonged to no nation; invited to teach in this or that city by prince or municipal council, he was the guest of the government and must go elsewhere when its policy changed. So Knox the foreigner had come to England, and so he went. Of course he feared death and fled because he feared it, but neither duty nor honour requiring him to stay. He had no cure of souls; he was deserting no flock committed to his care. His only commission was his royal chaplaincy, and that had been withdrawn. As to any private responsibilities, they were, if anything, an added reason for flight; his presence in England might compromise the Bowes family, but could not help them. As a landowner's daughter and a Privy Councillor's niece, Marjorie was safe; as a preacher's wife she might be in the gravest danger.

Perhaps there was another reason for flight. Knox had been in Kent, and on January 25th, just as he was leaving England, Sir Thomas Wyatt issued his proclamation of rebellion at Maidstone. A few days after he landed at Dieppe, the Kentish men were crossing the Thames and fighting their way from Hyde Park Corner to Ludgate. There is no scrap of evidence for the later story that he had fomented the rebellion, but he may well have known what was stirring, and he may have been suspected of complicity. That may have been the chief reason for the seizure of his letters. But he was not yet a rebel; that was to come later.

All this does not mean that he sought safety with a light heart. Throughout his life his unruly member was his conscience rather than his tongue. It was not for nothing that he had found a kindred spirit in Mrs. Bowes, and now his conscience was hardly less troublesome than hers. He had *appeared to play the faint-hearted and feeble soldier.* In the fever of those last weeks in England he had had no time to weigh his motives; he could only feel that *the fear of death was not the chief cause of my fleeing.* He comforted himself a little with a historical precedent. Jeremiah had bidden the inhabitants of Jerusalem go out and throw themselves on the mercy of the Chaldeans; only thus should they escape God's judgment on the unfaithful city. He had gone out from an England still more unfaithful, and it might be well if others would follow his example. *God's prophets has threatened and cried many plagues to fall upon England, but I hear not of many that prepares to flit. God grant that they repent not.* The advice was not so unpractical as it sounds; he was not thinking of an industrial proletariat living from hand to mouth on weekly wages, but of merchants and craftsmen who could emigrate from England at least as easily as the Glastonbury weavers from Strasburg. Many, in fact, did so. There were still cities of refuge in Europe; indeed, the tide of reaction, as we shall see, had turned in Germany. All the same, this was a rather artificial consolation; Knox probably found more comfort in completing his exposition of the sixth Psalm: *Have mercy upon me O Lord for I am weak. Lord, how long wilt thou thus intreat me.* That exposition he sent to Mrs. Bowes on February 28th, just as he was leaving Dieppe. *Seeing it is uncertain, beloved mother, if ever we shall meet in this corporal life, my conscience moveth me to write unto you, as though I should take from you my last good-night on earth.*

2

But in this month Knox's conscience had been busy with another problem: with nothing less than the right of rebellion. It was the result of these meditations that was to give him his place among those who have changed the course of history.

Hitherto, as we have seen, the leaders of the evangelical churches had been concerned to purge themselves from all taint of Hussism. From the beginning of the religious revolt they had taught, even more absolutely than the doctors of the old Church, the duty of political obedience. Rebellion against the secular powers was as the sin of witchcraft. Luther's advice to his Elector in 1521 had set the tone: "Obey the power that is over you. Let the Emperor dispose of life and property in your cities and your lands as the laws of the Empire shall allow. Repulse not authority nor resist it, nor procure others to resist or hinder it, even if it seeks to seize me or to kill me. For none may overturn or withstand authority, save he who has established it; in all others, resistance is rebellion, and rebellion against God." Fifteen years later Calvin elaborated what Luther had affirmed. "The Word of God requires obedience not only to the rule of princes who justly and faithfully perform their office, but to all those who exercise authority, in whatever way they may exercise it and however little they may perform that which belongs to their office."

But behind these seemingly iron admonitions, there lurked an ambiguity. It was not simply the old ambiguity that must always defy definition: the conflict between conscience and obedience. Luther and Calvin were both, of course, aware of that ultimate issue, and they did not pretend to settle it. There was something else, something inherent, not in the eternal facts of human nature, but in the special circumstances of the time. Granting that the Christian must bow to the authority of the State, where did that authority reside? In Western Europe monarchy had but recently emerged from the multifarious jurisdictions of feudalism; in Poland and in Central Europe it had not yet emerged. In Germany and Switzerland sovereignty was still divided, in theory as well as in fact, between the Emperor and the territorial prince, between the free city and its overlord. It was no rebellion against the ordinances of God for Luther to appeal to the German nobility or for Geneva to assert its independence against the Bishop and the Duke of Savoy. It was by no mere chance that these regions of divided loyalty had been the homelands of religious revolt. It was by no chance that the aristocratic anarchy of Poland had offered a refuge to heretics whom neither Catholic nor Protestant would tolerate elsewhere. And now, as revolt spread to Western Europe, its leaders were beginning to seek, here too, some escape from their own logic and to ask how far the new kings were justified in claiming an absolute sovereignty.

It was under the stress of persecution in France that, about this time, Calvin began to evolve his doctrine of the "lesser authorities." In principle he preferred aristocracy to monarchy. His teaching had found an audience, his followers a refuge, in the minor Courts of the day: in Italy with the Duchess of Ferrara, in France with the Queen of Navarre. Were not the French princes of the blood ordained of God, as well as the King himself; might not the struggling Huguenot congregations legitimately place themselves under the protection of local magnates?

The danger of this theory was to be terribly revealed in future years. It liberated the United Provinces, but for generations it disturbed their unity. As the watchword of the Huguenots, it led straight to the impossible dualism of the Edict of Nantes; if Richelieu had tolerated it, it would have destroyed France as a great power. If it had been applied more widely, it would have reduced every nation in Europe to the condition of distracted impotence in which Germany was to languish for three centuries. It was not, in fact, applied more widely, for the simple reason that the materials for its application did not exist. The kings had done their work too well; the "lesser authorities" were either unfit or unwilling to challenge them. But where that happened, what happened to the theory? For the theory was not simply that a noble might lawfully champion an oppressed people; it was that God would not leave His people without a champion. If that were true, and a people's natural leaders failed them, was God's choice limited to the aristocracy?

3

Calvin was to ask himself that question more than once, some six years later, when he had to deal with the vacillations of King Antoine of Navarre; but Knox was facing it now. His experience of England had shaken him profoundly. He might assure his *afflicted brethren* whom he had left behind him in England that God would raise up some Jehu to save them, but would He? Where was such a man to be found in the new nobility that the Tudors had substituted for the old? In the part of England that Knox knew best, the last Percy (as it then seemed) had died childless, seventeen years before, bequeathing his nephews' inheritance to the Crown. Of Dudley, who had appropriated so much of that inheritance, the less said the better; he was, after all, a type of the new order, son of the first Tudor's hated minister, without traditions and without scruple. Of the other old families, Dacre was a Catholic and Neville, as Knox knew to his cost, was a time-server. The new men, the Bowes, Wharton and the rest, were mere officials, bound servants of the Council and the Court. And as for Parliament, who sat among the knights of the shires but gentry of the same breed?

In truth, when we look back on the England of Edward VI and Mary, we get an impression of exhausted vitality. A nation must pay for a Henry VIII; new life could not grow in that shadow. In his son's reign the only signs of vigour were in the Church, and even its leaders, of both parties, belonged to the past. In 1553 Latimer was sixty-eight, Gardiner seventy and Tunstall seventy-nine. Sixteen years before, Tunstall had pleaded with Henry VIII to let him rest, for he was poor, old and hated. Hooper, it is true, was younger, perhaps fifty-five, but he, too, like the foreign refugees, belonged to the last generation, to the Lutheran or Zwinglian traditions of the German-speaking cities. It was to be the same with Mary's counter-reformation; it was heavy with old rancours and threadbare arguments. Gardiner still revolved the ancient dilemma between royal and papal supremacy; Pole, the returned exile, younger but even wearier, still strove to adjust old memories of the *Oratory* with old hatred of Henry VIII and all his works. In that counter-reformation there was no breath of the new life that was blowing through the Roman Church elsewhere. The legend of Gardiner's dying words, true or not, would fit like a glove the official England of that day: "I have denied like Peter, I have been converted like Peter, but I have not yet wept like Peter." England's Government had denied Rome and was being required formally to retract its denial, but it remained unmoved by any vigour of purpose or passion of feeling. The gentry kept their Church lands while three hundred or so craftsmen and preachers were burnt at the stake. In all that scene, the more we look at it, one figure stands out alone: Cranmer, timid and ageing, but still intent on the one broad purpose of his life, the fusing of Catholic tradition and evangelical discovery into a national Church. If he had a like-minded disciple, it was his former chaplain, Ridley, the youngest of the Edwardian bishops.

It was from these cold fallows that Elizabethan England grew, but the growth was slow and even in 1559 none could foresee the harvest. There could be no thought of it in 1554 when Knox sat watching in Dieppe. And he could gain little comfort by turning his eyes from England to Germany. There the nobility had just given an even more glaring example of their inadequacy. In 1552 the Lutheran princes had had a matchless opportunity. Henry of France, sure of England and Scotland, had thought it safe, for the moment, to throw over the Catholic cause. He would ally himself with the Lutherans and would hope, in the confusion, to snatch Cambrai from the Emperor as he had snatched Boulogne from the English King. So that spring Charles V was chased by the renegade Maurice of Saxony through the mountain passes to Villach. The battle of Lutheran freedom was won; the Peace of Augsburg was assured. And incontinently the German princes had fallen out among themselves; Duke Albert Alcibiades was showing how closely a German noble could imitate an Italian condottiere; and in the summer of 1553, while England was waiting for the death of her King, German anarchy had culminated in the battle of Sievershausen.

4

It was against such a European background that Knox was watching England. There he could only see apostasy and the re-establishment of false worship. And to him apostasy was not an affair of the individual conscience, to be accounted for at the Last Judgment. It was a matter of social life and death in this world. False worship had always led, could only lead, to one end: the destruction of the nation that practised it. It mattered not how many innocent might be found in such a people; as a nation it had sinned and as a nation it would be judged.

This view of history was no private fad of Knox's, born of Scots
dourness and overmuch study of the Books of Judges and of Kings.
It was the universal commonplace of the age, of Catholic and
Protestant alike. And it was this that gave the issue of rebellion so
sharp a point. God might be ruthless in His judgments, but He could
not be so ruthless as to provide no way of escape from them. True,
He was very patient, and men must be patient too. But when He
did strike, He struck very quickly; and was this the day of His
patience or of His wrath? Did not the agony of Europe show that
the time was short?

That was the query mark that Knox had reached in these days at
Dieppe. He could not yet venture an answer. He must seek that
among the fathers of the Church in Switzerland. But, so far as he
had got, he must announce his conclusions. On the same day, February 28th, on which he wrote to Mrs. Bowes, he despatched also
to some friend in England what he called *A Godly Letter of Warning
or Admonition to the Faithful in London, Newcastle and Berwick*. It was
an assertion of the imminence of God's judgment on the restored
idolatry, it pointed out, from the example of Jeremiah already
quoted, that *the prophets of God may sometimes teach treason against
kings*, but it stated quite definitely the old doctrine of non-resistance.
*Shall we go and slay all idolaters? That were the office of every civil
magistrate* (a terrible admission, forced on him by his argument, but
we shall have to consider that issue later); *but of you is required only to
avoid participation and company of their abominations*.

The treatise is mainly a descant on these last words, on the absolute duty of all the faithful to abstain from attending Mass. But the
background of this warning is a constant appeal to the experience of
history, to the irrevocability of lost opportunities. It is not the
marvels of Merlin that move him to prophesy, but *the plain truth of
God's Word, the invincible justice of the everlasting God, and the ordinary
course of His punishments and plagues from the beginning*. The Old
Testament shows many such precedents; but observe too the experience of Christendom: *The sun keepeth his ordinary course and
starteth not back from the west to the south. And so is it with the light of the
Gospel. Most evident it is that where the light of God's word for the un-
thankfulness of men has been taken away, that there it is not to this day*

*restored again. Witness whole Israel and all the countries of the Gentiles,
where the apostles first preached. What is in Asia? Ignorance of God.
What in Africa? Abnegation of the very Saviour, of our Lord Jesus. What
in those notable churches of the Grecians where Christ Jesus was planted by
Paul and long after watered by others? Mahomet and his false sect. Hath
God punished the nations forenamed and shall He spare us?*

A generation ago it was fashionable to call these beliefs obscuran-
tist. We can hardly take that smug view today. We too have seen
Europe in agony; we too think of that agony as a punishment. With
one difference, Knox's philosophy of history is ours also. We believe
that nations suffer for the sins of their rulers, but the sins we recognize are offences against man rather than against God. To us modes
of worship are trivialities and faith a mere personal opinion about
the unknowable; what matters is social justice and the material good
of the greatest number. The quality that offends us in Knox and his
contemporaries is their perpetual mumbling of the dead bones of
Jewish history, as if Christian civilization could learn either God's
will or its own duty from the turmoils of a primitive oriental
tribe.

Yet perhaps we are growing daily less cocksure even about this
point of difference. We have become conscious in recent years that
our distaste for the Old Testament has brought us into strange company. Obviously, it was as silly for Knox to harp on Jehu and
Jeremiah as it was for French revolutionists to invoke the shades of
Brutus and Aristogeiton. Any ignoramus can thus quote history to
his purpose. But, apart from the fact that the Old Testament was
necessarily the chief history textbook of that age, as much for
Raleigh writing his *History of the World* as for Knox dashing off his
pamphlets, is not our contempt for it at least as unscientific as their
credulity about it? After all, the Hebrew struggle for monotheism
is, for our western world, at least the greatest single fact in history.
It is, in truth, the only bridge between the old world and the new.
To it, and to it almost alone, we owe the very conception on which
we preen ourselves: that the essence of the State is not raw power
but moral duty. Now, in 1937, that conception has itself been challenged; it has become, once more, the central issue of European
politics; and we are beginning to look with new eyes on the dis-

credited chroniclers and prophets of Palestine. They were right enough, in their day, in thinking that the worship of Jehovah was more important than the balance of power between Egypt and Assyria; is it for nothing that, in ours, the records of this primitive tribe are intolerable to the propagandists of a purely political idealism?

And we are becoming conscious, too, that, if Jewish chroniclers and prophets were right in 750 B.C., Christian priests and preachers in A.D. 1550 may not have been far wrong. They were wrong, no doubt, from the standpoint of the pure Christian ideal, the ideal of "separateness". From that standpoint, the Christian's duty is not the Jew's. It is not his business to construct a godly polity out of the materials offered him by the State, or to use in his building the cement of State compulsion. But for 1,200 years Christendom had in fact been organizing itself on Jewish lines, and in the process Church and State had become inextricably entangled. The theologian may judge the Catholic and the Protestant of the sixteenth century for being enmeshed in that entanglement, but the historian cannot do so.

To the historian one thing is surely clear: in the sixteenth century the nations of Europe were, in truth, making an almost irrevocable choice, and the symbol of that choice, if not the essence of it, was the ancient issue of worship. As they then decided to worship, so for nearly four centuries would be, not only their religious, but also their political life. That choice was to determine immediately the character of their settled systems of government; it was to determine, more slowly, but no less inevitably, the reform movements that were to modify those systems or the revolutions that were to overturn them. Of course the choice was partly forced upon the nations by economic distress; of course, too, economic factors played their part in the developments of the succeeding centuries. But in this year, 1937, it seems more difficult to believe in Marx's philosophy of history than in Calvin's. We live once more in an age of creeds, and we know that though hunger may drive men to seek a faith, their faith once found will drive them to forget their hunger. It is not for nothing, again, that Marxists in Russia and in Spain have turned their first furies on the old Churches of East and West, or that the high priests of aggressive nationalism can profess Christ at Rome, but must deny Him at Berlin.

5

Knox's *Godly Letter* is subscribed *from a sore troubled heart, upon my departure from Dieppe, whither God knoweth*. Three weeks later he was in Geneva. In two months he was back in Dieppe, having *travelled through all the Congregations of Helvetia and reasoned with all the pastors and many other excellently learned men*.

The tenor of his reasonings we know from a record of certain questions which he put to Henry Bullinger, patriarch of Zürich, to whom Calvin had introduced him. Calvin himself had probably little time just then for this enquiring Scotsman. On October 27th of the previous year Servetus had been burnt, and it seemed for the moment as if that event might discredit Calvin as the Peasants' War had discredited Luther. And Calvin had made matters worse by his *Defence of the True Faith* published in January. All the cities of Switzerland were against him; his own friend Zurkinden at Berne had remonstrated with him in February. And now, this March, as Knox arrived in Geneva, his old antagonist, Castellio, had launched from Basel his *Treatise on Heretics* under cover of a resounding letter to the Duke of Würtemberg. "Are these in truth thy servants, O Christ, who devise these butcheries?" De Bèze, at Lausanne, Calvin's only faithful henchman, was busy over a counterblast, which would make matters worse still. No, decidedly Calvin was in no case to answer any more dangerous questions. The Scotsman had better go to Bullinger.

These questions which Knox took to Zürich were eminently practical. He had seen first Scotland and then England ruined by a regency; now the ruin of each was about to be completed by the marriage of a queen. He had seen Beaton and Hamilton and the Queen Mother; he had seen Dudley *ruling the roost by stout courage and proudness of stomach*. Now a King of France would rule in Scotland, a King of Spain in England. Ought these things to be? When the heir to a throne is a minor is he *to be regarded as a lawful magistrate and as such to be obeyed as of divine right? Can a female preside over and rule a kingdom by divine right and so transfer the right of sovereignty to her husband?*

Along this line, however, Knox could get small help from Bullinger. The reply was obvious. Edward VI was undoubtedly a lawful sovereign; and, as to the rule of queens and the rights of their husbands, that question must be decided by established law and custom, which good men should not challenge. There remained a second line of approach. If divine right could not be challenged *ab initio* on the ground of a sovereign's incapacity, could it be challenged subsequently on the ground of that sovereign's acts? Is *a magistracy to be obeyed when it commands idolatry; may nobles who are still in military occupation of towns and fortresses repel such ungodly violence;* if so, and it comes to civil war, what side should good men take?

Here Bullinger found himself on more definitely Scriptural ground; but here again he could give no definite answer. As before he had referred his questioner to the constitution of the particular State, so now he must refer him to his own conscience. Of course, laws contrary to God and His worship are not to be obeyed. Beyond that, there have been justifiable rebellions, but each case must be decided on its merits. Only let him who meditates rebellion beware of "precipitancy and corrupt affections." Prayer and repentance are the better way; "let us lift up our eyes to God, waiting for His deliverance."

There is no sign that Knox gathered any more definite advice on this journey, and when he returned to Dieppe his temper seemed to be Bullinger's. His *Godly Letter* was printed under date of May 8th; on May 10th and 31st, he despatched two new communications to England—*An Epistle to his Afflicted Brethren* and *A Comfortable Epistle sent to the Afflicted Church of Christ*. They are exhortations to patience and hope; only one sentence gives a hint of violence: *Hereof be assured, that all is not lawful nor just that is statute by civil laws, neither yet is everything sin before God, which ungodly persons allege to be treason.*

Nevertheless, Knox had made up his mind. He had resolved to take advantage of the largest loophole left to him by Bullinger's answers. Neither in England nor in Scotland could established law and custom be said to have affirmed the right of a queen to confer sovereign power on her husband. For practical purposes, such an event was unprecedented. Nor had Parliament itself any recognized right, in either country, to convey the people's assent to such an act. There was little doubt about popular feeling on the subject, at least in England. Knox had been in London on 17th November 1553, when the House of Commons had presented their Address to Mary, advising her to marry, but to marry one of her own subjects. He had doubtless heard of the scene that followed: how Mary, instead of replying through the Chancellor, had broken out herself in passionate reproof of their presumption. That had been the expression of the people's real will; that had been, too, the expression of the Queen's contempt for it. Approval of the marriage bill in April was hardly likely to impress a Scotsman who had known the packed Houses of Dudley's régime. Indeed, the Tudor Parliaments were to the royal power much what the House of Lords is to the House of Commons today; they could delay and soften policies, but they could not change them. This April of 1554 Parliament had boggled over the re-enactment of the old anti-Lollard heresy laws, but next winter it would pass them almost without a murmur. In the interval Mary had issued her mandates for the election of members "of a wise, grave and Catholic sort."

These recent events, coupled with the arraignment of Cranmer and Ridley at Oxford this same April before the doctors of the universities, showed clearly enough that Mary's policies were already Spanish policies. After all, she had been Spanish from the beginning. In her isolation, among the political adventurers and the gentlemen profiteers of the English court, her only adviser had been the Imperial ambassador, Renard. Knox must have know that too in London, and it was natural for him to assume that Renard's advice had been responsible for the forty-seven gallows erected in London after Wyatt's rising. He could not have known that Renard's advice to Mary was significantly milder than the policies pursued by his masters in their own dominions. On the other hand he could not have known that on this 3rd May 1554, Mary's Council was already asking the judges "what they think in law her Highness may do" to the bishops whom the universities had "judged to be obstinate heretics." If these things were done in the green tree, what would be done in the dry? Philip II was about to sail for England from Corunna, with his escort of one hundred and fifty ships. A Spanish King would, of course, persecute in England as he was persecuting in the Low Countries. That King's arrival in England must, therefore, be denounced as treason, treason by the Queen and her advisers against the people of England.

Perhaps another piece of news stirred Knox to action at this time. This April 1554 had been crowded with events, and not the least important had happened in his own country. On the 12th, at the Edinburgh Tolbooth, Arran had surrendered the regency to the Queen Mother, taking in return the French dukedom of Chatelheraut. So one more long-meditated step had been taken in the establishment of French rule in Scotland.

6

Knox's declaration of rebellion took a characteristic form. In June he sat down to write another pamphlet, this time *A Faithful Admonition to the Professors of God's Truth in England*. It was a sermon on Matthew xiv.: the feeding of the five thousand, the storm on Galilee and Christ walking on the water. And there never was a stranger mixture of other-worldliness and political incitement.

Like all his pamphlets, this was punctuated by topical invectives, and it is only the invectives which have attracted the attention of historians. Knox rings the alliterative changes on Mary's bishops— *wily Winchester, dreaming Durham and bloody Bonner*. He elaborates his old attack on Paulet: *Who was judged to be the soul and life to the Council? Who but Shebna? Who could best despatch business that the rest of the Council might hawk and hunt? None like unto Shebna. Who was most frank and ready to destroy Somerset and set up Northumberland? Was it not Shebna? Who was most bold to cry "bastard, bastard, incestuous bastard, Mary shall never reign over us?" Which of the Council, I say, had these and greater persuasions against Mary, to whom now he crouches and kneeleth? Shebna the Treasurer.* And Knox must needs branch off, too, into more than one ejaculatory prayer that the Lord will *repress the pride of these bloodthirsty tyrants. O Lord,*

151

consume them, consume them in thine anger, and let them never bring their wicked counsels to effect. Moreover, he leaves no doubt what this Scriptural language means: God is to *stir up some Phineas, Elias or Jehu, that the blood of abominable idolaters may pacify God's wrath that it consume not the whole multitude.*

In fact, however, in spite of these furious asides, the pamphlet is mainly a sermon, and in some ways a surprising one. It begins with a call to repentance, prefaced by a comprehensive confession of the writer's own shortcomings. And the call is precisely the reverse of what one might expect of a revolutionary. The faithful have sinned as the multitude sinned, who would have made Christ king. Richly fed in the days of Edward, they had *sought a carnal and worldly liberty.* It is for that reason that Christ has sent them out on a perilous voyage as He sent His disciples of old. Now they are in desperate straits, but deliverance will come, though not as they may expect it.

Here again, Knox is startlingly quietist. Christ saved His disciples by His presence alone. They might have desired some visible miracle, *to have had the heavens opened or else that the winds and raging waves of the sea suddenly should have ceased.* But the only sign vouchsafed by Christ was *His comfortable word and lively voice. It is I, your Master, yea, your Master most familiar. It is I whose voice and doctrine ye know, for ye are My sheep. It is I whose works ye have seen, although perfectly ye considered not the same. It is I who commanded you to enter into this journey and therefore am I come to you now in the hour of your trouble, and therefore be not afraid; this storm shall cease and you shall be delivered.*

Most surprising of all, Knox closes his sermon, not with an adjuration to martyrdom, but with a sympathetic address to tender consciences. The faithful may slip back into idolatry, but let them not despair. *God concludeth all under unbelief, that he may have mercy upon all. All Christ's apostles fled from him and denied him in their hearts. No man stood in greater fear than Peter when Christ's presence was taken from him. Yet neither were the disciples rejected for ever, neither was Peter permitted to drown in that deep.*

Yet into the middle of this long sermon of spiritual reproof and spiritual comfort, there is inserted one solid slab of political denunciation. It is short, hardly one-tenth of the whole, and almost seems to have been inserted after the rest was written. The printed pamphlet is dated July 20th, and possibly it first saw the light in print. That, curiously enough is also the date when Philip II arrived in Southampton Water and began his ride through the rainstorms of an English summer to meet his bride at Winchester. Knox could not have known this coincidence of dates, but he may well have heard of Philip's approach. If his attack was to be delivered, it must be delivered now.

Even this insertion, if insertion it be, barks rather worse than it bites. Knox does not say, as he has been sometimes quoted, that it would have been better if Gardiner, Tunstall and Bonner, and Mary herself, had been *sent to hell* in Edward's reign. In fact, he says the precise opposite. His argument is one against preventive execution. The wicked must be allowed to fill their cup: witness Athaliah and Jezebel. There follows a paroxysm of disgust at the profanity of London preachers who had spoken of the *virgin Mary*. Then comes the denunciation: Mary has *manifestly shown herself to be an open traitress to the Imperial Crown of England, contrary to the just laws of the realm, to bring in a stranger and make a proud Spaniard king—to the destruction of the nobility, to the spoil of them and theirs, to the utter decay of the treasures, navy and fortifications of the realm; to the abasing of the yeomanry, to the enslaving of the commonalty, to the overthrow of Christianity and God's true religion; and finally to the utter subjection of the whole public estate and commonwealth of England.* She has thus repudiated the promises which she had proclaimed at Framlingham when her throne was challenged by Dudley. *Under an English name she beareth a Spaniard's heart.* Her bishops have abetted her treason, and the worst of them is Gardiner, thirsting for the blood of Cranmer who had saved his life when Dudley would have killed him— Gardiner *son of Satan, brother to Cain and fellow to Judas the traitor.*

7

That is all—a mere defiance. It is open to anyone to interpret it as a mere fit of temper. At the moment it changed no events, it moved no man to action. The accusation, later levelled against Knox, that it provoked Mary to persecution is patently absurd. That summer the faggots were already laid for the rank and file of heretics, waiting only for an Act of Parliament to light them. Thereafter, Cranmer and his fellow-bishops would go to the stake so soon as the Pope, having received England back into his obedience, should give authority for their degradation. Not till Englishmen had seen those fires burning for two years would they finally take sides between the old Church and the new, and even then they would not rise. Knox had little need to preach patience to them; it would be nearly a century before they would begin speaking of a king's treason against his people.

Nevertheless, Knox's use of that language in 1554 marks an epoch. It was only a signpost, for it originated no new doctrine; but it warned the world that an old doctrine was becoming a new policy. In the hundred years between the *Admonition* and Milton's *Tenure of Kings and Magistrates*, men's idea of rebellion changed. What had been a moral right became a legal duty; a counsel of despair was converted into a normal principle of political action. According to that principle, political authority was the ordinance of God, but the magistrate exercised it by virtue of a covenant with the people. Therefore, on the one hand, the authority must not be lightly challenged; but, on the other hand, the covenant must at all times be enforced—if necessary, as a New England governor was to tell his citizens, "with the hazard of your very lives." If Knox's words did not start this movement of minds, his later action did. Having clarified his own mind, he was to become the first modern revolutionary.

But it is essential to an understanding of his later action to observe one thing. The curious dualism of the *Admonition* is significant. It corresponds closely with the dualism of his questions to Bullinger. In his crude way, Knox was drawing a real, though a fine, distinction between rebellion in defence of religion and rebellion in defence of *the just laws of the realm*. With the first, the citizens at large had nothing to do. Knox still believed what he had taught his congregation at Berwick, that *subjects* should not *pretend to defend God's truth or religion by violence or sword*. That was the duty of the "lesser authorities," of princes or captains, who, lawfully appointed, were in some measure responsible for national recognition or denial of God. Hence his invocations of Jehu and Phineas. Those men were not *subjects*; their utmost violence had the imprint of man's law as well as God's. Here Knox was invoking, not a popular rising, still less assassination, but a civil war proclaimed by *magistrates*. That was the meaning, too, of his passing reference, in the earlier pamphlet, to the duty of magistrates to slay idolaters. Again, he was invoking, not burning of heretics, but civil war.

So much for rebellion in defence of religion, but it was different with *the just laws of the realm*. These all citizens were called on to defend—the yeomanry and the commonalty, as much as the nobility. In so far as an established worship of God was part of those just laws, they must defend that too; but they must defend it on the ground of law, not on the ground of divine revelation. So, in the *Admonition*, Knox refrained from preaching political revolt to God's afflicted Church as such, and religious perversity was only one of many counts in his indictment of Mary. It could not be omitted, for the religious settlement had at least some place in the laws of England; but it came quite low down on the list.

Those who think this distinction a quibble are strangely mis-reading history, for it is only in the light of it that the different development of England and Scotland in the next hundred and fifty years becomes intelligible. On the whole, England preserved the distinction. Religion made her Civil War; it played a large part in making her Revolution; but in so far as the Puritans failed, they failed because they attempted a religious revolution, and in so far as the Whigs succeeded, they succeeded by treating the Established Church as only a part of the settled laws of the realm. In Scotland, on the contrary, the distinction became gradually blurred. There the same appeal was made, in the words of the National Covenant of 1638, to "the fundamental laws, ancient privileges, offices and liberties of this kingdom"; but that appeal was secondary, it was almost an afterthought. The dominant appeal was that made long before, eight years after Knox's death, in the Covenant of 1580, to "the true Christian faith and religion." The signers of 1580 undertook, first of all, to "continue in the obedience of the doctrine and discipline of this kirk and defend the same"; it was only "because we perceive that the quietness and stability of our religion and kirk doth depend upon the safety and good behaviour of the King's majesty," that they promised also to "defend his person and authority." The signers of 1638 subscribed to almost the same words, and when Montrose took seriously their more extended reference to the established laws of a "free monarchy," he had to part company with them. So, increasingly, the standard of Scottish political action became, not law, but revealed truth. For that development, some of Knox's later utterances were, as we shall see, partly responsible. But at this stage his attitude was English rather than Scottish, and he never really adopted the later Scottish doctrine. If he was the first modern revolutionary, he was not the first covenanter.

8

Even so, his was no doctrine for Englishmen in that age. He had, indeed, shrewdly touched their real feelings; they had resented a Spanish King even more than the restoration of Papal supremacy, and in comparison with those two issues they cared little for articles of faith or forms of worship. Yet it was not in England that Knox could have the chance of acting on his principles. Though he did not know it this July, the *Admonition* was to be the end of his English work.

He had loved England, but he had never understood her. Even then the most political nation in Europe, her politics had partly revolted and partly puzzled him. He could find no place for himself in London, either among the adventurers of the court or among the judicious compromisers of the Church. The beauty of Cranmer's church services meant nothing to him; the language of the Litany left him not only cold but shivering. He had fitted well enough into English provincial life in days of peace, for, as he said of himself long afterwards, *in quietness* he was *negligent*, willing enough to let things slide, like any Englishman. But *in trouble* he was *impatient*, *tending to desperation*, while *in the mean state* he was liable to be *carried away by vain fantasies*—and in these moods he played havoc with English reticences and sobrieties. Then as now, trouble deepened all the loyalties of England. In danger, Englishmen drew together, felt the more impelled to preserve the unity of their common life at the sacrifice of private opinions and even principles; they looked askance at this Scotsman running about and trying to raise their spiritual temperature. And now that this same Scotsman had, quite properly, taken his fervours abroad with him, who was he to warn them against the Spaniards? They knew that well enough, without being asked to read pamphlets whose discovery in their houses might mean prison or worse.

All this was still hidden from Knox, though he was to learn it in a few months' time. Meanwhile he could not stay indefinitely at Dieppe. The French Government was willing enough to receive refugees from a Spanish England, for Valois had been at war again with Hapsburg for two years. As the *Admonition* was going through the press the French armies a hundred miles to eastward, were drawing off from their invasion of the Meuse valley and were facing the imperialists round Cambrai. Still, the France of the Edict of Châteaubriand could hardly offer a safe asylum to a Protestant preacher. He could not settle down in this Norman town, with its Huguenot households beginning to draw together secretly into a congregation which four years later was to become a fully organized church. So this same July 20th he wrote another letter of farewell to Mrs. Bowes and set off for Geneva. *My own estate I cannot well declare, but God shall guide the footsteps of him that is wilsome, and will feed him in trouble that never greatly solicited for the world. If any collection might be made among the faithful, it were no shame for me to receive that which Paul refused not in the time of his trouble. But all I remit to His providence who ever careth for His own.*

CHAPTER XI

THE BREACH WITH ENGLAND
1554-55

I

THERE WAS to be a short postscript to Knox's English work—a sordid one enough. He had hardly arrived in Geneva when he received a letter from Frankfurt, dated September 24th. Would he come there as one of the ministers of a new Engish congregation, just established?

The invitation had a history. Some of the foreign refugees in England, who had emigrated back to the Continent on the accession of Mary Tudor, had settled at Frankfurt under the leadership of Pollanus, late minister of the Church of Strangers at Glastonbury. They had obtained leave from the magistrates to establish a church "in the name of all such as should come out of England for the Gospel." In June 1554 they had been followed to Frankfurt by a number of Englishmen. As Pollanus's services were conducted in French, the newcomers arranged with him and with the magistrates that they might form a separate congregation and use the church at times agreed on with the Frenchmen. It was a condition of this arrangement that they should subscribe the same confession of faith as the Frenchmen and, within fairly wide limits, should use the same general forms of worship. The limits were wide enough to enable them to use much of the Book of Common Prayer. Indeed, one may suspect that the magistrates would have raised no objection to the use of that book in its entirety, but the English refugees were mostly "left wing" evangelicals. Chief among them was one William Whittingham, scholar of Oxford and Student of Christ Church, more European than English, for he had only returned to England shortly before the death of Edward VI after three years on the Continent. Such men were glad enough of the excuse to get rid of versicles, litany and surplice, and to omit "as superstitious and superfluous" much of the Baptismal and Communion services. On this basis the congregation was finally established on July 29th and Knox was elected minister, together with two of his late colleagues in the royal chaplaincy, Haddon, then at Strasburg, and Lever, then at Zürich.

Lever accepted, but Haddon refused; and Knox would have been well advised to follow Haddon's example. For already the congregation were at odds with some of their countrymen in neighbouring cities. They had invited the English refugees at Strasburg and Zürich to join them, but the invitation met with a doubtful reception. They had been tactless in forming a congregation before they had a minister, and without consulting such leaders of the English Church as Grindal at Strasburg, another of Knox's late colleagues in the chaplaincy. Grindal, future Archbishop of Canterbury, had had a scheme for establishing a church at Frankfurt under John Scory, then at Emden, another future Elizabethan bishop. Whittingham had taken the bit in his teeth, and more responsible men were unfavourably impressed by his cavalier treatment of the Prayer Book.

Knox was the last man to handle this difficult position, not of his own making. In the past twelve months that troublesome conscience of his had been busy with the causes of God's judgments on England, and he had made up his mind that one of them was this same Prayer Book. He and so many others who had had *a good opinion of the Book* had thereby shown a sad *slackness to reform religion*. What was needed now was an *open defence of the Scriptures*; whereas the Book contained many things *superstitious, impure, unclean and unperfect*. Holding these views, he would be in a false position at Frankfurt. Probably he accepted the call against his better judgment, but he did accept it. He had not been fully informed of what had passed and he certainly did not come to Frankfurt in any fighting spirit.

2

He had hardly taken over his new work when he found himself in the thick of the controversy. Grindal came from Strasburg on November 28th to negotiate. He wanted *the substance and effect* of the

Prayer Book. The discussions seem to have been amicable enough, but they were inconclusive. Grindal returned to Strasburg and negotiations died away in an exchange of letters.

That, however, was not the end. The Frankfurt congregation itself was not happy about its forms of worship and its ministers were divided, Lever advocating a closer conformity to the English Prayer Book and Knox following Whittingham's lead. At Christmas, Knox and Whittingham asked Calvin's judgment on the Book, emphasizing their own objections to it. Calvin replied on January 20th in a letter which, like so many other religious documents of the age, was conciliatory in substance and irritating in form. The substance was that this "contention among brethren" was indecent. The Book was admittedly a compromise, forced on its authors by their English environment; wise men, freed from that environment, should surely find no difficulty in compromising upon a compromise. But this advice was sprinkled with remarks about the "foolishness" of many things in the Book which, as Calvin himself anticipated, were not likely to commend themselves to Englishmen who "perchance esteem me not so well that they will deign to accept counsel from such a source." Knox, however, showed himself conciliatory. On February 6th he agreed with Lever's proposal that an experimental order of worship should be tried out until the following Easter; though the agreed order was probably not all that Lever would have liked.

A month later, however, a new party of refugees arrived from England, among them two more future bishops of the Church of England, John Jewel and Richard Cox. Cox, as we have seen, had been one of the chief authors of the Prayer Book and his feelings of paternity were no doubt outraged by the Frankfurt compromise. He had also been Dean of Christ Church and probably had no love for this non-conformist Student of the college, Whittingham. But, as he subsequently avowed to Calvin, there was more in his mind than that. He may not have met Knox before, but he had an old feud with him; he had not forgotten his famous sermon of September 1552, nor the origin of the Black Rubric. Moreover, he had brought with him from England a copy of the *Admonition*, and was all afume at the trouble that this meddlesome Scotsman had made for sober

Anglicans. He had, in fact, made up his mind to drive Knox out of Frankfurt and it took him less than a fortnight to do it.

First he tried brawling in church, which provoked Knox to an indiscreet sermon. Then he turned to more constitutional action. The new arrivals applied to be admitted to voting membership of the congregation. Whittingham's party opposed the application but Knox decided to ride for a fall. He advocated admission and the motion was carried. Promptly the Coxians combined with the followers of Lever; Lever himself was won over and a motion was passed forbidding Knox to preach. Whittingham promptly went off to the magistrates and got an order forbidding any sermon that day. After some goings and comings and discussions, Cox, under official pressure, seems to have swallowed whole, not merely the compromise form of worship, but actually the form in use in by the French brethren, including sitting at Communion. Then, these preliminary skirmishes over, he unmasked his real guns. He produced his copy of the *Admonition* and delated Knox to the magistrates, accusing him *in nine articles of high treason against the Emperor, his son Philip, King of Spain, and the Queen of England.*

There was enough in the pamphlet to set the city fathers of Frankfurt agog. What caught their eye especially was that unlucky quotation from his sermon at Amersham when he had called the Emperor *no less enemy to Christ than was Nero.* This was no language for German ears at this moment, with the Diet sitting at Augsburg, on the eve of the Peace. They forbade Knox to preach. By that time the church was in an uproar; when Knox showed his face in it as a member of the congregation, Cox and his friends walked out. The magistrates were not anxious to prosecute him, but, if the Emperor heard of the business and required the city to surrender him, they would not be able to refuse. His friends were told to advise flight, and on March 26th he left Frankfurt for Geneva. The concluding scene is thus described by Whittingham: "The 25th March, Master Knox, the night before his departure, made a most comfortable sermon at his lodgings to fifty persons, or there about, then present; which sermon was of the death and resurrection of Christ, and of the unspeakable joys which were prepared for God's elect, which in this life suffer trouble and persecution for the testimony of His blessed Name. The next day, he was brought three or four miles on his way by some of those unto whom the night before he had made that exhortation; who with great heaviness of heart and plenty of tears committed him to the Lord."

3

It is not difficult to imagine Knox's feelings as he journeyed up the Rhine, and his own words show them clearly enough. Outside Switzerland Protestantism had now only one foothold in Europe: the Lutheran States and cities of Germany. These had been won back in the very hour that England had been lost. Scandinavia was too remote to be considered; moreover, Denmark had not proved too hospitable to some of John Laski's company who had landed there eighteen months before. And now Frankfurt had just shown how insecure was this foothold in Germany, how powerful Nero still was in the lands of the Empire.

That, however, was the least of it. Who had appealed to this persecuting Caesar? Who but his own brethren of the English Church, driven into exile by Caesar's son? This English Church itself could find no place for him. It was partly his own fault. On the whole, he had played the part of a peacemaker, but in his original discussions with Grindal and with Lever he had wounded suscepti-bilities by a curious pernicketiness about minor points. He could not abide the Litany, stickled about private baptism and the churching of women. To judge from all his writings, he attached little impor-tance to such points as these; but, once challenged, he could not stop expatiating. Bishop Ridley in prison, hearing of these arguments from Grindal, was at a loss to account for them. He regarded Knox (the phrase is worth noting) as "a man of wit and learning"; he was certainly "of an earnest zeal." But as for these prejudices, the bishop could only say, "I do marvel how he can or dare avouch them before the Englishmen that be with you."

That was the real trouble: Knox and his congregation were speak-ing different languages. He was talking European and they English. To him church unity meant a common confession and a common discipline; to them it meant a common worship. The Prayer Book

162

to him was a local peculiarity of English law; to them it was the one concrete achievement of the English Reformation, the sole cement of a national church. He thought of it as a book imposed by Dudley; they as the book forbidden by Mary. He took it for granted that men whom England had driven out would at least avail themselves of a freedom which England had denied them; they were resolved to preserve, as their common bond in exile, the worship which had been proscribed at home.

But these misunderstandings might have been reconciled. Knox did not leave Frankfurt, for any point of religion. What cut him to the quick, what finally demonstrated the incompatibility of temper between him and these Englishmen, was their appeal to the secular power. The secular power was *their old shot-anchor*. Because Parliament and Council had decreed their Prayer Book, they clung to it; because they had quarrelled with their elected preacher on points of worship, they *devised how to have me cast into prison* on a charge of treason. Impossible to resist the analogy between bustling ecclesiastical officials like Cox and the Pharisees of old; *they cried out against me: he is not Caesar's friend*. For Knox at this time was no Calvinist disciplinarian, but a Free Church congregationalist, profoundly distrusting the State and all its works. How could he be otherwise? All the States of Europe were bound to the Pope; the only evangelical government he had known was Dudley's gang; and here were the remnants of Dudley's gang in collusion with the Holy Roman Emperor.

One is tempted to linger over this incident, in spite of its pettiness, for it foreshadows a whole century of Anglo-Scottish mishandlings and misunderstandings. The English Prayer Book remained an essentially English growth; Scotsmen could never appreciate it, Englishmen could never realize the impossibility of transplanting it. The very idea of fixed forms of worship imposed by law seemed always to Scotsmen the worst form of Erastianism, the most abject confession of subservience to the State. They were wrong, but Englishmen were always confirming them in their error, above all the anglicized Stewarts of the seventeenth century. Those Stewarts must always be itching "to unite the three kingdoms in one form or God's worship and public devotions"; and their bishops were glad enough to support their policy. The English Church managed to steer clear of Erastianism as consistently, though often by as narrow a margin, as the English civil service steers clear of bureaucracy; but in her dealings with Scotland she had a fatal way of blundering into Caesarism. Cox would have many successors, not least in those unhappy times eighty years later when Scottish bishops, nominated from London, were showing their "want of temper and want of breeding" at the Council table in Edinburgh, and Laud, at the Council table in Whitehall, "never abated anything of his severity and rigour towards men of all conditions or in the sharpness of his language and expressions." From that too busy combination came the royal canons and liturgy of 1637, the riot at St. Giles, and the National Covenant.

4

But the final breach between Knox and the English Church prompts another and perhaps a deeper reflection. It represented a difference in styles of worship which was to have a profound influence on English and Scottish minds. That difference was soon to be crystallized in the Form of Prayers of the English church at Geneva, which became the basis of the Scottish Book of Common Order. Knox was not solely responsible for its drafting, but his hand is evident in it. He attached hardly less importance than Cranmer to a common order of worship; Cranmer was hardly less convinced than he that this common order should be a faithful reproduction of the Bible. But their methods differed: Cranmer's was distillation, Knox's amplified quotation. Who can estimate the effect of each on his nation: on the one hand the music of the Book of Common Prayer, on the other the piled-up eloquence of the Book of Common Order, with the whole tradition of extempore prayer which it originated?

Between these two, no impartial judgment is possible. Scotsmen have always feared the sleepy enchantment of that music, Englishmen have felt stunned by that eloquence. The truest judgment lies perhaps in the paradox that, on paper, the Scottish Order is more ritualistic than the English Book. Clarendon's famous judgment that presbyterian worship had not "the least appearance of any beauty of holiness" is typically English and exactly wrong. What is true is that the Scottish Order, rejecting external acts and decorations, strains to put all beauty and holiness into language; while the English Book, distrustful of prophetic fugues, relies on a certain dignity in action to give point to its economy of words. It is significant that the particular part of the English Book about which Knox and Cox chiefly quarrelled was the one where its style comes nearest to breaking down: the Morning Service where self-restraint in prayer has to be eked out, not by action, but by psalm-singing. The quarrel, in other words, was not between Low Church and High. In truth, then as ever since, the bare and unembroidered Book of Common Prayer has seemed to Scotsmen the least satisfactory of English compromises.

And, if Englishmen from Cox onwards have thus underrated the Scottish sense of worship, Scotsmen from Knox onwards have no less underrated the English sense of Scripture. It is another paradox that the English Book is more dependent on the Bible than the Scottish Order. Cranmer feared lest overmuch sermonizing might smother the gospel, and his warning is curiously illustrated by one of the chief complaints made by Knox and Whittingham to Calvin against the English Book. They pointed out that seven-twelfths of it was devoted to the Epistles and Gospels for Sundays and holy days. That criticism was significant; it marks one of the great watersheds in the history of Christian worship. In the Scottish Order the reading of the Word ceased to be a distinct devotional act. It was absorbed into the pulpit and, as every form of worship took on the pulpit tone, the Bible underwent a subtle process of fermentation. At its best the Scottish Order achieves grandeur, but achieves it at a dangerous cost. As every schoolmaster knows, recitation is no test of understanding; and, for the purposes of eloquence, the Old Testament is more quotable than the New.

But in these last days of March 1555 nothing was further from Knox's thoughts than the worship of a national Church of Scotland. He had left Scotland behind him long ago; now England had finally cast him out. Both were, to all appearances, irrevocably pledged to Continental Romanism, the Romanism of France and Spain. He was homeless; even the Geneva to which he was returning was an almost unknown city. He had no work there, but it offered at least a temporary halting-place where a man might find books and try to forget a failure.

IV. Geneva and Scotland
The Founding of the Congregations

CHAPTER XII

FROM GENEVA TO SCOTLAND

1555

I

KNOX SETTLED down at Geneva to *the rest of quiet study*, but the rest lasted only four months. By the middle of August he was journeying north again—to Scotland of all places. Yet his short residence coincided almost exactly with a moment of crisis in the affairs of this little town of no more than 13,000 inhabitants. A year ago he had visited it in an hour when Calvin stood at bay, defending the indefensible. Now he returned at the very instant of Calvin's final victory.

In the previous January 1555, the three Genevan Councils which shared between them the government of the city had at last made peace with the Genevan Church. They had themselves established that Church under Calvin's guidance. Fourteen years ago they had settled its constitution; but they had remained jealous of its authority. Its Consistory of six ministers and twelve elders might enquire into breaches of Church discipline, it might admonish offenders, but it must not punish. Though the elders were themselves members of the Councils, they could act only as *juges d'instruction*; they must refer culprits to the Councils themselves for trial and sentence. Calvin had approved this division of powers, expect on one point. He insisted that excommunication was an ecclesiastical, not a secular, penalty. On this point he had waged his last campaign with his liberal opponents, the party of Perrin. Now the Councils gave way; they recognized the Consistory's right of excommunication.

From that moment Calvin's power was established. Next month new elections gave him a secure majority on the Councils. He had now the support of the growing colony of refugees from England,

Scotland and Italy, as well as from France. Between the middle of April, when Knox arrived from Frankfurt, and the middle of May, no less than sixty Frenchmen were admitted to citizenship. But in May the men who had opposed Calvin's dictatorship for years made a last effort to assert themselves. They appealed, as they had often done before, to local patriotism: Geneva was being flooded, her citizen body diluted, by alien immigrants. On the night of May 16th discontent broke out into a minor riot. It was not serious, but it gave the Calvinist majority their opportunity. Perrin and the other opposition leaders fled the city; on June 3rd they were sentenced to death in their absence. There were wholesale arrests, a liberal use of torture, four executions and a number of sentences of banishment. By August, when Knox left for Scotland, Calvin could feel that he had finally eliminated his enemies.

It is worth noting that this was Knox's first experience of Geneva. He was only an onlooker, not yet a citizen nor even a minister; and what he witnessed was the registration of an accomplished fact. He had not known the city in its long years of struggle and persecution. He had not seen the hysteria of the plague years, with their witch-hunts and warlock-burnings. He had not watched Calvin's way with rival preachers and insubordinate laymen: how he had brought Pighius into line, jostled Castellio and Bolsec into flight, and executed Gruet. Nor had he experienced the growth of Calvinist "discipline" in a loose-living community. Controversy will always rage round this discipline, with its petty inquisitions, it minute regulation of morals and conduct. Some will denounce it as a new evangelical reign of terror, blasphemously established in the name of Christ; others will discount nine-tenths of it as reproducing only the familiar features of all municipal administration in that age. But however it may be judged, by this summer of 1555 it had done its work. The city Knox knew was the tame Geneva of the refugees.

And it was tame with the tameness of a provincial city. Its metropolitan days were still to come. It was a *school of Christ*, but an elementary school. It was not a centre of learning like Basel; higher education was represented only by Calvin's occasional lectures. Nor was it yet a missionary centre; the five scholars whose burning at Lyons in May 1553 had shocked the conscience of half Europe had come thither, not from Geneva, but from Lausanne, where de Bèze was still teaching. The famous College and Academy of Geneva were not founded, under de Bèze's rectorship, till 1558; not till then did the city begin to become the theological seminary of western Protestantism. In 1555 it was cosmopolitan, but not oecumenical. The Huguenots of France were only beginning to form local churches; Calvin was deep in correspondence with them, but he had not yet organized Geneva to help them. Frenchmen came there, not to enlist in a gospel army, but to seek a shelter. The great years of missionary enterprise, the farewells to preachers as they passed out of the city gates to Paris or Normandy or Poitou, the gallantries of martyrdom, the stir of the coming wars of religion—all this lay in the future. In these "years between" the city by the lake was a place of rest rather than of action. The popular picture of Knox, issuing aflame from this hearth of fanaticism to conquer Scotland for Calvin, is oddly out of focus. In truth, it might have been better for him if he had surrendered himself longer and more consistently to this atmosphere of comparative peace.

2

That, however, was not his destiny. He had hardly installed himself and opened his books when he received a letter from Mrs. Bowes. Sir Robert, presumably the chief obstacle to Marjorie's marriage, had died in late February or early March. Sir Richard, no longer captain of Norham, had (we must suppose) withdrawn his opposition. Let Knox therefore return. They could meet at Berwick; and, if England could not offer a home to Marjorie and him, perhaps Scotland would.

The venture did not at all appeal to Knox. It was *most contrarious to his own judgment*. Nevertheless he set out. If he had received any communications from Scotland itself suggesting his return, they did not weigh much with him. Mrs. Bowes alone, he said, had *drawn him from the den of his own ease*.

His reluctance was natural. He had had few influential friends in Scotland. His connections there had been only with the Lothian lairds and with the company of St. Andrews. To the lairds he was known as little more than an upper servant; but among the company of St. Andrews he had enjoyed a rather surprising prestige. He had been Balnaves's confidant; he had played oracle to the rougher members of the gang. With only two of these, however, had he had any touch since his release: with two whom, in a way, he had helped to escape. The prisoners at Mont St. Michel and Cherbourg had disputed whether they might break prison. Old Kirkcaldy at Cherbourg thought not; it might make the lot of the other prisoners harder. Knox, called on to arbitrate, replied *that such fear proceedeth not from God's spirit*; let them by all means break prison provided they did not *shed any man's blood for their freedom*. Young Kirkcaldy and Carmichael at Mont St. Michel acted on this advice, escaped on the eve of Epiphany 1549, and, after many adventures, met Knox in London on his arrival there three months later. They were both on the Border, at least within reach of Berwick, at the end of that year, with other Scots pensioners of the English Government.

There, too, Knox must have met his three friends of Haddington days, Cockburn, Douglas and Crichton. All three were on the English pension list. They had been serving with the English forces since Pinkie, but by the previous summer of 1548 the English commanders had lost confidence in two of them. Crichton was "showing more goodwill than service," Douglas was become "one of our most sovereign enemies"; among the Lothian gentry only Cockburn remained staunch. Of the three, then, he was the only one from whom Knox could expect any welcome; and he was not in Scotland. He had been arrested at Norham early in this year 1555 for some minor offence, sent to London and committed to the Fleet prison. It was the same with Balnaves and Kirkcaldy. Both were still abroad; like the rest of the St. Andrews leaders, their forfeitures were not removed till the following year—Cockburn's and Crichton's, indeed, not till 1558. Kirkcaldy, after playing the spy in France for Dudley in 1551–53, was now fighting in the French army. Knox had need of new friends and better protectors, if he were to venture into Scotland.

And in these eight years he had had little opportunity of making such new connections. In his days at Berwick and Newcastle, after peace had come in 1550, he must have heard plenty about Scottish affairs, but there was little in them to interest him. Scotland was in a state of precarious convalescence, and invalids have no history. In the summer of 1551 a Scots clergyman of the English church, one John Willcock, came to Berwick in Dorset's train and he probably met Knox then for the first time; but Willcock had severed connection with Scotland as much as Knox, and in 1555 he, too, was abroad at Emden, where Laski also had settled down for the moment. In November 1551, while Knox was preaching his All Saints' sermon at Newcastle, Mary of Guise was at Hampton Court, returning from a year's sojourn in France. She passed through Northumberland a fortnight or so later. The Scots gentlemen whom she had taken with her to France went north about the same time, among them Cassilis; but Cassilis, like the rest of the former English party in Scotland, was now a pensioner of France. Towards the end of 1552, however, while Knox was in London, he did make one new acquaintance, and a momentous one. James Stewart, Prior of St. Andrews, passed through London at that time on his way from a French visit, and this was the beginning of the later friendship between the two men. For the rest, in 1553 Knox's own brother William, a merchant licensed to trade between Scotland and England, was with him at Newcastle. That, with any conjectures we may like to make about the Scots in his Newcastle congregation, is all we know about his possible Scottish connections during all these years.

In 1555 he was returning to a new Scotland. The men who were to take the lead now were not Lothian lairds or St. Andrews gangsters. But, in closing this old chapter, Knox's biographer can hardly say good-bye to the company of St. Andrews without a passing salute to their leader, Beaton's chief assassin. We know little good of Norman Lesley, but he did not come to a bad end. On 14th August 1554, as Knox was travelling south from Dieppe, the French and Spanish armies, under the command of King and Emperor, came into skirmishing touch near Cambrai, and Lesley "on a fair grey gelding" rode out of life in a shimmer of gallantry beneath the eyes of Montmorency, Constable of France. One of the Constable's staff, a fellow-Scot, watched the galloping figure as, with only seven followers, it breasted the slope of the Spanish position. It was a conspicuous figure, red bonneted, with a coat of armour and sleeves of mail worn above black velvet and, for badge, two broad white crosses on back and breast. It drove, with levelled spear, at the Spanish horse and culverins, unhorsed five men, dropped its broken spear and passed into a flurry of sword-play. Then, as another Spanish troop came up, it turned and came spurring back, to collapse almost at Montmorency's feet. The grey was dead; Lesley, desperately wounded, was carried to the King's tent. Fifteen days later he died, and "no man made more lamentation than the Laird of Grange who came to the camp the next day after."

CHAPTER XIII

THE SCOTLAND OF 1555

I

THE EPISODE of Lesley's death is not irrelevant to our story. For one thing, it had a direct effect on the fortunes of the other leaders in Beaton's murder and the St. Andrews insurrection. Moved by Lesley's death, the French King interceded for them; two years later they were pardoned; Kirkcaldy, returning home in March 1556, was to play a leading part in a more successful rising. But the episode is significant in another way; it is almost a symbol of the revolution that was coming upon Scotland.

In these middle years of the sixteenth century she was still, in most things, a mediaeval country, and modernism was about to flood her unprepared. The fifteen century had dug no channels in her national life which might receive the inundation. Alone of western European countries her social structure was still cast in the most primitive of all moulds: the mould of the Three Estates. She had her warrior caste, her priestly caste, her "labourers to burgh and land"; but she had neither a king to dominate them nor, as yet, a middle class strong enough to break them up from within. Of the Three Estates, the fighters were the first to be overwhelmed. Eight years of war with England had already demonstrated the inefficiency of their feudal organization. In 1548 an old-fashioned patriot pictured them under an allegorical figure: Scotland's eldest son "in harness, trailing a halberd behind him, being all affrayit and fleyit for dreddour of his life."

The great nobles would survive this collapse—nobilities always do. Experience of power has given them training of a sort; when their military traditions are outmoded, they can turn politician. But for many of the best among her gentry, her natural leaders, Scotland would find no place for long years to come. Less experienced and less adaptable, they would take their loyalties and their gallantries abroad—no longer, as in old days, simply to enlist in the Scottish guard of the French kings, but as gentlemen adventurers in all the armies of Europe. They would accustom Scotland to the bad habit of living on romance. Some, like Lesley, would find death or fortune in foreign service; others, like Kirkcaldy, would return to fling all away on forlorn hopes at home. For the laird of Grange was less fortunate than his friend; six years later he was to have his hour of glory as the captain of the Congregation; twelve years after that he was to hang for a cause which he espoused only when it was lost. Both deaths were magnificent; but they were not war.

2

What of the other two Estates in this year 1555? It is difficult to answer the question without exaggeration; and it becomes more difficult the more one reads the contemporary writings of Scotsmen. The Scots language of the period had a queer trick of hyperbole, even in official documents. In 1535, said a sober Act of Parliament, the burghs were "wasted and destroyed in their goods and policy and almost ruinous." That was before the English war, and the words can hardly be taken literally. Since then real calamity had come upon the country. The Scotland of the later Middle Ages had had little part in the agony of Europe; now she had been initiated into it by eight years of concentrated misfortune. All the melancholy, all the mystic forebodings, which Europe had begun to shake off in a fever of action, descended on her suddenly in these years of post-war reconstruction.

The worst prophets of woe were not new gospellers, but old conservatives, like the allegorist already quoted, who marshalled all sorts of learned pedantries in support of his conclusion "that the world is near an end." The old Church had adorned Scotland with "divers sciences divine and human, with many charitable acts and supernatural miracles"; but now her appearance was so "altered from the first fashion that no man could extract any profitable sentence nor good example from any part of it." She held the book of learning in her hand but "the clasps were fast locked with rust." And the Third Estate was "worst grathit and spoilt than the other two; all the green trees, corns, bestiality, mechanic crafts and ships and merchandise were destroyed, and the earth was become barren and sterile so that no ordinance of policy could be preceived in it nor esperance of relief." The "old enemy of England" had wasted the country; the decay of the national character left no hope of restoration. Another conservative, Sir Richard Maitland, pointed the moral, thinking perhaps of his house of Lethington burnt by the English, and of a curious preacher called Wishart whom his neighbours had brought to stay with him some years before:

> How should our commonwealth endure?
> God to offend we take no cure;
> And none presses their life to amend
> For no trouble that God will send,
> As though plagues came by aventure.

But all this, of course, is exaggeration. The melancholy was in itself a significant symptom, but the pessimists were not faithful reporters. The truth is rather that the new Scotland of 1555 was passing through one of those periods of apparent deadness which are so apt to deceive the ordinary run of politicians. Old power was decaying, new power was stirring beneath the surface; but on the surface all that seemed needed for reconstruction and restored prosperity was a reasonably efficient administration. Such an administration Mary of Guise was determined to provide. She had all the ordinary political talents, a sound administrator, a winning diplomatist, hard-working and practical. Even before she took over the government in 1554, Arran, with her help, had been active enough in pacification. Together they had quartered the country, holding their justice eyres in Inverness and Aberdeen, in Glasgow and Ayr and back by the Borders to Edinburgh. But in money matters Arran was a family peculator of the old school; not till Mary took control did the government begin to pull itself out of the pit of bankruptcy.

Remarkably enough, it was the Second Estate that seemed to take the lead in this work of administrative reconstruction. If the passing of resolutions could bring about reform, the Church would have forestalled the coming revolution. In a series of Councils between August 1549 and January 1552, the bishops, abbots and doctors had made an imposing parade of their good intentions.

The statutes which they passed in 1549 were prefaced by a frank confession: the two main "causes and roots" of dissensions and heresies were "the corruption of morals and profane lewdness of life in churchmen of almost all ranks, together with crass ignorance of literature and of all the liberal arts." They adopted the decrees, a century old, of the Council of Basel in regard to "the incontinence of churchmen" and the "punishment of open concubinaries." They adopted the recent decrees of the Council of Trent "in the matter of instruction heretofore neglected and preaching of God's word." They resolved on their own account that "neither prelates nor their subordinate clergy shall keep their offspring born of concubinage in their company," and "that rectors and bishops should preach in person four times in the year." They ordained the appointment of "more worthy masters" in the old grammar schools, the restoration of decayed schools and the foundation of new ones. They laid on monasteries the duty of sending "two religious or one to the nearest university to remain for the space of at least four years in the study of theology and holy Scripture." They emphasized the need for the proper appointment of parish curates and allotted benefices "for the maintenance and permanent establishment of preachers of the word of God." They issued regulations for reforming procedure in Church Courts. And, having thus professed to set their house in order, they decreed the appointment of diocesan "inquisitors of heretical error" and the holding of "general inquisitions four times a year and special ones as often as the occasion shall arise." Next year they acted on these fulminations by burning on the Castle Hill at Edinburgh one Adam Wallace, after trial in the Church of the Black Friars before a bench of bishops and lords of session, under the presidency of Argyll, hereditary Justiciar of the kingdom. Significantly enough,

Wallace was Knox's successor as tutor to the Cockburn children at Ormiston. But this was an isolated act of persecution, and eight years were to pass before it was repeated.

In January 1552 these statutes were confirmed and seventeen new ones passed, two of which are worth mentioning. One decreed the "severe punishment" of "all who wilfully absent themselves from the parish Mass on days of obligation" and gave as the reason for this enactment that "the greatest neglect of the divine mysteries has prevailed among the subjects of the realm within these last few years, so that very few indeed out of the most populous parishes deign to be present at the sacrifice of Holy Mass on the Sundays and the other double festivals appointed by the Church, or to attend the preaching of God's word." The other ordained the issue of a Catechism to "rectors, vicars and curates as much for the instruction of themselves as of the Christian people committed to their care." This was the famous "Archbishop Hamilton's Catechism," mainly drawn up, it is said, not by that questionable prelate himself, but by Winram, Sub-Prior of St. Andrews. It was a remarkable document, reflecting for the first time in Scotland the new spirit of the Roman Church.

This Catechism, indeed, was the one serious fruit of all these deliberations; though there are some signs of a real revival in the grammar schools, notably at Linlithgow where one Ninian Winzet was appointed master in 1552. But that was all. The Church was far too weak to reform itself. It was not only that the moral decrees of these Councils excited popular derision when contrasted with the private lives of their authors and, above all, of the Primate of St. Andrews. The Councils felt that themselves and expressed their fears as politely as they could. They exhorted the bishops "as well as the rest of the prelates and the incumbents of benefices in the realm to reform their life and morals to better purpose, lest the very persons who are themselves implicated in notorious offences should rashly proceed to the rigorous correction of the morals of others." But the evil went deeper than that. The historians of four centuries have expended themselves in denunciations of the Scottish church, but, in fact, its corruptions were the same as those which were then in process of reform in every country of Europe. In no country was the Church able to reform itself except under the stimulus and with the constant reinforcement of the secular power. The trouble in Scotland was that the secular power was as weak and as corrupt as the ecclesiastical.

4

Indeed, the trouble went further. In a very real sense the old Church in Scotland was weak because, before the Reformation began, it had already been sapped by the worst features of the Reformation movement. The kings and nobles of Scotland had been plundering the Church haphazard long before Henry VIII of England or Gustavus Vasa of Sweden had set themselves to systematic confiscation. So far as one can date such things, this process had begun in the reign of James III eighty years before; it had been greatly intensified during the minority of James V. Royal nominees were pushed into monasteries and bishoprics, or, often mere laymen, received ecclesiastical benefices *in commendam*—a convenient type of trust imposing no obligations on the trustee. Two of James V's bastards sat as commendators in the Council of 1549; three more held the priories of Holyrood, Coldingham and Perth. The system not only sucked the Church's wealth; it diluted her government. When she was called on to face the shock of revolution, she was already half laicised. Of the twenty priors and abbots in the Reformation Parliament of 1560, no less than fourteen were commendators.

But the Church was not only plundered from without; her own prelates were intent on dissipating her capital. They, too, could amass commendatorships for themselves or others. They could amass parish benefices also; perhaps two-thirds of all the parishes had become annexed to monasteries or bishoprics, and were served by mere curates. They must provide for their friends, their relations, their sons; they must raise money for their own swollen expenses; they must buy the goodwill or the protection of their neighbours. Scotland evolved her own peculiar way of doing this: the "feuing" of land to hereditary tenants. The system had mixed origins and purposes, but in the hands of the Church it became the rake's road to dilapidation. It had, moreover, the same effect as enclosures in England; it dispossessed the poor tenant in favour of the richer gentry:

How prelates heights their tithes it is well known
That husbandmen may not well hold their own;
And now begins a plague among them new,
That gentlemen their steadings takes in feu.

From 1530 onwards the process had been hastened by Papal grants of Church subsidies to James V. From 1535 the Church was paying an annual subsidy to the Crown; twenty years later Mary of Guise could only balance her budget by obtaining a double subsidy from Rome. The Council of 1549 legislated against the alienation of glebes by "infeftments or leases in feu-farm, or tacks for a long time"; but the enactment remained a dead letter.

Naturally, this financial dependence of the State upon the Church still further weakened the States' capacity for Church reform. In 1556 the clergy still far surpassed the laity in wealth. The income of the religious houses alone has been estimated at over £200,000, at a time when the royal lands brought in only some £17,000 and customs little more than £3,000. To put it dramatically, in a nation of perhaps half a million, 3,000 clergy and members of religious communities, or commendators holding their lands, owned at least half the wealth of the country, and their income from tithe and ecclesiastical dues alone was at least double the revenue of the Crown.

In a poor country, it is dangerous for a Church to be wealthy, but it is fatal for a wealthy Church to have lost control of her own wealth. That was the state of the Scottish Church, and she did not know it. The Councils of 1549–52 showed no sign of realizing it. The statute agains feus was their only attempt at economic legislation, and that was designed rather for the preservation of Church property than for the protection of tenants.

5

Insensitiveness to economic evils was, indeed, the fatal defect of Scottish statesmanship. Her Third Estate was in a bad way, but its plight was not due to the English wars. They had, indeed, devastated the best corn lands of Scotland, but a poor agricultural country recovers rapidly from such disasters. Primitive farm implements and turf huts are soon replaced; living at best from hand to mouth, the husbandman has reconstructed his life as soon as he has gathered his first harvest after peace. What held the Scottish tenant down in this poverty was the social organization of his own country.

He had three main grievances. The first, the least serious but perhaps the most resented, was against the Church: the burden of tithe and other ecclesiastical dues. There was the "silver commonly called the Church rights"; there were the "Easter offerings which are taken at Easter from men and women for distribution of the sacrament"; there were, above all, the "corpse-presents, the cow or the uppermost cloth," exacted at a death in payment of a year's masses for the soul of the departed. Perhaps what hurt most in these exactions was not the actual loss, but the quality of the compulsion; the churchmen would "not only fulminate their sentence of cursing" against defaulters, "but also stop and debar men and women to come to the ready using of the sacraments of Holy Church."

The second grievance was against the burghs: their monopoly both of markets and of crafts. The Scottish burghs made their way to wealth and power, not by winning local charters and developing self-government on individual lines as in England, but by lobbying for general legislation. King and Parliament had made them a separate estate of the realm with special privileges. That process robbed Scotland of village industries and village markets. Between 1517 and 1570 only one legal market was authorized outside a royal burgh; up to the end of the century at least, the royal burghs were active in prosecuting "the workmen in clachans." Here as elsewhere, royal policy coincided with class privilege; the burgh merchants' monopoly ensured the easy collection of the royal customs dues.

But such monopolies had not yet made the burghs strong. They were tiny in size; Edinburgh had only some 9,000 inhabitants, Glasgow only half that number, and Aberdeen less than 3,000. Living conditions were bad; the plague at Dundee in Wishart's day was a common experience; "the most part" of the citizens "ends their days in their green youthhead." These little communities were torn by dissensions between the merchant and craft guilds, and between craft guilds and "unfree" craftsmen. They lived largely on an export trade in which they were mere middlemen; nearly 80 per cent of the country's exports consisted of agricultural produce. They were not even independent; the local gentry interfered in the "abusion and confusions" of their politics; in 1544 Ruthvens and Lesleys had fought a pitched battle in the streets of Perth for the provostship of the city.

But these grievances of the countryside against Church and burghs were as nothing in comparison with the central evil of Scottish agricultural life: the husbandman's insecurity of tenure. Here again one must beware of exaggeration. There were "kindly tenants," like Knox's own family, who enjoyed an almost hereditary security, though the "gressum" payable on inheritance might be as high as twelve times the rent. For other tenants leases were often as long as five years, and, especially on Church lands, were probably renewed readily enough, for a "gressum" equal to one year's rent. But for at least a century past, as the feuing movement grew, the tenure even of these relatively fortunate farmers had become increasingly insecure. "Great fines on renewal of leases" became a steadily deepening grievance; under pressure of such fines, it was not difficult to buy out a tenant's "kindness" at a cheap price. And a very large number of tenants were farming on mere annual leases. By the evidence of sober Acts of Parliament, evictions were constant and riotous. In 1469 there were "great gatherings and disorders upon the solemn days of Whitsunday and Martinmas" caused by "distraining for rents and annuals and incasting and outcasting of tenants." In 1546 the evil continued. In 1555 it was still the custom for armed bands to "run in harness to cast out the countrymen."

In spite of these hardships, the Scottish cultivator of the sixteenth century was not the oatmeal-eating pauper of later English legend. The evidence is strong that, on the contrary, he lived mainly on meat, in contrast to the peasants of Europe. It was cereals that he lacked. On the other hand, there were grain-producing districts where a harvest failure spelt ruin—and these were precisely the battlefield of the English wars. The best evidence of conditions in these districts is the impression that they made on a foreign observer —no less than Mary of Guise herself—and this impression perhaps gives the key to the later legend. In November 1549, protesting to her brothers in France at the behaviour of the French cavalry in the country out of which the English had just been driven, Mary described the condition of the peasantry even in times of peace: "You must know that our peasant owns nothing himself: he stays only five or six years on the same land and in this time the poor fellows must get what bare livelihood they can. So they are but sojourners, and must pay their masters for their hired plots in wheat and barley; they keep nothing for themselves but the oats, on which they live."

6

In face of these evils and discontents, Mary's policy as regent was, within its limits, sound. No Scottish sovereign had ever been strong enough to attempt reform against both nobility andChurch; least of all could she afford such an adventure. But she could do two things: she could restore the government finances and she could keep the peace. Four years of economy and begging from France and the Church at length achieved a balanced budget. If economy entailed the replacement of Scottish by French officials, that might well seem a price worth paying. A law of 1555 requiring landlords to give fifty days' notice of change of tenancy, and empowering the sheriff to enforce such notices, could not give security to tenants but might at least remove the scandal of riotous evictions. Mary might well think that this modest policy would be sufficient. Her subjects were busy on the work of reconstruction; they had little time for agitation; the Church Council of 1552 had some ground for its belief that the "frightful heresies" which had afflicted the nation in recent years had "now at last been checked and seem almost extinguished." But there is one heresy more dangerous to governments than any religious creed or party programme: the belief that no change can be for the worse. When that belief is combined with regret for old times, revolution is near; for then conservatism itself turns radical. Such a feeling was growing in the Scotland of 1555. Revolution would not come from the masses, but they would watch it without fear and without disfavour; and when revolution can count on such an audience, its victory is already half assured.

Nevertheless, if Mary had had no policy but sober reconstruction, she might have won through. Unhappily reconstruction was only her method, not her aim. Her aim was to set a French King on the Scottish throne. There was no concealment about this; it was her elementary duty. She was determined to do it by kindness; she insisted that all Frenchmen serving their King in Scotland "should take trouble to be popular, that they might win the people to take him as their future prince." But she must be in a position to use force, and therefore the gateways of the country—Leith and Inchkeith on the east and Dumbarton on the west—must be fortified and garrisoned with French troops. That was an open secret; in the summer of 1551 it was the common talk of the French court, it was reported from Scotland to the Venetian Senate. Moreover, Scotland must not only be assured to France; she must be equipped to play her part in French world politics. Mary herself may not have been the bitter anglophobe depicted by Mason, the English ambassador in France, the egger-on of her Guise brothers and the advocate of French interference in Ireland; but in the eyes of the French court her daughter was not only Queen of Scotland but heiress to the throne of England, and her daughter's husband was to sit on both thrones. She was the agent of that policy and it was as its successful agent that, in Mason's words, her "service in Scotland is so highly taken here as she is in this court made a goddess."

In 1555 she had been playing her cards carefully for five years and she seemed to hold a winning hand. Peace once made with England, her first step had been to make sure of her ground in France. On 8th August 1550, she "shipped at Leith with six galleons of France." She took with her all the nobles who might have made trouble in her absence: the Catholic Huntly, Chancellor of the kingdom; the half-Protestant Cassilis; Maxwell who, two years before, had been playing fast and loose with the English; her step-son James Stewart, as yet known only for his youthful dash in repelling an English raid on Fife; and a number more. For a year she stayed at the French court, while her Scots escort hung round impatiently, trailing behind her from Blois to Tours and from Tours to Angers.

Her first concern was the regency; her daughter must be declared fit to appoint her own representative in Scotland as soon as she reached the age of twelve. Her next was money, to pay off the war debt and to win the support of the nobles against Arran. She played the "importunate beggar for herself and her chosen friends"; the revenues of Guienne and Brittany were charged with Scottish subsidies; the Receiver-General of Brittany "wished Scotland were in a fish-pond." When she sailed for Portsmouth in October 1551, she had got what she wanted; six months before, the Senate of Venice had heard that "in France there is neither Scottish duke nor lord nor prelate nor lady nor dame but who is munificently bribed by the Most Christian King."

There followed two years of careful diplomacy. Mary travelled Scotland with Arran, supporting him in public and undermining him "quietly and in secret." She won the five chief earls: Angus, Huntly, Argyll, Athol and Cassilis. Arran was left without a party and yielded with what grace he might. But Mary had no sooner won the regency in April 1554, than she made the almost fatal mistake of dropping her diplomacy. Reconstituting her Council, she gave both the comptrollership and the vice-chancellorship to two Frenchmen, Villemore and de Rubay. She allowed d'Oysel to take the same place in her counsels as Renard was taking in the counsels of Mary Tudor. She was astute enough to keep Cassilis on her side by giving him the treasureship, but otherwise, as one of her admirers confessed, she "utterly neglected the Scots nobility." Then, proceeding from neglect to positive offence, she disgraced Huntly for failure in an expedition against a Highland clan, fined him heavily, transferred his chancellorship, in fact if not in name, to de Rubay and his government of the Orkneys to another Frenchman. His disgrace reflected on Argyll, who had participated in his failure. No doubt her motive was exasperation at Scottish inefficiency; no doubt, too, ill-health made her irritable. "You must make allowances for my anger," she had written to her brothers five years before, after three days of pain; "you know that gouty people are not patient." But this was no way to treat the "perfervid temper" of Scotsmen; she would need to tread more carefully in future if she were to keep the advantage she had won.

7

So opened the year 1555. It ran an uneventful course till, *in the end of the harvest*, John Knox landed quietly somewhere between Forth and the Border. This time his journey must have been easy enough. The war between France and Spain had reached a deadlock in Flanders; no clash of arms to the eastward, such as he had heard the year before, troubled him on his way to Dieppe. England was at peace with France, for the marriage treaty between Philip and Mary had stipulated that she should not be dragged into her new King's European wars. Nearly two years were to past before that promise was broken. Meanwhile the narrow seas were open, even for the man who had been exiled from Scotland and had written treason against the English throne.

CHAPTER XIV

THE SCOTTISH MISSION
1555–56

I

THE SCOTTISH visit of 1555–56 is the core of the Knox legend. He arrived, hesitant still, distrustful of himself, a repressed evangelist half ready to turn politician. He passed some days at Berwick with Marjorie and her mother, and was cheered a little by what he saw of his old congregation, *perceiving that in the midst of Sodom God had more Lots than one and more faithful daughters than two.* Then, still more hesitant, he ventured to Edinburgh and lodged with a burgess of the name of Syme. There, to his astonishment, his presence was no sooner known than people began to flock to the house. Towns-people came with their wives, among them the Dean of Gild himself, head of the Edinburgh merchants and chief officer of the burgh council. Another visitor was an old acquaintance of Lothian days, David Forres, at whose house Wishart had slept on his way to Haddington. Above all, Wishart's wisest friend, Erskine of Dun, came to make Knox's acquaintance. Even more welcome, perhaps, was the unexpected appearance of his fellow-preacher, John Willock, who had come to Scotland earlier that year on a diplomatic mission from the Duchess of Friesland to the Queen Regent, and had been spying out the land. He could confirm what Knox was beginning to see: that in the last eight years men's minds had turned definitely from the old Church to the new.

From that moment Knox was carried away. Politics dropped from him for the time; his sense of mission revived. He had been guilty of *slothful coldness*; God had permitted him against his will to *behold the fervent thirst of our brethren, night and day sobbing and groaning for the bread of life. If I had not seen it with my eyes in my own country, I could not have believed it.* He would not, as he had intended, return to Berwick. He was called here and now, not only to preach, but to found a church.

He began, indeed, by harping on his old chord: the deadly sin of idolatry. *The trumpet blew the old sound.* It was not lawful for Scotsmen *to give their bodily presence to the Mass or yet offer their children to the Papistical baptism.* He trumpeted that message *till private houses of indifferent largeness could not contain the voice of it.* And he urged it specially on his more influential visitors. Erskine collected a supper party for him. Besides Forres and Willock, Knox met at this party young William Maitland, whom he may have seen ten years before, when Wishart's party slept at his father's house of Lethington the night before the Haddington sermon. That young man was already the rising politician of Scotland. A typical *politique*, in the contemporary French phrase, he was naturally opposed to Knox's quixotry. What, after all, was the harm of treating old ceremonies with decent respect? Had not St. Paul himself paid his vows in the Temple at Jerusalem? Knox overbore such arguments with Johnsonian vehemence; if he did not convince Maitland, he at least reduced him to silence.

2

But there was a new tone now in Knox's passion against the Mass. His reasoning pointed to a new conclusion. If his countrymen, the depth of whose conviction he had only just realized, must thus cut themselves off from the ministrations of the Church, they could not rest content with such self-excommunication. They must create a communion of their own. Here Knox's own deepest conviction flooded his mind. He could not take Calvin's colder view about the sacraments. As a matter of Church order, indeed, Calvin was pledged to the ideal of a weekly celebration of the Lord's Supper; but he had not only concluded that his church in Geneva could not live up to that ideal, he was inclined to discourage the struggling churches of France from aiming so high. They must not organize churches prematurely and hanker after regularly appointed ministers, just in order that they might celebrate the Supper. Knox felt differently. It was, above all, his task to restore *the right use of the Lord's Table.* For *the Son of God, who is the wisdom of the Father hath commanded us to assemble together in His name; He hath appointed His holy Word to be preached and His Sacraments to be ministered and received; which Sacraments He hath sanctified to us with His own precious blood, and remembrance whereof He hath straitly commanded us to celebrate to His ganecoming.*

In this spirit he set out to organize congregations of the faithful. Early in November Erskine brought him north to his house at Dun, between Dundee and Brechin, *where he remained a month, daily exercised in doctrine, whereunto resorted the principal men of that country.* Crossing Forth again, he settled at the one house in Lothian which was still open to him, Calder, the seat of Sir James Sandilands, Cockburn's father-in-law. There he found a more distinguished audience: no less than two future Regents of Scotland, James Stewart, the future Earl of Moray, and his uncle Erskine, the future Earl of Mar, then Governor of Edinburgh Castle. With them came James's half-brother-in-law and Erskine's cousin: Archibald Lord Lorne, Argyll's heir. They began to discuss whether, instead of secret meetings, Knox might not preach publicly. Till after Christmas he was back and forth between Calder and Edinburgh, and then passed into Ayrshire to make acquaintance with Rough's and Wishart's old disciples among the county families. They were all there as of old—Lockharts Campbells and Chalmers, with the Wallaces and Andrew Stewart, Lord Ochiltree.

Then, a little before Easter, came the climax of these missionary journeys. It began with an invitation from by far the best brain in the Protestant party at that time, Alexander Cunningham, the former Lord Kilmaurs, who had succeeded his father in the earldom of Glencairn seven years before. He sent for Knox *to his place at Finlaston* near the banks of Clyde, *where after doctrine he likewise ministered the Lord's Table.* Thence Knox retraced his steps, establishing the Sacrament as he went in the congregations already prepared. In mid-April he was back at Calder *where divers from Edinburgh and from the country about convened as well for the doctrine as for the right use of the Lord's Table, which before they had never practised. From thence he departed the second time to the Laird of Dun, and, teaching there in greater liberty, the gentlemen required that he should minister like-*

wise unto them the Table of the Lord Jesus, whereof were partakers the most of the gentlemen of the Mearns.

3

That was the climax of Knox's mission—perhaps the climax of his life. What followed seemed more exciting, but in fact it was bathos.

Knox, in his *greater liberty*, had now come into the open, and the authorities must take notice. Nothing like this had happened since Wishart's day. Already the Regent had been asking if it were an Englishman who was preaching in Ayrshire; and *a prelate, not of the least pride*, had told her, *nay, no Englishman, but it is Knox, that knave.* Mary did not want to interfere; she probably did not realize the danger. Not so the bishops. Their authority had been openly challenged, and they were determined to act. They summoned Knox to appear before them at the Blackfriars' Church in Edinburgh.

A more foolish move could hardly be imagined. They were giving Knox precisely the opportunity that Wishart had wanted and that Beaton had forestalled. He had not to rely, like Wishart, on any uncertain tryst with followers from the other end of Scotland; the summons reached him at Dun where the *gentlemen of the Mearns* had just *banded themselves to the uttermost of their powers to maintain the true preaching of the evangel of Jesus Christ.* He came to Edinburgh, but not alone; Erskine with *divers other gentlemen* came with him. No one had bargained for this: the summons was hurriedly withdrawn.

But Knox had (presumably) already surrendered himself to the keeping of the Bishop of Dunkeld, and he saw no reason to move from that prelate's *great lodging.* He preached there twice a day for ten days to *a greater audience than ever before he had done in that town.* Glencairn came to hear him, bringing the Earl Marischall. They were eager to exploit the opportunity. The Regent herself was thought to have taken Knox's side and rebuked the bishops. She was no friend to the Hamilton who was Primate of St. Andrews, nor he to her. He was the only backbone of that spineless clan; he had laboured for years to bring his half-brother, the new Duke of Chatelheraut, to the sticking point; he had urged him, not only to keep the regency, but to aim at the throne; he had spoken of the little queen in France in language unfit for polite ears. Now that the duke was gone to his new French estates, might she not be ready to bring him and his whole pack of bishops to heel—to undertake the reform of the Church as every other monarch in Europe had undertaken it?

For one moment Knox seemed to catch the infection of these hopes. He sat down and wrote to Mary, pompously but moderately. He must, of course, lecture her; he must talk of Josiah and Jehoshaphat, those *most godly princes*; he must even mention Rahab among those whose hearts God had moved *of very pity and compassion to save his people*. But, however elephantine his eloquence might be, the substance of his plea was reasonable. More, it was very much to the point. It hit off exactly Mary's main weakness; her pre-occupation with the formal enforcement of order—or, as she herself expressed it, "the bringing of a young people into a new subjection to those who desire to see justice reign." That, Knox argued, with curious insight into her character, was not enough. There was in Scotland a *universal defection as well in religion as in manners*. A reformation in manners was clearly urgent; *a justice inflexible against murderers and common oppressors*. But he would leave such admonitions to others; his duty was to urge an even plainer truth. *Vain is it to crave reformation in manners where the religion is corrupted*. Of course it was *dangerous to innovate anything in matters of religion*; of course, too, Mary's power to initiate *a public reformation* was limited. But it must be attempted; and it must be attempted by the secular power. *The negligence of bishops shall no less be required of the hands of magistrates than shall the oppression of false judges*.

The letter was despatched. Glencairn delivered it to the Regent; but, if he saw anything of its reception, he did not tell Knox of it. And then suddenly, on this pinnacle of excitement and expectation, Knox announced his intention of returning to Geneva. He despatched Marjorie and her mother to France; himself he left Edinburgh, and proceeded to pay a round of farewell visits to his congregations. From Ayrshire he went to Castle Campbell, to visit old

Argyll, the official president of at least one tribunal that had sent evangelists to the stake. He saw a new field of work in the Campbell country, and Campbell of Glenurchy urged him to stay; but he insisted that his duty called him to Geneva. And so, *in the month of July he left this realm and passed to France.* He joined his family in Dieppe and went straight to Switzerland, arriving in Geneva on September 13th.

4

Why this anticlimax? Knox's most admiring biographers have shaken their heads over it. Had his nerve failed him again?

He had a good enough excuse for going. Soon after he had left Geneva, some of the English at Frankfurt had moved there, with Whittingham at their head. They had been allowed to form a congregation and, on 1st November 1555, they had elected Knox minister. He had been notified of the appointment; he could not temporize about it indefinitely; he felt, no doubt, some responsibility for *the little flock* which had followed him to Switzerland. But could this be much more than an excuse? After all, the congregation at Geneva was not pastorless; they had elected two other ministers, Goodman and Gilby, both able clergy of the English Church. The new Scottish congregations, on the other hand, had as yet no ministers except a certain Harlow, who had begun life as a tailor in Edinburgh. He had been evangelizing quietly in Scotland for two years past and was now beginning to preach publicly; but, though full of *zeal and diligent plainness in doctrine*, he was not a well educated man and his only ordination had been that of deacon in the English Church of Edward VI. Willock had gone back to Emden. As between rival calls there could surely be little doubt which was the more compelling.

It is useless to speculate about Knox's motives, for we have no evidence. We know only that, on this occasion, his unruly conscience did not appear to trouble him. That, in itself, may be significant. But, whatever his motives, no decision could have been wiser. It was wise as a matter of political calculation; it was wiser still from the point of view of the future health of the Scottish Church.

Scottish politics at this time were a whirlpool of cross-currents, more confusing than the old family feuds or the recent alignment of loyalists against English. The rock round which the eddies swirled was a fact so simple that historians hardly mention it. Scotland, with her poverty and her aristocratic anarchy, could never be governed by an absentee; yet that was the form of government to which she was pledged. The fatal miscalculation of the Valois and the Guises was that they proposed to keep the Queen of Scots permanently in France. Married to the future King of France, she was to be the pledge of Scotland's obedience to him. They did not see that what they had thus taken in pawn was the linch-pin of the Scottish cart; without that pin the cart could never be driven, even on menial errands. But what they did not see, Scottish patriots and Scottish brigands saw only too clearly.

A perpetual regency might not be distasteful to the brigands, provided it were weak; they had made their profit out of regencies before. But to the patriots the prospect was intolerable. At the moment when Mary Stewart should wed the Dauphin, she would, in effect, resign the Scottish throne. The only question was: who should reign after her? There would, of course, be no abrupt usurpation. The Queen Mother was a convenient stop-gap; eventually she would give place to some Scots Lieutenant-General of the kingdom. He would have time to choose his policy; he might found a new dynasty, or Mary might have more than one Valois-Stewart son and the younger might be offered her Scottish throne, or the old project of an Anglo-Scottish union might be taken up again. It was known now that Mary Tudor would die childless; her sister's accession would open up new possibilities.

It is these calculations that explain the attitude of men like Cassilis to the Queen Regent's administration and to the French marriage. The marriage was inevitable, but in countenancing it they were not accepting the French obedience. Rather, they were saying good-bye to a queen to whom, after all, they owed little more than a sentimental loyalty. That good-bye said, sooner or later they would have to shift for themselves. Meanwhile they would use her name and her mother's authority to keep the country in some sort of order and, perhaps, to pave the way for a change of government.

There was one Scotsman, above all, whose mind was at work on these calculations: James Stewart, Prior of St. Andrews. That young man, still only twenty-four in 1556, is one of the secret figures of history. Two things only seem certain about him. In religion and in private life he was a puritan, with the puritan's personal rectitude and a good deal of the puritan's hardness; in politics he was a man of public spirit, in the strict sense of that hackneyed phrase. That probably was his real secret. In an age and a country where politics were predominantly an affair of personal ambitions and predilections he had, like the English Cecil, the purely governmental mind. He was, first and last, a politician, with an infinite capacity for holding his hand. He spoke not very much and he wrote less; in diplomatic correspondence he had a terseness of style which amounted to genius. But, unlike Cecil, he had a touch of the dangerous charm that makes a leader; and, unlike him too, his religious convictions were real and compelling.

Much ink has been spilt on the question whether James was, at this time, a traitor to his half-sister, his country's queen. Of course he was, if it was treason to distrust romantic imperialists like the Valois and the Guises, to foresee the breakdown of their schemes and to make preparations against that breakdown in advance. In that sense he had probably been already a traitor four years earlier, when he had visited Edward VI on his way from France. Moreover, it was doubtless with such treason in mind, as well as from religious conviction, that he and others, like Glencairn, had been encouraging Knox in the past few months. If he was to save Scotland from the evils of absentee government, he must have a party in the country, more secure than family combinations. And Knox seemed to be creating just such a party.

5

Knox's appearance in Edinburgh marked a definite stage in these calculations. It coincided with another crisis. There was one practical alternative policy to that of James Stewart and his friends, one way in which an absentee sovereign might govern Scotland. That was the creation of a standing army, predominantly French. This was the Queen Regent's policy. It was also the policy of her Council, largely French, from which she had excluded most of the men who represented native Scottish ideals and prejudices. She sprung it on the Scottish Parliament about this time. She proposed a sort of Doomsday survey of "the possessions of the shires and every man's gear," and a special tax for the maintenance of a mercenary army. Immediately the gentry were up in arms. Three hundred of them assembled at Holyrood and deputed old Sandilands to remonstrate with the Regent. Scotland must remain a feudal country, defended by feudal levies. Mary gave way, and her conciliatoriness raised their hopes.

After Knox's tour there was little doubt whither the mind both of gentry and burghers was moving. There was a new spirit in his congregations. Sandilands was a symbolic figure; he represented a decaying feudalism, but he represented also a new religious conviction. The gospel and the Sacrament might change the ancient *Scottish kindness* between landlord and tenant into something both steadier and more formidable. This new communion might be at the service of a likeminded Regent in the future, when he had to steer his judicious course between a nominal sovereign in Paris and the nobles of his own country. But first it must be freed from the prohibitions and repression of the old Church. And, for that purpose, the old Church must be bridled. Might not Mary herself be ready to do the bridling? The concourse in the Bishop of Dunkeld's lodging was hardly less impressive than the gathering of gentry at Holyrood. Might she not listen to the one as she yielded to the other?

Of course there could be no question with her of any Protestant revolution. But that was not necessary. There had, as yet, been no such revolution in any country, except in a few Swiss cities. In Lutheran Germany, even in England and Scandinavia, the old Church had been changed into the new without any very violent transition. The Scottish Church, was after all, a half-empty shell; gospel preachers had found no difficulty in walking into empty pulpits. If Mary could be induced to grant the new congregations freedom of worship and to limit the priests' power over men's lives, the rest might follow naturally.

This was no wild dream. If Mary of Guise had been a little less clever than she was, she might well have fallen into the trap; if she had been as indifferent to religion as Catherine de Medici, she would have walked into it with her eyes open. At this moment statutory toleration was the right policy in Scotland, as it was the right policy in France five years later, when Catherine actually tried it. And it was perfectly feasible. There was no great Catholic family in Scotland, like Mary's seven Guise brothers in France, who could wreck such a policy. Moreover, in Scotland, as in France, the outcome of such a policy was by no means certain. It might prove a trap, not for Mary, but for the Protestant lords. The new congregations had as yet struck no deep roots, except perhaps in Dundee and Ayrshire; they might have been killed by a little temporizing kindness, if simultaneously Mary could have brought in the new Jesuit preachers and enlisted the support of the gentry for a reform of Church abuses on the old Spanish model. But Mary had not the imagination for such a policy. Instead, she set herself to gain time by leading the Protestant lords to believe that she might fall into their trap. "I am forced," she wrote next January to her brother, the Cardinal of Lorraine, "to keep up many pretences until I come to the proper time." The Protestant lords, on their side, muted their demands, asking no more from her than a good Catholic might grant.

But in this sort of politicians' game, Knox was a mere hindrance. In his present mood he, too, might mute his demands, assuring the Regent that the *victory* of God's *chosen children standeth not in resisting, but in suffering*, and adjuring her only, as regards Church reform, that *albeit suddenly ye may not do all things that ye would, yet shall ye not cease to do what ye may*. But he could not help using language to which no Catholic could listen, speaking of *damnable idolatry* and quoting: "*all plantation that My heavenly Father hath not planted shall be rooted out.*" He would never be able to accept even a temporary compromise that recognized the full ritual of the Mass. When men began to think of such compromises, he was better out of the way.

6

That was the political aspect of the choice that Knox made that summer. But there was another aspect of far greater importance to the future life of Scotland—indeed, to the future life of Europe. The calculations of the politicians were to be ironically upset by fate. Scotland was not, after all, to have an absentee sovereign; five years later her Queen was to return to her, a childless widow. For four years after that, until her tragedy began, that queen was to govern among counsellors who had lost their bearings. Historians have puzzled over their motives and their aims, but the truth is that they had none. They had planned for what they thought was the inevitable; they were improvising to meet the wholly unforeseen. Not so the congregations that Knox had founded in 1556. Untouched by the revulsions of politics, they took charge of the nation, moulding it in their image. What that image was, its excellencies and its deformities, we know only too well; but in 1556 its features and its spirit were as yet unformed. They were to be formed in the next two years; would they be better fashioned if Knox were to stay or go?

For indeed, in this Scottish summer of 1556, the whole future of Christendom hung on a knife edge. The Protestant Reformation was being offered its last chance of achieving something more than a social revolution. Luther had failed; Calvin had pre-condemned himself to failure before his European mission was well begun. Faith had taken refuge again in law; the Purpose of God was already being cramped into politics. But in the interval between these two failures, for one moment Knox's new congregations seemed to recapture something of the old simplicity. It is impossible to mistake the language in which Knox wrote to them. In his farewell letter of July 7th there was no word of politics or discipline; no demand even for freedom of worship. First and last, let them study the Bible, privately, in their households and, where possible, in weekly *assemblies of brethren. Let them especially be frequent in the prophets and in the epistles of St. Paul. In households once a day at least let family and servants be partakers in reading, exhorting and in making common prayers; in assemblies let there be confession and invocation of God's Holy Spirit, thanksgiving and common prayers for princes, rulers and magistrates; for the liberty and free passage of Christ's evangel; for the comfort and deliverance of our afflicted brethren; and for such other things as the spirit of the Lord Jesus shall teach unto you.* They had known *fellowship and participation with the Lord Jesus in his body and his blood;*

let them not *change* the *nature* they had thus received; but, reading and praying in secret, let them *patiently abide the glorious apparition and coming of the Lord Jesus.*

Such had been the worship in which Knox had led them. And from these intimacies, from the solemnities of the restored Sacrament, celebrated behind closed doors, he had been called to the tumults of Edinburgh, to an armed bodyguard of gentry, to the crowds pressing round the doors of the bishop's lodging, to the calculations and hesitations of the politicians. The trumpet note crept back into his voice, and all that he had created in the last six months began to totter.

The storm-signal was hoisted in that single sentence of his letter to the Regent: *the negligence of bishops shall no less be required at the hand of magistrates than the oppression of false judges.* We cannot call this doctrine wrong; but it contained the germ of all the errors that had degraded the Reformation, Protestant and Catholic, and were to degrade it again. In any Christian State the secular power must have some duty to restrain abuses of ecclesiastical authority; in the Jewish organization of sixteenth-century Christendom this duty had necessarily become one of the main functions of government. Preached by Catholic doctors to Catholic sovereigns, who could measure their reforms by accepted canons of faith, the doctrine actually operated to restore the balance between Church and State. But preached by Protestant evangelists, who had rejected the canons, to Catholic sovereigns or to revolutionary governments, it became the catchword of every form of political insubordination and party strife. We know from his later writings that Knox realized the danger. No spiritual ideal could live in such thunder weather. Yet, so long as Knox remained in Scotland, these electric storms would continue to roll up. He was a magnet for them. He was too public a figure; his reputation would not allow him to turn pastor, however much he might desire it. If the new spirit was to have free course, he was better away.

We know the sequel. He did go, and his going perhaps postponed the storm for a few months. But not for longer. The Reformation missed its last chance; once more, and finally, quietism appealed to the law and took the sword. Yet it is well to remember that this happened in Knox's absence, and at least not under his direct leadership.

7

Again Knox travelled south in peace. There was honeymoon weather in Europe that autumn for his family party. It had been a brilliant summer of great heats, and it had been a summer without war. The Truce of Vaucelles in the preceding February had suspended hostilities between France and Spain, and in this space of quiet the chief figure in Europe disappeared. Four days after Knox arrived in Geneva, Charles V, his abdication completed, set sail from the Netherlands for the monastery of St. Just. His brother Ferdinand had taken over the Empire; his son Philip had entered successively into the possession of Milan, of the Netherlands, of Spain and Naples. Now it was for them to decide whether the long Hapsburg-Valois feud should be waged on or finally closed.

Philip was to close it, forming a united front with Henry of France against the heretics of Europe. But not yet; two and a half years were to pass before a final peace. A new storm was blowing up in Italy. Old Caraffa, who had ascended the Papal throne at last, eighteen months before, at the age of seventy-nine, was reverting for a moment to the habits of his Renaissance predecessors. He had revived his old Neapolitan family feud with the Hapsburgs, and had thereby incautiously defied the best soldier in Europe. This same September, the Duke of Alva, Philip's Viceroy in Naples, was invading the Romagna, and Caraffa was summoning help from France. Two months later, the Duke of Guise crossed the Alps in "as sharp a winter as men remember to have seen." He was to meet with no better fortune than previous French armies in Italy. Next year the storm was to spread back to the frontiers of the Low Countries, to Calais and to the Scottish Border. It would not be so easy for Knox to retrace his steps, if he should receive a new call from the north.

And with this Papal war the fortunes of Scotland were closely linked. In the previous December 1555, while Knox was at Calder, a letter had gone to the Pope from Blois, in the name of the Queen of Scots, praying him to grant a Church subsidy to the Regent and to consider certain proposals for Church reform which would be submitted to him by "our cousin the Cardinal Sermoneta, the protector of our suits with your Holiness." The Cardinal's memorandum drew a picture of immorality in nunneries, of Church property alienated and decayed, of clerics immersed in secular affairs and trade. It prayed the Pope to appoint a commission of Scottish bishops to restore order. This diagnosis of Church abuses was defective and the remedy hardly impressive; for, if the commission suggested did not include the Primate of St. Andrews, it included Hepburn, bishop of Moray, the father of nine children in whose interests he had become a flagrant collector of benefices and dilapidator of diocesan property. Still, the programme was at least something. But Caraffa himself was too deeply immersed in secular affairs to consider such schemes. Almost two years passed before he took action, and all that time the sands of Scottish patience were running out.

CHAPTER XV

THE HESITATIONS OF A MISSIONARY
1557–58

I

KNOX'S FIRST thought after leaving Scotland was characteristic. He wrote from Dieppe to one of his *sisters* in Edinburgh. It may have been to Elizabeth Barron, wife of the Edinburgh Dean of Gild, who, like other ladies before her, had *delighted much* in his company *by reason that she had a troubled conscience*; or to her sister Janet Macgill, wife of the Clerk to the Registry; or to Janet Guthrie, whose husband was Clerk of the City of Edinburgh. He wrote also, then or soon after, to his *merchants' wives* in London, Mrs. Locke and Mrs. Hickman. The advice offered in the two letters was significantly different. The wife of the Edinburgh official was adjured in the old tone to have no part with idolaters; but Mrs. Locke and Mrs. Hickman were advised *to flee the present idolatry* by leaving England.

Knox has been often accused of counselling his friends to run risks which he refused to face himself, but the accusation is hardly just. In the summer of 1554, when he was issuing his manifestoes to the faithful in England, non-attendance at Mass, might hurt a man's social or political prospects, but did not yet endanger his freedom or his life. It was the same in Scotland in 1556. That was the point of Erskine's supper party. For Maitland, soon to be the Regent's secretary, nonconformity meant the sacrifice of ambition, but it meant nothing worse. The wife of an Edinburgh official, too, might feel it politic to *avoid danger and displeasure both to herself and to others*, especially to her husband, but she was as safe from actual persecution as Knox himself. On the other hand, by that time merchants in London, notoriously the focus of English Protestantism and therefore of persecution, were in a very different position.

For them and their families flight was the only safety. *My heart weeps and my eyes are not dry in requiring this of you, but very love compelleth me thereto.*

Both Locke and his wife appear to have taken this advice. On November 19th, Knox was writing to Mrs. Locke, hoping soon to see her, and bidding her expect a further communication *against the market in Frankfurt.* From another letter written three weeks later, it would appear that both were in Frankfurt—Locke content to remain there, but his wife anxious to go on to Geneva. In the following May she went there, with her son and daughter.

Knox recommended Geneva to her as *the most perfect school of Christ that ever was in the earth since the days of the Apostles. In other places I confess Christ to be truly preached, but manners and religion so sincerely reformed I have not yet seen in any other place.* And that is really all we know about Knox as minister of the English congregation in Geneva. The congregation had its printed and published Form of Prayers and Ministration of the Sacraments; its ministers preached, after the manner of Geneva, at least three times a week, conducted their house-to-house visitations in preparation for the quarterly Sacrament Sundays, and conferred with their fellow ministers at meetings of the Consistory. Of Calvin himself Knox probably saw little; in these months the patriarch was immersed in his diplomatic correspondence, and more intent on the organization of the new churches of France than on the government of Geneva.

Indeed, Knox owed to Geneva little but happy memories. He learnt there the elaborations of predestinarian doctrine and could repeat them from the lips outward, but they had little effect on his mind. At the request of his friends he wrote a treatise on the subject before he left the Continent in 1559, but the book does not seem to have found its way across the Channel till some twenty years later, after his death; and to all appearances he took little of these elaborations home with him. He learnt, too, at Geneva an admiration for disciplinary order in the congregation, to the pedantic delight of Theodore de Bèze. He used Calvin as a reference book on all matters of doctrine, but on the most important point about which he consulted him he diverged, as we shall see, widely from Calvin's teaching. In truth, Geneva to him was not a school but a retreat.

2

In May 1557, Knox had other visitors than Mrs. Locke. Barron and Syme arrived from Edinburgh, bringing a letter signed by Glencairn and by the three nobles who had attended his preachings at Calder—Erskine, Lorne and James Stewart. It was an invitation to return to Scotland, "where ye shall find the faithful that ye left behind you, not only glad to hear your doctrine, but ready to jeopard lives and goods for the forward setting of the glory of God." The political situation was unchanged, but there was no sign of active persecution and the friars were "in less estimation both with the Queen's grace and the rest of the nobility."

Barron and Syme were the bearers of other verbal messages from these lords. There has been much unnecessary guessing as to what those messages may have been; they presumably outline the same policy which had been discussed the year before and was actually undertaken a year later. The Regent and Parliament were to be asked to undertake the reform of the Church, and meanwhile freedom of worship was to be demanded for the Protestant congregations. Knox consulted Calvin, *with other godly ministers, who all with one consent said that he could not refuse that vocation unless he would declare himself rebellious unto his God and unmerciful to his country.* In fact, however, he waited four months before leaving Geneva and did not reach Dieppe until the end of October. In the meantime he wrote a series of letters to the congregations in Scotland to which, owing to the *troubles of these wicked times,* he received no answer.

His delay has occasioned much head-shaking among historians, but it is not difficult to account for it. Barron and Syme could hardly have arrived at a less opportune moment. Marjorie's eldest son was born in May and christened on the 23rd. Mrs. Locke, his old friend and his guest, had lost her daughter immediately after her arrival. It was reasonable that Knox should delay a little at such a moment. Moreover, the state of Europe was even less favourable than his private circumstances. Already, as the two Edinburgh burgesses travelled south, they must have seen signs of approaching war. The Truce of Vaucelles was over; Picardy and Normandy were filling up with bands of cavalry; Coligny, Admiral of France, was there and the Prince of Condé; on April 27th, the English ambassador in France reported that "some invasion was meant into England; the passages are stopped or shall be shortly." A month later naval preparations were in full swing; sixteen sail were ready at Havre and twenty rigged out at Dieppe. And now, on June 7th, under pressure from Spain, England at last declared war on France, and the Scottish Regent, with d'Oysel at her side, was planning to break off her conferences with the English commissioners on the Border. It would be no easy task for Knox to find a passage from Dieppe to Leith.

It might not even be easy for him to pass through France at all. At the King's request, the Pope had just authorized the establishment in France of an Inquisition on the Spanish model; on April 25th he had appointed the Cardinal of Lorraine as chief Inquisitor. The Parlement at Paris had refused its consent, but on July 24th the King issued the new Edict of Compiègne against heretics.

Nor was it merely a question of difficult travel or possible arrest for heresy. Again, we do not know Knox's motives, but, in fact, the lords had no sooner sent off their invitation than, under the influence of the new war, the whole political situation began to change. The war had two results in Scotland. First, it led Mary of Guise into her third capital mistake. She had alienated the nobility by her new-broom reorganization in 1554; she had alarmed the gentry by her proposals for a standing army in 1556; now she upset the whole nation, still hardly more than well launched on the work of post-war reconstruction, by her attempt to commit Scotland to active hostilities against England. And, secondly, the fighting in Flanders went badly for the French. On August 10th at St. Quentin, the French army was overwhelmingly defeated; the Constable of France was taken prisoner; for a moment there was nothing between the Spanish army and Paris. Defeat gave Scotland a new and more urgent value in the eyes of the French King. The project of a Franco-Scottish union must be brought into effect at once. The marriage between the Dauphin and the Queen of Scots must be pushed on. So Henry wrote to the Regent.

Henry's letters were despatched on October 30th, a week after

Knox arrived in Dieppe. And, meanwhile, something else had happened. The Regent's war plans had gone well enough up to a point. She had lured England into war by an unsuccessful raid across the Middle Marches and by beginning the fortification of Eyemouth at the very gates of Berwick. She had assembled an army at New-battle and had marched it to the Tweed for an attack on Wark and Norham. But the army and siege guns had no sooner been concentrated at Maxwellheuch than the nobles executed a time-honoured manœuvre, as they had done fifteen years before with James V; they refused point blank to cross the Border. They would defend their own country but they would not venture into England. This feudal mutiny was a turning-point. Mary was furious; she never forgave it. That is the explanation of much that was to happen in the next eighteen months. She abandoned all hope of real co-operation with the leaders of her adopted country. She could, per-haps, gain their support for her daughter's marriage, but, that marriage once celebrated and the "crown matrimonial" secured for the Dauphin, the French Government must reduce their new territory to obedience.

Accordingly Parliament was summoned for December to con-sider the letters from France.

3

Knox, arriving at Dieppe on October 24th, found word of some of these things in two letters from Scotland. One told him that *new consultations was appointed for final conclusion of the matter before pur-posed*; the other warned him that the writer *had communed with all those that seemed most frack and fervent in the matter, and that in none did he find such boldness and constancy as was requisite for such an enterprise.* Knox was in no state of mind to receive such news with equanimity. This was a pretty ploy: to bring a man half across Europe in time of war, strung to a dangerous adventure, with the touching farewells and admiring praises of his flock still in his ears—and then to bid him wait for a more convenient opportunity!

Nor, perhaps, was this the only cause of his exasperation. On his way to Dieppe, through Paris or its outskirts, he had been forcibly reminded of the insecurity of the times. After St. Quentin, panic had taken hold of Paris, and its first result had been an attack on the Huguenot congregation there. Its meeting-house in the Rue St. Jaques had been attacked on the evening of September 4th, when the members were assembled for a celebration of the Supper. After a tumult in which many of the men fought their way through the mob, a hundred and twenty women and children, with a few men, were arrested and imprisoned. On the 27th two men and a woman were burnt in the Place de Grève, and two more men a week later. It was the first threatening of the wars of religion, and the Cardinal of Lorraine had taken the lead in urging wholesale executions. His sister in Scotland would show no less zeal if half-hearted politicians allowed her the opportunity.

In these circumstances, it is not to be wondered at that Knox should have reacted violently to the news from Scotland. He wrote a passionate letter of expostulation, too passionate to be intelligible. *Only for this cause are ye called princes of the people: not by reason of your birth and progeny, but by reason of your office and duty, which is to vindicate and deliver your subjects and brethren from all violence and oppression to the utmost of your power. Thraldom and misery shall apprehend your own bodies, your children, subjects and posterity whom ye have betrayed and presently do fight to betray, them and your realm, to the slavery of strangers. The war begun (although I acknowledge it to be the work of God) shall be your destruction, unless that betimes remedy be provided. God open your eyes, that ye may espy and consider your own miserable estate.*

This letter was the outburst of a man who had lost his bearings. He sat down at Dieppe to recover them, and, as was his habit, he did his thinking on paper. By December 1st he had completed a letter to *His Brethren in Scotland*. A week later he finished translating, with additions of his own, a French Huguenot *Apology for the Protestants who are holden in Prison at Paris*. Ten days after that, on December 17th, he despatched another letter to the *Lords and Others professing the Truth in Scotland*. From these documents his estimate of the situation in Scotland is clear, and the estimate was not far wrong.

The reforming politicians in Scotland, whose calculations we have already sketched, had two ends in view; to humble the bishops and to eliminate the Regent. But they had no intention of taking on both these opponents together if they could secure the help of one against the other. Nor was the elimination of the Regent, in itself, a matter of any urgency; they could push her aside at their leisure; and for the moment she might be positively useful to them. In March they were still of the same mind as when Knox had left Scotland: they thought that they could enlist her in at least the first moves of a campaign against the bishops. In this they were shrewd enough. We have seen that schemes for Church reform were in the air; and if the Pope at this moment, amid the ruins of his Italian policy, was a broken reed, the Regent might be the more ready to accept moderate Protestant support.

But, as the year went on, James Stewart and his friends were gradually driven to revise their policy. In the first place, they had reason to doubt the strength of the Protestant congregations on which they were relying as the core of their future party. Already these congregations were troubled by internal dissensions. The semi-anabaptist element which was to play so curious a part in Scottish Protestantism was already beginning to emerge. It showed itself first in a puritan revolt against the moral laxities of the faithful. There were laxities enough; in Scotland, as earlier in Germany, emancipation from the bondage of Church law was producing very mixed results. Here, too, as elsewhere, puritanism grew into pharisaism and pharisaism into spiritual pride. The faithful could and should become saints, freed from sin, no longer needing either confession or forgiveness. And, as usual, the claim that men could become Christs verged on the assertion that Christ was no more than man. This at least, from what he heard, was Knox's estimate of the state of his congregations. The reforming politicians would be foolish to identify themselves with such ambiguous support.

Moreover, there was a strong anti-clerical party whose alliance they desired, but who would have nothing to do either with Knoxians or with sectaries. This party was not prepared to go further than a Catholic reformation; the most they would demand, beyond the reform of abuses, was worship in the vulgar tongue. Above all, the determining influence in the change of policy was the Regent's war policy. By it, she had brought the issue between the nobles and herself to a head at a moment when the issue between the reformers and the Church had not yet been fairly joined. Unless, therefore, the reformers were to fight both Regent and Church at the same time, they must fight the Regent before they fought the Church.

And at this moment the French marriage proposals offered them a golden opportunity for turning the Regent's flank without any frontal attack. The marriage involved the fixing of the succession. If Mary died childless, who should be King of Scots? The Valois and the Guises, of course, intended that the succession should pass to her husband, but Scotsmen would be united in opposition to that solution. The only alternative candidate for the succession was Arran, now the Duke of Chatelherault. He could be attracted to the reformers by that offer, and he would bring over with him his half-brother of St. Andrews, followed by at any rate more than one of his fellow bishops. Then, once designated as heir presumptive, he would be the obvious lieutenant-general for an absentee queen; Mary of Guise could not, in the long run, assert her regency against his claims.

There was a flurry of intrigue before the reformers settled down to this policy. Mary attributed her defeat at Maxwellheuch especially to Chatelheraut, and James Stewart seems to have thought it politic to play upon her resentment. There was talk of bringing Lennox to Scotland again, to play his old part as an anti-Hamilton pawn. But we need not pause over these obscure moves. When Parliament met in December, the main policy was put into execution. The marriage was approved, the succession settled on Queen Mary's children and, failing them, on the Duke. Commissioners were appointed to go to France and conclude the marriage treaty on these lines.

5

All Knox's instincts revolted against this policy. It offended his downrightness. It awakened all his old memories of the year 1543. Then, too, magistrates and people had set their hand to a reformation of the Church, to a new freedom of worship; then, too, the impulse had died away in political manœuvres. And the leader in these manœuvres had been this very Hamilton, now a French duke. He had braved Beaton and then truckled to him, just as the reformers were doing now in 1557. There had been the same question of war or peace with England, the same dickering about a royal marriage. Glencairn's father and Cassilis had been isolated then; they would be isolated again now, with James Stewart and the rest, if they would insist on playing politics instead of driving at the central issue.

But, above all, these manœuvres collided with the central principle to which Knox still held: the Protestant's reverence for the secular authority. He held to it more than ever now, when the whole future of the Huguenot church in France depended on its assertion. *How are princes blinded*—so he wrote of the Paris persecutions—*that they persecute their true subjects who, next to God's glory, do principally maintain the cause, honour and authority of their princes? For the chief cause why the Pope and his kingdom do hate and persecute us is that we affirm that no power on earth is above the power of the civil ruler.* How was it possible to reconcile this principle with an obscure alliance between reformers, anti-clericals, bishops and the Hamilton family against the duly constituted representative of the Queen of Scots?

This being his mood, Knox set himself, in his letters to Scotland, squarely against current tendencies. He rebuked the congregations for their loose living and warned them against sectaries who *promise such perfection in this life that unfeignedly we need not to say: remit to us our offences for we are unprofitable servants.* To the lords after much "prolix" sermonizing, he addressed the most emphatic of all his political utterances, which deserves quotation almost in full.

I hear in these parts uncertainly that contradiction and rebellion is made to the Authority by some in that realm. My judgment, and commandment which I communicate to you in God's fear and by the assurance of His truth, is that none of you that seek to promote the glory of Christ do suddenly disobey or displease the established Authority in things lawful. But in the bowels of Christ Jesus I exhort you that, with all simplicity and lawful obedience, joined with boldness in God, and with open confession of your faith, ye seek the favours of the Authority, that by it (if possible be) the cause in which ye labour may be promoted, or at the least not persecuted. Which thing after all humble request if ye cannot attain, then, (with solemn protestation of your obedience to the Authority in all things not plainly repugning to God) ye lawfully may attempt the extremity, which is to provide, whether the Authority will consent or no, that Christ's evangel may be truly preached and His holy sacraments rightly ministered unto you and your brethren. And further, ye lawfully may—yea, and thereto are bound—to defend your brethren from persecution and tyranny, be it against princes or emperors; providing always that neither yourselves deny lawful obedience, neither yet that ye assist nor promote those that seek authority and pre-eminence of worldy glory. I mean of him—and the exordium ends in a bitter denunciation of Chatelheraut, *who began to profess Christ's truth but, suddenly sliding back, became a cruel persecutor of Christ's members.*

A prophet has seldom talked sounder sense than this, yet half-hidden in it was the seed of danger which prophets seem doomed to sow in the field of politics. The statement marks a subtle shift in Knox's revolutionary position, the sort of shift that always comes when high principle is applied to practice. Three years before, when he had preached revolution to Englishmen, his doctrine had been the same, but his emphasis had been different. Then, when there was no sign of a Jehu raised up to suppress idolatry, his emphasis has been on political rebellion as a popular right, the remedy for a sovereign's treason against established law. But now, in Scotland, the position was reversed. No accusation of treason could fairly lie against the Queen of Scots or her representatives: but, on the other hand, Jehu had appeared. Revolution by the "lesser authorities" in the name of religion, which he had preached before, as a theoretical duty, now became a practical policy. And immediately the narrowness of the theoretical distinction between such a revolution and a more popular rising in the name of religion began to be revealed. For in Scotland Jehu was a corporation, he was the whole body of armigerous gentlemen. There the "lesser authorities" had time-honoured methods of enforcing what they regarded as their lawful rights: their "bands" between earl and earl, their "bonds of manrent" be-

tween the earl and his neighbour "barons," their "kindness" between landlord and tenant. Their methods in defence of religion
would be the same: the band would be concluded in the name of
"Christ's Congregation," manrent and kindness would seem to be
hallowed and confirmed by the communion of the Lord's Table
itself. It would not be long before the new democracy of a Congregation in arms would become indistinguishable from a popular
rising.

6

It would be too much to say that Knox detected this flaw in his
own position; but there is no doubt that his letters failed to satisfy
his own mind. They failed by the standard that the man of action
instinctively sets himself: they gave him no guide to his personal
conduct. He could not bring himself to continue his journey; early
in the new year he decided to return to Geneva. He was ready to
risk his life; *my own motion and daily prayer is, not only that I may visit
you, but also with joy I may end my battle amongst you.* But if he were to
hazard all it must be *for the manifestation of Christ's glory*, and how
could that glory be manifested when all minds were absorbed in the
twists and turns of politics? *Shall Christ, the author of peace, concord
and quietness, be preached where war is proclaimed, sedition engendered
and tumults appear to arise?* Were not things come to such a pass that
public life itself was a sin for Christians? *The regiment of princes is
this day come to that heap of iniquity that no godly man can brook office or
authority under them.*

Knox was thoroughly ashamed afterwards of these compunctions.
On his way south and on his arrival in Geneva, he confessed them
naïvely to the ladies in Edinburgh who acted as intermediaries for
his informal letters to his friends. These had been the temptations of
Satan: he ought to have gone to Scotland and he had *fled the battle.*
In fact, he had committed precisely the sin which he charged against
the politicians who were always accusing the faithful of *indiscreet
rashness*; he too, had feared lest *by foolish and young counsel we mar all.*

It was characteristic of his itch for moral introspection that he
never pleaded external events as a ground for his decision. He drew
no picture of Normandy that December, when Dieppe was a base

of naval operations, and the French army was concentrated, just to eastward, round Calais and Guisnes. For the days of English rule on French soil were numbered. The Duke of Guise, recalled from Italy, was in charge of the campaign and on January 9th Calais surrendered to him. Mary Tudor still thought of reconquest, but her transports had been scattered by stormy weather and, for the moment, she had lost command of the narrow seas. Five companies of infantry from France had slipped through to the west coast of Scotland in early December and now a larger expedition might be despatched any day in that direction. D'Oysel was urging an attack in force on Berwick; if that fortress were once "brought under the obedience of their Majesties," the sovereigns of France and Scotland, "the kingdom of England would be completely uncovered." De Rubay was instructed to urge this project on the French Court when he left Scotland early in February. Such a state of war was certainly not favourable to missionary enterprises.

Nor was this all. Another event made a missionary journey at this moment to Scotland a flat absurdity. On February 9th the Scottish commissioners for the Queen's marriage sailed for France with de Rubay. Among them were the two men on whose support Knox must chiefly rely: James Stewart and Erskine of Dun. Cassilis went too, with Rothes, Fleming, Seton and the Bishops of Glasgow and Orkney. They were not to return until the following autumn. It is tempting to suppose that Knox saw Stewart and Erskine at Dieppe before he left, but there is no evidence of such a meeting. Another of the men who had signed the original letter of invitation to Knox could not now be counted on: Erskine who, as Governor of Edinburgh Castle appointed by Parliament, had probably already decided that his official trust bound him to neutrality. There remained only Glencairn and Lorne, the one a man of small wealth and merely local influence, the other still only his father's son. They, with the gentry of Kyle, Lothian and the Mearns, were good enough backing for local preachers, but hardly for a national figure like Knox.

It would have been better for Knox if he had been less honest in his self-examination and had justified his action to himself on these quite reasonable grounds. As it was, this abortive journey to Dieppe marked the second turning-point in his political life, the second and final phase of his revolutionary education.

There is one more word to be said before we close the story of these months. Knox was not the only missionary at this time whose mission seemed to peter out in futility. In September 1557, while he was on his way from Geneva, the Pope had made peace with Spain. At last he remembered the petitions of the Queen of Scots. In October, as Knox arrived in Dieppe, he put his signature to a brief, authorizing visitation of all churches and religious houses in Scotland "to reform them both in head and members, to restore property wrongly alienated, to see that the fabrics of churches of every sort be repaired and restored, and to ordain all other things necessary for the restoration of ecclesiastical discipline." This document he despatched to Paris in December by his legate to the Court of France, who was to appoint the visitor after consultation with Henry II. But nothing whatever happened, Henry thought himself betrayed by the Pope and would have nothing to do with the legate. Again, for another year, the sands were allowed to run.

Chapter XVI

THE REVOLUTIONARY GOES FURTHER

1558

I

KNOX ARRIVED back in Geneva about the middle of March 1558 in a dangerously logical frame of mind. His conscience had set him thinking; his temper had been touched by two reports which had reached him. Some time in the last months he had learnt what Mary of Guise had said when Glencairn had handed her his famous letter in the summer of 1556. With typical French inability to resist an epigram, she had passed it to the Archbishop of Glasgow with the words: "Please you, my lord, to read a pasquil." The other piece of news was less wounding to his pride, but it was a challenge to his public credit. The Scottish bishops had *summoned him and for non-compearance burnt him in effigy at the Cross of Edinburgh.* There is some doubt when this event occurred. Knox himself, writing some years later, dates it immediately after his departure from Scotland in 1556; but the absence of any reference to it in his public or private writings for nearly two years after this date seems to indicated that at least he did not hear of it until some time later. Now, once more settled at Geneva, he determined to take notice of it.

This summer of 1558 he published four manifestoes. The earliest, perhaps largely written at Dieppe, was the famous *First Blast of the Trumpet against the Monstrous Regiment of Women.* The second was a *Supplication* to Mary of Guise, embodying his letter of 1556 with a running commentary. Closely connected with this, and printed almost simultaneously, were two other publications: an *Appellation* against his condemnation by the bishops, addressed to the *Nobility and Estates of Scotland,* and a *Letter to the Commonalty of Scotland.* These four documents contained a formal and final statement of his political principles. They were his old principles, but he had added something to them. Finding that they had led him into the *cul de sac* of Dieppe, where their logic seemed to inhibit all action and to set him at odds with all parties, he sought a logical way out. The result was disastrous. He added to his creed two new and fatal articles which toppled him over the edge of unlimited revolution and were to work havoc in the English-speaking world for centuries to come.

2

The popular idea of the *First Blast* is that Knox, the petted confidant of devout ladies, vented his personal spleen against Mary Tudor and Mary of Guise and betrayed his secret contempt for women in a wild invective against queens. In fact, there is little in the *Blast* that might not have been written by the most uxorious anti-suffragist of the twentieth century. It is merely a treatise, not more violently phrased than was the fashion of the age, on a theme which was the universal commonplace of that age. Government by women was "a deviation from the original and proper order of nature, to be ranked, no less than slavery, amongst the punishments consequent upon the fall of man." That had been Calvin's judgment when Knox had consulted him on the point a year before. That was Knox's text and those who censured him later for his rashness did so on the ground, not that he had been personally violent, but that, on the contrary, he had "swerved from the particular question to the general."

Knox was topical, as always; but he was here concerned, above all, with a general principle and his particular application of it was to the sins of Englishmen and Scotsmen rather than to the crimes of either Mary. Both Marys were God's judgment on *the proud rebellion and horrible ingratitude of the realms of England and Scotland*. For when God had offered them, fifteen years ago, *the means by which they might have been joined together for ever in godly concord, then was the one proud and cruel and the other unconstant and fickle of promise*. Volumes of carefully written history have hardly bettered that judgment on the events of 1543.

But what was Knox doing with the "original and proper order of nature"? That was a new note in his political teaching. In religion his standard had been Scripture, but in politics it had been the laws and customs of the particular realm. Rulers were bound to defend and promote the Church whose creed and discipline accorded with Scripture, but they derived their authority direct from God, who had ordained them by sanctioning the human laws which regulated their succession. That had been the distinctive Protestant attitude. It had given Knox ground four years ago for claiming that Mary Tudor had forfeited her people's allegiance; but he did not feel that it justified the same challenge to Mary of Guise. He looked for some clearer principle of action, and he found it in an unexpected quarter.

Catholic doctrine had tended to follow a different course from Protestant. It had inherited the Law of Nature from the schoolmen; and that idea was to prove a powerful weapon against kings. Calvin, learned in the schools, accepted the idea in theory, but rejected it as a ground of political action, for in matters of government fallen man was under the law of his fallen nature and he could not appeal to the absolute law of his innocency, which he had rejected in Eden. Catholic doctors, on the contrary, were even then deducing a whole abstract theory of rebellion from the conception of natural law. In doing so, they were preparing the way for Rousseau and the continental philosophy of revolution.

In a fatal hour, Knox borrowed this conception. Female government was *monstrous*, a queen a *monster*, not in the language of invective, but in the strict sense of being unnatural. To some extent he modified the conception in a Protestant direction. Avoiding abstract speculation, he identified natural law, not with the inherent rights of man, but with the recorded commandments of God. It was *the Law Moral, the constant and unchangeable will of God, to which the Gentile is no less bound than was the Jew*. But while this modification might limit the just occasions of rebellion, it tended to convert rebellion on just occasion from a right to a duty. The Law of Nature was permissive, but the *Law Moral* imperative. Overriding all constitutional law, it absolved the officers of state from their duty, the nobility and the estates from their covenants, the people from their oath of obedience. *For neither may the tyranny of princes, neither the foolishness of the people, neither wicked laws made against God, neither yet the felicity*

*that in this earth may hereof ensue, make that thing lawful which He by
His Word hath manifestly condemned.*

And then came the practical application. The *Law Moral* ordained
that no woman might reign. That Knox proved from Scripture to
his own satisfaction. God was above His own ordinances and might
raise up a Deborah *against His ordinary course;* but men had no right
to presume on such exceptions. *To reign over man can never be the
right to woman.* Therefore a queen might convey no authority to her
husband, for *from a corrupt and venomed fountain can spring no wholesome water.* Therefore it was the duty of all citizens to *repress her in-
ordinate pride and tyranny, to remove from honour and authority that
monster in nature,* and *to execute the sentence of death* against any who
might *presume to defend* her sovereignty. No oaths they might have
sworn could be cited against that duty; on the contrary, *as the
beginning of their oaths was sin, so is the obstinate purpose to keep the
same nothing but plain rebellion against God.*

It would be difficult to exaggerate the responsibility assumed by
Knox when he wrote these words. Their particular application to
female government was a side-issue; it was no worse than a political
blunder. Knox was to discover that it is unwise in politics to blurt
out what all men think. A year later Cecil, who in private yearned
no less than he for "a masculine succession," gave him the hint by
shrewdly parodying his habit of prefixing scriptural salutations to his
letters. "Master Knox," wrote that hardened politician, "there is
neither male nor female, for all, saith Paul, are one in Christ; blessed
is the man who trusteth in the Lord." But the blunder had no permanent influence on events. The real point of the *Blast* was that it
translated a continental doctrine into English terms. Neither Englishmen nor Scotsmen have ever taken kindly to the Law of Nature;
but transmuted into the *Law Moral,* with Scripture cited as witness,
it was to weave a thread of alien fanaticism into all their future
constitutional struggles. Knox was the first to take the step to which,
as we have suggested, Calvinism was foredoomed by its own logic.
Horrified though he would have been by the accusation, he had in
fact imported into British politics what Bacon called "the anabaptists and other furies." Not only in Britain but in America, the *Law
Moral* was to prove as dangerous a guide as the "inner light."

3

But if this was to be the effect of the first new article in Knox's creed, the effect of the second was to be even worse. He had found a doctrine which justified the deposition, not only of Mary the Regent, but of Mary Queen of Scots and of the Dauphin her husband. Now he turned to look for a doctrine which might give the congregations in Scotland the same right to wage war against idolatry that he had hitherto claimed for magistrates and "lesser authorities."

His first step towards this—first obviously in order of thought, though not in order of publication—was his *Letter to the Commonalty*. Few nobler statements of Christian democracy have ever been penned; few have shown so clearly by what gradations an ideal of brotherhood may pass from love to hate. *Albeit God hath ordained distinction and difference betwixt King and subjects, betwixt rulers and common people, in the regiment and administration of civil policies yet in the hope of the life to come He hath made all equal. Of the Prince doth God require that he refuse himself and that he follow Christ Jesus; of the subject He requireth the same. Neither is there any of God's children so poor but that he hath thus much to bestow upon the ornaments and maintenance of their spiritual tabernacle; neither yet is there any so rich of whose hands God requireth any more.*

Thus equal in their membership of the Church, all must be held equally responsible for its organization and defence. *Ye, although ye be but subjects, may lawfully require of your superiors that they provide for you true preachers and that they expel such as, under the name of pastors, devour and destroy the flock. And if in this point your superiors be negligent, most justly ye may provide true teachers for yourselves. Them ye may maintain and defend against all that shall persecute them. Ye may, moreover, withhold the fruits and profits which your false bishops and clergy most unjustly receive of you.*

And then the permissive "may" hardens into a commandment. This is no mere assertion of political rights; it is the *loving calling of your Heavenly Father*. Those that despise that calling are without excuse before God and *shall drink the cup of His vengeance. It will not*

219

avail you in the day of His visitation to say: we were but simple subjects, we called for reformation; but Lords' brethren were bishops, their sons were abbots and the friends of great men had the possessions of the Church, and so were we compelled to give obedience to all that they demanded. These vain excuses I say will nothing avail you in the presence of God, who requireth no less of the subjects than of the rulers and doth not only punish the rulers, but with them doth He damn the consenters to iniquity.

Thus the argument comes back to the central dilemma of the age: if God judges nations for the sins of their rulers, what is the way of escape for the innocent? Knox, alas, had now decided on his answer to that question. He propounded it in the *Appellation*.

The *Appellation* was an appeal to the nobility and Estates of Scotland from his condemnation by the bishops—a demand to be confronted with his judges, that he might purge himself of heresy and convict them of idolatry. *In the name of God I require of you that the cause of religion may be tried in your presence by the plain Word of God; that your bishops be compelled to desist from their tyranny; that they be compelled to make answer for the neglecting of their office, for the substance of the poor which unjustly they usurp and prodigally they do spend, but principally for the false and deceivable doctrine which is taught by their false prophets.*

In support of that plea he set out the full doctrine of God's judgments. Horrible as it might seem *to the carnal man*, God had laid it on Israel to root out the idolaters of Canaan; *He commanded the whole inhabitants of that country to be destroyed and all monuments of their idolatry to be broken down.* That command was the mirror of His eternal purpose; *in such cases will God that all creatures stoop, cover their faces and desist from reasoning, when commandment is given to execute His judgment.* In such judgments only those can escape who, in the words of Ezekiel's vision, *mourn and lament for all the abominations done in the city.* And passive confession of national sin will not be enough to save them, *for no man can mourn for those things which he will not remove to the uttermost of his power.* The conclusion is evident. *The punishment of idolatry doth not appertain to kings only, but also to the whole people.*

4

It is often said that Knox asserted the right and duty of every Protestant to kill any Catholic, and there are plenty of sentences in the *Appellation* which may be quoted in support of that charge. He had a dangerous habit, which few preachers wholly escape, of saying more in the development of his text than he intended to assert in the application of it. It is to be hoped that theological colleges warn their students against this habit, for the *obiter dicta* of preachers, at any rate in matters affecting the relations of Church and State, have done more harm in Christendom than any positive false teaching. But this was not, in fact, Knox's argument. Better, perhaps, if it had been; hooliganism is less dangerous than a philosophy of revolution. And it was such a philosophy that Knox was concerned to announce.

It was not, he explained, for the individual citizen of a Catholic country to rise against his papist rulers. The apostles never taught insurrection against pagan emperors. Rebellion must have a constitutional foundation. That foundation was the *covenant and league* made between God and a Christian people. Such a people were no less covenanted to God than the Jews. There might be *universal defections* from that covenant, *such as this day be in papistry.* Where that happened, the citizen must possess his soul in patience; *no ordinary justice can be executed; the punishment must be reserved to God.* But the citizen's duty was different *wheresoever Christ Jesus and His evangel is so received that the magistrates and people have solemnly avowed and promised to defend the same.* Such a covenant had been made in England under Edward, *and therefore I fear not to affirm that it had been the duty of the nobility, judges, rulers and people of England, not only to have resisted Mary, that Jezebel, but also to have punished her with death, with all the sort of her idolatrous priests, what time she and they openly began to suppress Christ's evangel and to shed the blood of the saints of God.*

So was born the doctrine of the Covenant. It emerged, as such things will, not by sudden discovery, but by an almost natural transition of thought. The just authority of rulers was based on national law and custom; it might therefore fairly be described as a covenant between king and people. Knox had reached that position,

the distinctively English one, four years ago. The tenor of that
covenant was a question of facts in each realm. But in all realms an
established religion was certainly one of those facts—had been so in
every Christian country for centuries. What more natural than to go
one step further and to identify this covenant between king and
people, on the Jewish analogy, with a covenant between both and
God? What more natural, but on the other hand what more revolutionary? For the tenor of this divine covenant could not be a
mere question of fact. God being a party to it, its terms must be
presumed to be agreeable to God's unchangeable decrees, as revealed
in Scripture. It must be interpreted, it must if necessary be over-
ridden, by the *Law Moral*. So interpreted, it must take precedence of
any covenant based on national law and custom. Hence the distinctively Scottish doctrine; hence that conflict with the English
doctrine which ninety years later was to be brought to an issue between English and Scottish revolutionaries on the field of Dunbar.

Knox himself did not draw these conclusions. As we have said, he
was not himself a covenanter. It was enough for him to have
thought out a principle which would give the commonalty the
same right and duty as magistrates, not only to enforce the law and
customs of the realm, but to reform religion. Yet, here again, he
must bear the responsibility of those who set men's minds moving
in a new direction. Bacon has pronounced judgment on him: "For
as the temporal sword is to be drawn with great circumspection in
cases of religion, so it is a thing monstrous to put into the hands of
the common people."

5

Knox was saved from the logic of his own principles by an element in his character which has been too little recognized. In spite of
his perpetual insistence on God's dealings with nations, high policy
meant little to him, either in Church or State. His measure of
national godliness was the parish congregation. He asked of the
civil power little more than that it should create conditions in
which such a congregation, with its minister, could worship un-
disturbed and enforce upon its members its own spiritual discipline.
For that purpose, the civil power must suppress certain extremes in

religion: superstition which *imposed upon the consciences of men* and lawlessness which rejected church discipline altogether. The centre of such superstition was the Mass, which must therefore be forbidden by law, together with *vows of chastity, forswearing of marriage, superstitious observance of fast days, difference of meat for conscience sake, prayer for the dead and keeping of holy days of certain saints.* The quotation is from the *Book of Discipline* of 1560, and it will be observed that the demand is mainly for the prohibition by civil law of what civil law had previously enforced.

Beyond this, it is hardly too much to say that, in Knox's view, the less Church and State had to do with each other, the better. *Let none that be appointed to labour in Christ's vineyard be entangled with civil affairs, be he never judged so apt for that purpose.* So ran the *Book of Discipline.* At the end of his sojourn in Geneva Knox's experience there did, indeed, prompt him to suggest to his friends in England that, in a properly reformed Church, *execution of discipline must be done in every city and shire where the magistrates and ministers are joined together,* but he seems to have abandoned this municipal device as soon as he returned to Scotland.

Above all, though he held firmly that *the reformation and purgation of religion appertains chiefly and most principally to the civil power,* he had a horror of State-enforced uniformity. There was a cant phrase among the English politicians in Edward's day which he never forgot: "the King's proceedings." It was their name for the enforcement of the Act of Uniformity and the Prayer Book. In these months of cogitation and writing in 1558, he returned to that phrase again and again. *What then was heard as concerning religion but, the King's proceedings, the King's proceedings must be obeyed?* That is from the *First Blast* and this is from a letter to his old congregations in Berwick and Newcastle, written on November 10th, seven days before Mary Tudor's death: *How oft have ye been partakers of the Lord's Table, prepared, used and ministered in all simplicity, not as man had devised, neither as the King's proceedings did allow, but as Christ Jesus did institute!* After that experience his main desire was that, as he told his English friends at this time, kings themselves should *be subject to the yoke of discipline* if they *would usurp any other authority in God's religion than becometh a member of Christ's body.* Here he was speaking with the authentic voice of the Scottish Church, long after she had shaken herself loose from leagues and covenants.

Of course these views are not wholly consistent; of course, too, Knox's subsequent conduct did not always conform to them. But most of his vagaries were those of a man labouring to cope, not with a settled order, but with a transition. He was to be involved in the anxieties of that transition to the day of his death. But in his irritabilities and his violences throughout the coming years, there was to be more of the frustrated parish minister than of the domineering ecclesiastic. He had had enough of courts and politicians; he would not even undertake the diocesan responsibility of a Superintendent; he asked nothing better than to end his days in the pulpit of St. Giles.

6

But this is to run ahead of our story. After the publication of the *Appellation* in July 1558, Knox remained six months in Geneva. In November he wrote the letter to his old congregations in England from which we have already quoted. It is a long drawn lamentation over their apostasy. At the end of that month his second son was born. That month, too, arrived letters from Scotland for both him and Calvin, urging his return. Then came overwhelming news: the death of Mary Tudor and the accession of Elizabeth. On January 12th Knox despatched another letter to England. *When in dolour of heart I wrote this former letter, I neither looked nor could believe that the Lord Jesus would so suddenly knock at thy gate.* Soon after, he left Geneva alone and hurried on his old road to Dieppe. Peace had returned to that road; on the frontier of the Netherlands at St. Pol, the commissioners of France, Spain and England were bringing their long negotiations to an end; on April 2nd the Treaty of Cateau Cambresis was to open a new era in Europe. Arrived in Dieppe Knox wrote for leave of passage through England and waited impatiently for a reply.

CHAPTER XVII

THE EVE OF REVOLUTION
1558–59

I

WE HAVE followed Knox through a year of pamphleteering. During that year his Geneva writings cannot have materially influenced events in Scotland. The sequence of those events is by no means clear. The account we are about to give seems the most reasonable interpretation of the confused records; but whatever interpretation is put upon them, Knox's influence from Geneva can hardly be detected. Yet his Scottish congregations were taking almost precisely the same steps in action as he was taking in thought. There are few more curious examples in history of the real relation between the thinker and the man of action. Often the pen is mightier than the sword only in the sense that it rationalizes emergency measures to the confusion of future generations.

Knox's letters from Dieppe may, indeed, have started these events upon their course. On 3rd December 1557, ten days before the opening of the Parliament, the first Covenant was signed, in response, perhaps, to his October expostulations. Of those who had urged his return in the previous March, Erskine did not sign this Common Bond, nor did James Stewart, that cautious lover of the background. In their place appeared Erskine of Dun and old Argyll —and a third who enters our story for the first time: James Douglas, son of the Sir George we know, Earl of Morton by right of his wife and effective head of the house of Douglas by guardianship of his young nephew Angus. Old Angus had died in 1557, Sir George earlier in 1552. What these men signed, together with Glencairn and Lorne, was a joint pledge, taken "before the majesty of God," to promote "the most blessed Word of God and his Congregation," to provide "faithful ministers" for the people, and to "defend them, the whole Congregation of Christ and every member thereof at our whole powers and waring of our lives, against Satan and all wicked power that does intend tyranny or trouble against the aforesaid Congregation."

This was not an isolated act. Consultations were held and a programme drawn up under two heads. The policy to be urged on the Government was the adoption of the Second Prayer Book of Edward VI, to be read in every parish church each Sunday; meanwhile, in the reformed congregations, preaching and study of the Bible were to be carried on "in quiet houses without great conventions of the people thereto." Argyll acted on the second half of this programme by taking home with him a preacher, one John Douglas, *alias* Grant, who made Castle Campbell a preaching centre, in spite of the expostulations of the earl's half-brother-in-law, the Primate of St. Andrews. Then old Sandilands of Calder was deputed to carry out the first half. In the name of the Congregation he presented to the Regent a five-point petition: freedom "to convene, publicly or privately, to our Common Prayers in our vulgar tongue"; freedom to interpret the Scriptures in such conventions; the administration of baptism and the Lord's Supper in the vulgar tongue; communion in both kinds; and reform of "the wicked, slanderous and detestable life of prelates and of the State Ecclesiastical." The Regent gave a soft answer, holding out the hope of a Parliament which would consider Church reform and asking only that, meanwhile, there should be no public assemblies in Edinburgh or Leith. That, at least, was the petitioners' interpretation of her reply, and they claimed that they had complied with her condition by discountenancing public preaching in the two cities.

2

All this was in the spirit of Knox's letter of December 17th, and the reformers prided themselves on their moderation. Nevertheless, they had committed themselves to a course which must mean open war. Just as the position taken up by Knox in his letter of December 17th was forcing him to evolve a doctrine of religious rebellion, so their policy in action was forcing them to challenge the lawfulness of established law. Their whole position was illegal; so far as the law could run at all in a country where executive power was so weak, its full rigours might be enforced against them at any moment. Argyll's chaplain, as the Primate reminded him on 25th March 1558, was "an infamet person of the law," more especially as he was an ex-friar, a "man-sworn apostate." So was another of the preachers who had recently appeared, Christison; so was Willock, who returned to Scotland six months later. The life of these men was automatically forfeit, without the intervention of any secular tribunal. The whole process of law, indeed, had drifted into the Church courts. James V had sought to counteract this tendency by establishing the College of Justice in 1532; but, even so, eight senators of the College were ecclesiastics. And for the execution of renegade priests there was no need to go through any of the ordinary processes of law.

This was the real point of what happened in April. An old priest, one Mill, over eighty years of age, was suddenly arrested and accused of apostasy at St. Andrews. The Primate probably had nothing to do with his arrest and would have been glad enough to escape the odium of his condemnation. But condemned he was, under conditions verging on lynch law, and on the 28th he was burnt. Where a harmless renegade was thus proved to have no rights at law, what security was there for active apostates like Douglas?

In these circumstances, the congregations were demanding nothing less than a revolutionary change in the whole structure of national law, a change which could only be carried out by the joint action of Crown and Parliament. And they had not the slightest prospect of such joint action. They had thrown over the only policy which offered any chance of a peaceful solution: the policy of James Stewart and Cassilis and the other "temporisers," the policy of changing the regency before attacking the Church. They were determined to present to the existing Regent a tangle which she was powerless, even if she were willing, to untie; they had therefore committed themselves, sooner or later, to cut through that tangle with the sword.

Nor was this all. There was a second reason why the congregations were necessarily committing themselves to armed revolt. The language of their Common Bond may have been just an example of fashionable rant: "we forsake and renounce the congregation of Satan and declare ourselves manifest enemies thereto." But this document, which had begun perhaps as a private contract, rapidly became a public manifesto. By this summer of 1558 they were hawking it round Scotland for signature by gentry and burgesses. More, they were appealing to the commonalty as a whole. They had unloosed a popular movement. The main plank in their platform was the protection of the preachers who were inciting that movement; and some of those preachers were not of the gentry, but of the people. Besides the ex-friars, there were Harlow the ex-tailor and Paul Methuen the ex-baker—"and other proud clatterers unlearned." The bond became, not merely a political manifesto, but a pulpit text.

With such a following, technical and necessary illegality plunged rapidly into active lawlessness. That is the plunge which religious democracy has always taken and must always take when it turns to political ends; and always the depth of the political plunge is in proportion to the genuineness of the religious fervour. In the Scotland of 1558 lawlessness naturally took the same form as in Wittenburg thirty-seven years before, the same as in Lyons and Orleans four years later: it found its outlet in image-breaking and window-smashing. Naturally, for the congregations met in half-disused parish churches, with none to hinder; "monuments of idolatry" were all around them and, the sermon ended, they pulled them down, as a crowd issuing from a Communist meeting may throw a stone at a passing top hat. At this stage there was no organized iconoclasm, that was to come a little later; but, apart from sermon riots, popular temper was rising. Already an Edinburgh crowd had burnt the image of their patron St. Giles, after throwing it into the North Loch, and the burgh council had refused to replace it, though the Archbishop's curate "cursed them black as coal."

So the summer passed. The Bond was widely signed; disorders grew. At last, in July, the clergy took up the challenge. At a meeting held in Edinburgh certain preachers were summoned. Armed bands of their adherents answered the summons. The Regent ordered them south to patrol the Marches, where the English war still flickered aimlessly. But there were gentry of Kyle among them, who had just come off Border duty. They forced their way into the Regent's presence; Chalmers of Gadgirth defied the bishops to her face *and therewith every man put on his steel bonnet.* The Regent promised that the summons should be cancelled, and so far got her way that the only sentence passed on the preachers was that they should make a public recantation at the Edinburgh market cross on St. Giles's day, September 1st.

The day came round, but no preachers appeared. Instead, the customary procession in honour of the saint was mobbed and *a marmoset idol borrowed from the Grey Friars* was tumbled in the gutter. Next month Willock arrived in Edinburgh and, though seriously ill, held meetings in his bedroom, even Lord Seton, Provost of Edinburgh, just returned from France, attending to hear him. At the beginning of November the bishops called another meeting and Paul Methuen was "put to the horn." That was a declaration of war, not only against an individual, but against a party, for it involved penalties on all who should harbour the outlaw or supply him with the necessities of life. It seems probable that the same sentence was pronounced on Willock.

3

But now Parliament time was come, the Parliament of which the Regent had spoken in the spring. Now, it seemed, the conflict might be brought to a constitutional issue. The leaders of the Congregation submitted a petition to the Queen for transmission to Parliament. All Acts conferring powers on ecclesiastical courts for the trial of heresy were to be repealed, a secular court was to be substituted, proceeding under due forms of law, and the test to be applied by such a court was to be "the manifest word of God." But there was other business before that Parliament. Four of the Scottish commissioners for the Queen's marriage had returned from France: the Archbishop of Glasgow, James Stewart, Seton and Erskine of Dun. On November 29th, when Parliament met, they were to make their report.

They had duly signed the marriage contract at Paris on April

19th; on April 24th the marriage had been solemnized; they had, as the French King noted complacently, "sworn fealty" to the Dauphin as "their true and natural lord"; on July 8th the Parlement of Paris had registered the royal decree according full rights of French citizenship to the subjects of the new King of Scots. But then came a hitch. The French court wanted one thing more: that the Scottish "crown matrimonial" should be sent to Paris. As to that, said the commissioners, they had no instructions. They could only present the request to Parliament on their return.

All this they reported on November 29th; they reported also that one of their colleagues, the Bishop of Orkney, had died at Dieppe on their way home and that three others, Cassilis, Rothes and Fleming, were still there. As a matter of fact, two of these, Cassilis and Rothes, had died the day before, November 28th. Fleming had returned to Paris to consult the doctors and died there on December 15th. It was small wonder that men began to talk of foul play.

What the commissioners did not report, because they did not know it, was that on April 4th, a fortnight before the marriage contract was concluded, the Queen of Scots had repudiated it in advance. She had signed three papers, appointing her husband to succeed her if she died without issue, pledging the kingdom of Scotland to the French King until the expenses of her education were repaid to him, and pronouncing null and void any contrary deed which she might subsequently execute. There have been many comments on this transaction, but the briefest is the best: "We may find excuses for the girl; but, if treason can be committed by a sovereign, she was a traitor."

With the business of the "crown matrimonial" on hand, the Regent could not afford to offend the bishops. Once more, and for the last time, French policy sacrificed the substance for the shadow. For seven years Henry II had postponed the assertion of his authority in Scotland for the sake of the Hapsburg-Valois feud. At any time in those years he could have made Scotland a French province with a tithe of the forces that he had wasted on the Rhine, on the Meuse and in Italy. Out of all these adventures he had won nothing but Calais and a strip of territory or two in the debatable lands of Burgundy. The wars were ending in disaster. On July 13th the Spaniards under Egmont had crushed his last army at Gravelines, assisted by the guns of the English fleet. He had kept the Papal legate hanging round his ante-room and had burked his proposals for Scottish Church reform. Now his representative at Edinburgh was missing the last chance of settlement.

She got what she wanted for the last time. In deference to her representations, the Congregation withdrew their petition but substituted for it a rather harsher Protestation. They claimed freedom in matters of religion, pending a "just reformation," and immunity from prosecution either for exercising this freedom or (the words are significant) "for violating of such rights as man without God's commandment or word hath commanded." Underlining that ominous sentence, they protested "that, if any tumult or uproar shall arise amongst the members of this realm for the diversity of religion, and if it shall chance that abuses be violently reformed, the crime thereof be not imputed to us." They asked that this Protestation should be registered in Parliament, but again the Regent put them off. The Act conferring the "crown matrimonial" on the Dauphin was passed, James Stewart and Lorne were appointed as commissioners to carry it to France, and Parliament adjourned. Lorne was now Argyll; the old earl, that late but significant convert, had died some four months before, *most constant in the true faith of Jesus Christ, with a plain renunciation of all impiety, superstition and idolatry.*

4

But the commissioners never started. The year 1559 opened blackly. Again, in the last days of December, the bishops summoned the preachers to "a day of law" at St. Andrews on February 2nd; again, under the threats of the gentry, the Regent induced them to withdraw. Then, in the first days of January, came one of those mutterings of storm which, even when manipulated by stage managers, give warning that there is thunder about. One night a paper was nailed *to the gates and posts of all the friars' places.* In the name of "the blind, crooked, bedrels, widows, orphans and all other poor," it summoned "the flocks of all friars within this realm" to "remove forth of our hospitals, betwixt this and Whitsunday next, so that we the only lawful proprietors may enter thereto." Scotland had never known a peasants' revolt; was she to be initiated now into this phase also of the agony of Europe?

But the Regent had no ear for notes like this. The best reading of her character is that she was insensitive to imponderables. She was nobly "determined to see justice take a straightforward course," and she thought that she still had to deal only with the old Scottish love of license and hatred of "French laws," with which she had been contending for sixteen weary years. She had few troops, but enough to challenge this sort of discontent. And it was time to challenge it. She was ill, some thought her dying. Certainly she was tired out. And she had done her work; Scotland was now legally subject to the future King of France. In a few weeks peace would be signed with England; the French envoy for this purpose arrived in Scotland in mid-April; the treaty was to be concluded at Upsettlington on May 31st. All this done, she could at least take a holiday. She had meant to be in France the Michaelmas before, or at latest by this Candlemas. She would wind up quickly, and then go. In the name of law and order, she would force the issue.

This being her mood, it is little wonder that the manner of her challenge was a series of miscalculations. She prefaced it by a wanton piece of nepotism, in the worst traditions of the Church she wished to reform. In January, on the death of her eldest bastard step-son, she assigned the benefices of Kelso and Melrose to (of all people) her brother, the Cardinal of Lorraine. Then she opened fire. On February 9th she issued a proclamation forbidding on pain of death, interference with the ceremonies of the Church and the eating of flesh in Lent. The retort was immediate. If the Regent intended to keep Easter in her way, the preachers would keep it in theirs. Methuen was at work in Dundee, where the new doctrines had taken hold fifteen years before. Something like an official city reformation was carried out there, and from there the infection spread. Methuen "preached in sundry gentlemen's places in Angus and also Fife and ministered the sacrament of the communion in Lundie and in Cupar in Fife and caused the images thereof to be cast down and abolished the Pope's religion, wherever he passed and preached."

Then, at the beginning of March, came the next step in the Regent's campaign. A new Church Council met in the church of the Dominican Friars at Edinburgh to isolate the evangelical extremists by satisfying the moderate reformers. It re-enacted and reinforced the statutes of 1549 and 1552, it appointed commissioners to reform the lives of the clergy, it regularized and reduced "mortuary" charges. On paper, in fact, it met all the demands of "some temporal lords and barons" who had submitted a programme of reform—except one. It would not authorize "common prayers with litanies in our vulgar tongue." And, having once more professed to set its house in order, it fulminated "the greater excommunication and other penalties enacted by law" against "Paul Methuen, William Harlow, John Grant, John Willock, John Patrick and several other apostates from the Catholic faith," together with all parents who should have their children baptized by them and all who should receive "the sacraments of the eucharist or of marriage" at their hands. The ban was proclaimed by the Regent on Holy Thursday, March 23rd. At the same time, or soon after, the preachers were summoned to appear at Stirling on the Wednesday before Whitsunday, May 10th.

This was to take the very step which the Regent had repeatedly discountenanced in recent months. It was to invite an armed assembly. But it seemed the only way to force the issue; she had tried to get Methuen arrested quietly at Dundee, but had failed. Probably, too, she was misled by an apparent accession of strength at this moment. She was at Glasgow, within easy reach of Stirling; at her back was Dumbarton, with the Scots companies in French service who had been sent from Brest fifteen months before. James Stewart and Argyll were both with her; both seemed on her side. She might think that they had been alienated by the extremists; and, if that were so, she could afford to give a tart answer to Glencairn and the Sheriff of Ayr who came to remonstrate with her. These Ayrshire gentry were cut off from their evangelical brethren in Angus, Mearns and Fife; she could, if necessary, crush them at leisure. In fact, however, James and Argyll were surely acting on James's old policy. The Regent was almost eliminated; why risk a violent revolution when she was perhaps dying and certainly on the point of leaving the country? In that mood they would be effective mediators, but poor allies. She could have used them to restrain

Methuen; instead, she called on them to fight, and she only discovered her miscalculation too late.

Moreover, she had made a military miscalculation. The preachers were assembling their congregations in Dundee, and in the path which they must take if they obeyed her summons was Perth, the only effectively walled town in Scotland. She had not the men both to occupy this strategic point and to overawe Ayrshire; and at this moment she heard that Perth itself had caught the evangelical infection. She sent for Ruthven, almost hereditary provost of the town, but he would promise nothing. Perhaps it was then that she began to realize the forces against her; she complained later that, "through the negligence of prelates," she had been "left in ignorance." But it was too late to draw back. On May 3rd she received another piece of news from the agitated bishops still assembled in Edinburgh. That morning a messenger had burst in on them in the Black Friars "and assured them that John Knox, who was new come out of France, had been all night in that town. At which news they rose suddenly from the board where they sat and passed forth to the yard, altogether abashed."

5

For nearly three months Knox had been stamping and champing at Dieppe. Twice he had written for leave to pass through England. His head was full of the conclusions he had reached in these last months; full, too, of all he would say to his old congregations in north England as he passed through, and of the diplomacy he might transact in London with Cecil whom he had known *familiarly* in the old days.

He was beginning this diplomacy, after his own fashion, in Dieppe itself. He was not the only missionary who started from Geneva in these early months of 1559. Word was going round the Huguenot congregations in France, now nearly fifty in number, summoning the first Synod of the French Protestant Church for May 26th in Paris. A year before Calvin had estimated the strength of the faithful at no less than 300,000. In the last eighteen months Coligny, Admiral of France, had joined them, following his younger brother d'Andelot, an earlier convert. Antoine de Bourbon, King of Navarre, had

234

come over too, followed by his brother Condé. A year ago,
d'Andelot had been proselytizing in Brittany, defying the Edict of
Compiègne. There were all the materials of revolt, and Knox did
what he could to light the fire. The congregation at Dieppe was
pastorless; he probably ministered to them, as he had done on
earlier visits, and he told them what he thought of female government and the right of rebellion. The French King must not find this
Norman town too comfortable a base of operations if he wished to
send an army to Scotland. Perhaps we may guess, from the agitated
reports sent to Calvin by the Huguenot pastor in Paris, that he was
recommending Whittingham as a suitable minister for Dieppe; it
would be no bad thing to have a personal friend at this key point.

But while he thus fluttered the Calvinist dovecotes in France, no
reply came from London. All that reached him was private information that *my first blast hath blown from me all my friends in England.* On
January 25th his old antagonist Cox had preached Elizabeth's
coronation sermon. It was even difficult for him to find a messenger
who would carry his letters across the Channel; returning exiles
fought shy of him and his "fond assertions." He vented his grievance
on Mrs. Locke, who had written him a fussy letter from Geneva,
asking how far, when she got back to England, she might lawfully
attend baptisms and communion, if these sacraments were celebrated according to the Second Prayer Book of Edward VI. He
brushed all these scruples aside. What mattered was not *Mr. Parson's
pattering of his constrained prayers*; the only question was, did he preach,
did he preach? *None can be a lawful minister of Christ's sacrament who
first is not a minister of His blessed Word.* For his part he would preach,
in season and out of season, whatever men might say. The crisis had
come; *our captain Christ Jesus and Satan His adversary are now at
defiance.*

And accordingly, four days later, he indited a sermon to Cecil
himself, the most brazenly tactless of all his letters. Cecil had been a
time server; he was *worthy of hell* for his *horrible defection from the
truth* in Mary's reign. Let him beware now how he joined *the
troublers of God's servants*; unless he repented he would share the fate
of the Dudley gang to which he had once belonged; like them, he
would be *as the dust which the wind tosseth* and would *not long escape*

the reward of dissemblers. So let him issue Knox's passport without delay. As for Elizabeth, God had raised her up, *albeit that nature and God's most perfect ordinance repugn to such regiment.* Knox would obey God's will, but let her do the same; she could base her claim to rule only on this *extraordinary dispensation,* not upon *consuetude, laws and ordinance of men. Only humility and dejection of herself before God shall be the firmity and stability of her throne.* Let Cecil tell her that; if he did not, *I will make it patent to the world that thus far I have communicated with you.*

Knox kept this exordium back till April 22nd and then despatched it. But this time he did not wait for a reply. He took passage for Scotland and was in Edinburgh on May 2nd.

There was more than tactlessness in his message to the Queen of England; there was a new note of authority. Arrogance, perhaps, but there was power behind it, of a sort. At this point we part company with Knox the thinker and the arguer. Henceforward the pace of our story must quicken. He had sown the ground of his own mind; now he and the world were to reap what he had sown. In these last months he had chosen, half-consciously but irrevocably, between private vision and public policy. In his letter to Mrs. Locke, we see the private vision dwindling into the background, the pulpit taking position in front of the Sacrament table. In these weeks at Dieppe he had completed his refutation of anabaptist objections to the doctrine of predestination, closing with that invective against *those that hate and detest all lawful powers* from which we have quoted in an earlier chapter. But as he wrote, as he sent off his manuscript to the friends in Geneva who had commissioned it, his feet were set on the same road as those whom he condemned. For when once a man sets out to establish the Kingdom of God as an earthly polity, it matters little whether he defies the State or invokes its aid, whether the sword he plans to take is the rebel's or the king's. In either case, however much he may flatter himself that he has drawn the sword only as an emergency measure, he can never sheathe it again. Those who appeal to force for the limited ends of mere social order can limit their use of it—not so the man who appeals to it as an instrument of perfection. The man who takes that sword is happy if he can perish by it; if he lives, he will be bound slave to it all his days.

V. Scotland
The Patch of Glory

CHAPTER XVIII

CAVALCADE

1559 MAY–JUNE

I

KNOX LANDED in Scotland on Tuesday, May 2nd. He slept two nights in Edinburgh. On Thursday, Ascension Day, he left for Dundee. On Saturday he was outlawed by proclamation at Glasgow. Within the next forty-eight hours he set out for Stirling—"quietly," says a hostile witness—with the other preachers and an escort of local gentry. There was no great noble with them—only the Master of Lindsay, Erskine of Dun and some well-known lairds like Wishart of Pitarrow. Willock was not among the preachers; he was with Glencairn in Ayrshire.

The Thursday following, the outlaw was preaching in St. John's Church at Perth; thirty days later he read out his text beneath the remembered spire of St. Andrews; twenty days after that he stood in the pulpit of St. Giles itself. The leaderless lairds who gathered at Dundee on Ascension Day, marched into Edinburgh eight weeks later, six thousand strong, with a king's son and three earls at their head; they were met there by two earls more, with the levies of Ayr and Lothian. In those eight weeks they had twice faced the Regent's forces in the field and twice imposed a truce; and on all the roads from Dundee and St. Andrews to Stirling, and thence through Linlithgow to the capital, they had left hardly a religious house unsacked, hardly a church unpurged of images. No wonder that onlookers and opponents ascribed this transformation scene to Knox. At the age of forty-five he had become a legend.

And, on the whole, the legend is true. In all Scotland at this time, indeed in all Europe, there were just two people who saw that, now at last, there could be no compromise between Regent and Congregation. The two were Knox and the Regent herself. From the moment that the marchers left Dundee, it was almost a personal battle between these two.

2

The march opened with an attempt at compromise. Erskine of Dun went ahead to Stirling, to assure Mary that the marchers came in peace. Let them halt at Perth, said Mary; Erskine sent them word accordingly and they halted. Then on Thursday morning (probably), Erskine himself rode into the town, angry in spite of his *most gentle nature*. Mary had outlawed the preachers after all, because they had not appeared the day before. The lairds were at dinner after sermon; they gathered in the church again to hear Knox preach against idolatry. The sermon over, riot broke loose; the church was gutted, the houses of the Black and Grey Friars and the Carthusian Abbey were sacked, the inmates expelled. "Within twenty-four hours they made bare buildings." The mob, *the rascal multitude*, no doubt got out of hand, but the violence was deliberate. The abbey was attacked only after the lairds had held an evening council at the town bridge, had listened to Knox praying for God's guidance, and had summoned the prior "to leave idolatry and to live according to the written will of God." Ruthven watched the work from his castle; many thought that he approved. That Whitsunday no Mass was celebrated in Perth; the town council had prohibited it on pain of death.

So revolution was declared, but still the marchers did not know what they had done. Most of them went home, but Knox stayed, while the Regent concentrated her troops and called out the levies of Stirlingshire, Lothian and Clydesdale. James Stewart and Argyll were with her; Chatelheraut took command. On Monday the 22nd her army was at Auchterarder, fifteen miles from Perth, and the lairds, summoned back in haste, were taking position a mile or two outside the town. They had between four and five thousand men; Chatelheraut perhaps between seven and eight thousand. Next day, Ruthven slipped out of Perth, leaving dismay behind him. But Knox was ready. In these last ten days he had been drawing up the manifestoes of the revolution, in the name of *the Congregation of Christ Jesus within Scotland.* He was not alone in the work, but he was the draftsman. There was a letter to the Regent, there were letters to d'Oysel and his French officers; above all there was an address to the nobility, Catholic and Protestant, and a declaration of war on *the Generation of Antichrist, the Pestilent Prelates and their Shavelings within Scotland.* Now copies were struck off and sent out broadcast.

Of these, the address to the nobility must have been sent out some days before the 22nd, the date of the letter to the Regent. It appealed to the Catholics for moderation: *Stay yourselves, and the fury of others, from persecution of us, till our cause be tried in lawful and open judgment.* But it commanded the Protestants, who *sometime have professed Christ Jesus with us and yet have left us in our extreme necessity, or at the least look through your fingers in this our trouble,* to come out and join the Congregation, on pain of excommunication. In support of that sentence, it asserted baldly the apostolic right of *our Church and the true ministers of the same* to forgive sins or retain them. And the purpose of this summons was defined in the manifesto to the bishops: *we shall begin that same war which God commanded Israel to execute against the Canaanites; contract of peace shall never be made till ye desist from your open idolatry and cruel persecution of God's children.* Even the letter to the Regent announced that, unless she could restrain those that *pursue us for the matter of religion,* the Congregation would *be compelled to take the sword of just defence* and to appeal, not only to the Queen and Dauphin, *but also to the Princes and Council of every Christian Realm.*

This was not the language of a minister of the gospel, but it sent up the temperature of the Congregation. They swore to fight to the death against the French, and "in sign and token the most part put six quarters of tow about his neck, that if he fled he should be hanged therewith and if they overcame the Frenchman they should hang them therewith." And in another quarter Knox's voice found an even stronger echo. It brought the men of Ayrshire together in the church of Craigie; Glencairn overbore their hesitations and, with Willock for preacher and Boyd, Ochiltree, Gadgirth and the rest for lieutenants, he appeared in Glasgow with some 2,500 men. Lyon Herald summoned them to disperse; the bridges above Stirling were occupied or destroyed. Forced thus to take a more westerly and rougher road than that by which, eighty-six years later, Montrose was to skirt Stirling on his way to Kilsyth, they marched *through desert and mountain* and were within eight miles of Perth by the end of the week.

But the battle was not to be joined. On the Wednesday, Argyll and James Stewart had come to Perth as mediators; on Sunday, the 28th, after goings and comings, an arrangement was signed. The Congregation was to evacuate Perth, but the Regent was to put no Frenchmen in the town. These terms settled nothing; they merely threw on the Regent the responsibility for a new breach. That was why Knox accepted them. What had really happened in these goings and comings was that Stewart and Argyll had changed sides. Glencairn and Willock had been at them; Knox had spoken to them in his new Elijah tones. On Thursday he had delivered to them a solemn message for the Regent, admonishing her that she was fighting against God. He had bidden them consider, for themselves, not only the religious issue, but the fate of their country exposed to French invasion. They had considered. They asked only that before they turned their coats the impossibility of compromise should be proved.

3

It was proved within a week. The Congregation had made no promise save evacuation. On the Monday afternoon they marched out "every man to his own house," with Knox's voice in their ears assuring them that the war was but begun; "and as they passed, where they found in their way any kirks or chapels, incontinent they purged them, breaking down the altars and idols in all places where they came." That same evening the Regent entered a town whose council had forbidden the only form of church worship permitted by the law. She was bound to vindicate the law, to appoint a new council and to leave a garrison to protect them. For garrison she had only Frenchmen and the Scottish companies in French pay. She put in four of the latter and was immediately accused of bad faith. To make matters worse, her troops had fired off their muskets in the streets and killed a child.

That was proof enough for those who wished to be convinced. Glencairn, Boyd, Ochiltree and young Campbell, the Sheriff of Ayr's son, had stayed in the town. On Wednesday, the 31st, Stewart and Argyll signed another Band with them, in the name of the Congregations of the West Country and of Fife, Perth, Dundee, Angus, Mearns and Munross. Next day the brothers-in-law left Perth. The Regent sent after them; they answered with a defiance. They rode to St. Andrews, set themselves to raise Fife, and sent word to Dundee and Angus. There was need, for the Regent recalled her French troops from Stirling and advanced with Chatelheraut and d'Oysel to Falkland. D'Oysel's French numbered perhaps 2,000; Chatelheraut had perhaps 1,000 more. Knox was preaching in Craill and Anstruther, to the now usual accompaniment of breaking images. He joined the Lords in St. Andrews on Saturday, June 10th, but the Primate, with some courage, was there before him and threatened him with *a dozen culverins* if he presumed to preach. But preach he did the next day, with all the fervour of a dream fulfilled. St. Andrews must be purged of corruption as Christ had purged the Temple of old. Again the cathedral was gutted, the houses of the friars sacked and a bonfire of images made in "the same place where Walter Mill was burnt."

But the town was in greater danger than from its Archbishop's culverins. The Regent was pushing her outposts to Cupar ten miles away and the musters of the Congregation had not arrived. Stewart and Argyll decided to seize Cupar before her, and did so on Monday evening; but they had only a hundred horse. The gamble just came off. That night the town bands of St. Andrews marched out and the musters began to arrive, not only from Angus but from Lothian. Fife was rising; Rothes, the sheriff, came in and the provost of Falkland itself. Best of all, Ruthven rode in from Perth. *It appeared as men had rained from the clouds.* Early on Tuesday morning the Congregation occupied rising ground on Cupar Muir, behind the Eden stream, and the musters, marching in during the forenoon, took up position as they could.

The day broke misty. D'Oysel's horse, coming into contact with Ruthven's cavalry screen, could see on the slope beyond the stream only the spears of the Angus and Fife contingents. That force they could easily contain; they began to edge round it towards St. Andrews. Then at noon the mist lifted, and showed artillery coming into position to command their line of advance and, in another part of the field, the massed town bands of St. Andrews and Dundee. By that time the forces were nearly equal. A halt was called.

D'Oysel had not bargained for a pitched battle. Never had he known a people "so easy to rouse and bring into the field," nor gentlemen who changed sides so quickly as Ruthven, "in the morning with us and after dinner with them." Moreover, James Melville had just arrived in Falkland from Paris, with messages from the King and the Constable of France. They promised help to the uttermost if the rebels were challenging the royal authority; but, if it was a mere question of religion, they counselled moderation and tolerance. Appeasement would be impossible if Chatelheraut and his nephew Argyll were forced to open blows. So a flag of truce was sent, and an armistice concluded. The Regent's troops were to retire to Falkland; for eight days "exclusive" they should not "invade, trouble or inquiet" the Congregation; the Congregation, on their side, "should enterprise nothing nor make no invasion"; meanwhile, the Regent and Council would arrange a peace conference.

4

The truce was a mere manœuvre of extrication. The Regent intended to negotiate, but the inside of a week was useless for the purpose. She must first retreat from an untenable position. She withdrew all her troops, except the Perth garrison, to the neighbourhood of Edinburgh, leaving even Stirling uncovered. While this operation was in progress, she probably gave the Congregation to understand that she might accept peace on the basis of the *status quo*, pending the assembly of Parliament.

But the Congregation were not content with the *status quo*; they followed up her retreat. Before the truce was over they sacked the Abbey of Lindores. On Saturday the 25th they arrived at the walls of Perth; on Sunday they entered it after no more than an exchange of artillery salvoes with the garrison the evening before. On Monday the men of Dundee marched out to Scone, to pay off old scores with Hepburn, Bishop of Moray, whom they regarded as chiefly responsible for the burning of Walter Mill. Their provost and Stewart hurried after to stop them, for the bishop had promised to join the Congregation, and a Hepburn (as we shall see) was worth winning. But that night Stewart was called away. News came that the Regent was about to re-occupy the Forth bridges. With Argyll he made a dash for Stirling, and was just in time. Behind them the Abbey and Palace of Scone were sacked, though Knox, summoned from Perth to take Stewart's place, did his best to restrain the mob. In the next three days the religious houses of Stirling and Linlithgow, the Abbey of Cambuskenneth, the Black and Grey Friars at Edinburgh, the Abbey and (according to one account) the Palace of Holyrood itself, all suffered the same fate. By the morning of Friday, June 30th, Stewart, Argyll, Ruthven and Rothes had ridden into the capital; Glencairn followed them, having "purged" Glasgow on his way; Maxwell escaped from Edinburgh Castle; Morton came in to meet them. The next day Knox was preaching at St. Giles.

The Regent was at Dunbar, where d'Oysel confessed himself at his wits' end, amid a hostile population with troops half-starving and mutinous. The French ambassador in London urged his master at Paris to send his son and daugher-in-law to Scotland as the only hope of appeasing their subjects' passions. But as he wrote his master lay dying. On June 29th he had been wounded at a tournament; by July 10th he was dead.

CHAPTER XIX

INTRIGUE

I

THESE TWO months of cavalcade might well intoxicate the faithful, but Knox was uneasy. The Congregation were weaker than they appeared. They lacked two things: territorial influence and regular troops.

The balance of forces in Scotland was hardly more favourable than it had been in 1543–47. Now, as then, Huntly the Catholic could dominate the north for the Regent; badly as she had treated him, he was offering her his services in exchange for the earldom of Moray. In the west she had lost the Campbells, but they could always be held in check by M'Connall and his Irish; on the other hand, she had gained the Kennedies, for the new Cassilis, dominant in Wigtown and Carrick, was a Catholic. The Maxwells might be against her, but again they could be held in check by the gentry of the Western Marches, and their leader, Sir John, was a prisoner in Edinburgh Castle. Erskine, the Castle Governor, was with her; Morton, with his Douglases, was undecided; in Lothian and the Middle Marches she had the young Earl of Bothwell, son of Wishart's arrester, with all the Hepburn influence; above all, she had Chatelheraut and his Hamiltons in Clydesdale.

Chatelheraut was the weakest link in this loyalist chain. He must be won, and the way to win him was clear. His son, Arran, had been living on his father's French estates for nine years past and had recently turned Huguenot. If the young man could be brought back to Scotland, he might turn the scale. He might even marry Elizabeth —at least that was a bait to be dangled before his father's eyes. For the rest, territorial influence in the north and on the Border might to some extent be counteracted by popular preaching. More preachers were needed; Knox's Geneva colleague, Goodman, must be summoned to Scotland; the English Government must be urged to appoint a good pulpit propagandist at Berwick—*a learned and godly man, with license also to preach within Scotland*. Congregations must be established at Jedburgh and Kelso. These—Arran and preachers— were the first two points in Knox's programme.

But the Congregation were not only weak territorially, they were unable even to use the forces they had. Twice it had proved impossible to keep their volunteers together; twice their hasty reassembly had been almost too late. Even now, for the third time, they were melting away. Many had gone home as soon as they heard that the Regent had evacuated the capital. Among their leaders there was not a single man of any wealth; they could not pay mercenaries. If d'Oysel at Dunbar was telling the French Government that he could not restore order without money and reinforcements, Knox was even more sure that the Reformation could not be established without both military and financial help from England. Those—money and men—were the third and fourth points in his programme.

2

But Knox could do little himself to carry out this programme. He was busy with his own kind of propaganda both in France and England. He was urging the Huguenots in Dieppe to carry out an open reformation of their town on the Scottish model; he was using Mrs. Locke in London as his intermediary for news and begging letters. He was asking her where Goodman was, and sending directions for his journey. Now and later he wrote to her of the Congregation's financial straits—not without some success, for Hickman lent money to Glencairn. But all this was of little use. Cecil, and Elizabeth herself, must be induced to move, and Cecil would not answer his letters, while Elizabeth would not have his name mentioned in her presence. Whom could he find to speak for him?

On the morrow of Cupar Muir he found what he thought a convenient mouthpiece: his old acquaintance, Kirkcaldy. That soldier of fortune had been serving the Regent on the Border for the last two years, but was home now at his house of Grange, about to change sides once more. He and Knox put their heads together and decided to sound the Government in London. Kirkcaldy had some credit there, for he had been an English agent in France, and in the last two years he had made himself well known to the English officials on the Border. These were a new set since Knox's Northumbrian days. Sir James Croft was Captain of Berwick, with Knox's brother-in-law, George Bowes, as Marshal. The Percys had been reinstated by Mary Tudor: two brothers, nephews of the last Earl of Northumberland, sons of the Thomas Percy who had led the pilgrimage of Grace. Thomas, the new earl, honest Catholic and most unpractical politician, was Warden of the East and Middle Marches; Henry, a lively schemer of no particular religion and no scruples at all, was his active deputy. Croft and Henry Percy would at least be able to act as a post-office for letters from Kirkcaldy for Cecil.

Thus opened a rather clumsy negotiation. Between June 21st and 28th, Kirkcaldy wrote three times to Cecil and Knox twice. When they reached Edinburgh they both wrote again on July 1st. The letters were little more than a general appeal for co-operation and for an opportunity to talk things over.

Cecil jumped at the chance, but not too hastily. The Arran scheme was not new to him. At this very moment, Noailles, the French ambassador in London, was informing him that Arran had been making "infinite scandal" in Poitou, that orders had been issued for his arrest and that he had disappeared. Noailles added that he was thought to be making for England and, if this were so, demanded his extradition as a rebellious subject of the King of France. Cecil professed bland ignorance, but sent out an emissary who traced the fugitive to Switzerland and brought him north through Germany. For the rest, it was too early to talk of military help, but a subsidy might be possible, if Cecil could loosen his mistress's grip on her purse strings. But, though Croft and Percy might usefully talk to Kirkcaldy, business of this kind could not be transacted with gentlemen-amateurs. Could Croft and Percy find out how far the Lords of the Congregation were really to be trusted and how far they were really prepared to go?

Accordingly, Kirkcaldy, meeting Percy at Norham, was told that the English Government were interested but wished to know for whom he spoke. He and Knox passed on to the Lords this straight tip from London, with all the pride of volunteer diplomatists; Knox drafted letters for them to send to Elizabeth and Cecil. From that moment the Lords found themselves balancing on the most insecure of tight-ropes. The intrigue has been repeatedly described by historians and its dishonesties exposed; but the trees are so many that it is easy to miss the wood.

3

The one real issue in the mind of all parties was the approaching French invasion of Scotland. That invasion was about to take place; there was no shadow of doubt about that. But the French did not want to send more troops than would be necessary to keep Scotland in allegiance to the French crown. They did not propose to engage in a religious war. They had enough trouble of this kind in their own country. At the Synod of Paris in May the Huguenot Church had adopted a national constitution. Early in June, the Parlement of Paris had protested, to Henry II's face, against the Edict of Compiègne; Henry had imprisoned four of them and had sworn to burn their leader, du Bourg. But if Valois and Guise were going to fight down this rising menace at home, they must let Scottish Calvinism go its own way for the moment. They were assured by d'Oysel that the revolt against the old Church was general; if Scotsmen were to be brought back into the Pope's fold, it must be by persuasion and Church reform. On the very day of his fatal accident, Henry II wrote to the Pope, throwing on him the whole responsibility for the long delay in Church reform, and proposing that the Bishop of Amiens should now be despatched to Scotland as Papal legate. A few days later another French emissary, Béthencourt, the same who had just returned from concluding the Peace of Upsettlington, was sent back to the Regent, with renewed promise of troops but also with renewed advice to handle religious dissent *doucement, et par moyens*.

The Queen of England's attitude was not very different, except that she had no wish to see a successful Papal legate at Edinburgh. She, too, insisted that the subjects of the Queen of Scots should not rebel against their lawful sovereign. She not only hated rebellion in principle; she was bound by her just-concluded treaty with France not to countenance this particular rebellion. Just because she disliked French troops near her frontiers, she would be the more angry with the Scotsmen whose rebellion should provoke so unwelcome a visitation. The one chance of inducing her to intervene in favour of the Congregation was to play on a particular grudge which she bore against the King and Queen of Scots. No sooner had peace been signed than they had quartered the English leopards with the Scottish lion on their coat of arms. That was no empty gesture, for the French negotiators at St. Pol had referred to Mary Stewart as the rightful Queen of England. If Elizabeth could be sure that the Congregation would work consistently for an Anglo-Scottish alliance, she might support them against foreigners who "do falsely pretend title to the crown of England."

Thus far, then, it was to the interest of the Congregation to expatiate on their obedience to lawful authority, to protest their friendship for England, and to insist that they were only defending their religious liberty. But Cecil's view, the view of almost all Elizabeth's officials, was almost exactly the opposite. These asseverations of loyalty were too reminiscent of the fiasco of 1543. If England were to give money or men again to help Scottish lords, she must be assured that a Stewart or a Campbell would not make sudden peace with Frenchmen as a Hamilton had done sixteen years before. More than ever was this necessary now that Henry II was dead. Now the King of France was King of Scots, and England's one aim was to clear Scotland of Frenchmen. That could only be done by rebellion. Religion was a convenient cry for rebels, but it was the rebellion that mattered. "In any wise do your endeavour to kindle the fire," wrote Cecil to Croft. That being so, the Congregation, while it publicly talked religious freedom for Elizabeth's benefit, must privately talk rebellion for Cecil's.

Up to a point, Knox was only too well qualified to play this double game. His trade was words; he could formulate either policy with convincing eloquence. In fact, he had done so repeatedly in the last few years, for he genuinely believed in both. More, there was, in truth, no real distinction between the two. From whichever end the case might be argued, the conclusion was the same. To no one at that time did religious freedom mean the abandonment by the civil power of responsibility for religious order; at most it meant the substitution of local option for national uniformity. But how could local option be enacted in Scotland without a "change of authority"? Whatever a Scottish Parliament might enact, could the King and Queen of France, or their representative in Scotland, sanction laws which would exclude the Roman Church from the capital and all the chief burghs of their Scottish realm, and from every country district where the lairds might take possession of the parish church in the name of a local congregation? No responsible person in 1559 thought such a solution possible, especially now that, since July 10th, the Guises were assumed to be in full control of their niece's policy. And, in fact, as we shall see, the Scottish Reformation of 1560 was never legalized until that niece's fall seven years later. What was the difference between rebellion and a fundamental change in national law, enacted in the name of an absentee sovereign, but without her consent?

But while Knox was thus an ideal publicity agent for a tight-rope-walking Congregation, he was a hopeless performer when he tried to walk the diplomatic rope himself. The author of the *First Blast* was irretrievably suspect to Elizabeth; no letter that he wrote would be allowed to reach her, if Cecil could help it. He knew this, yet he insisted on writing: *I am become so odious to the Queen's Grace and her Council that the mention of my name is unpleasing to their ears; but yet I will not cease to offer myself.* That was to Cecil on June 28th. On July 19th he "offered himself" again to Cecil, in a letter which harped once more on the danger of defending female government in principle, *whereof already we have seen the danger and felt the smart.* The next day he "offered himself" to Elizabeth, assuring her of his respect for her authority, yet admonishing her in tones of almost sublime offensiveness: *forget your birth and all title which thereupon doth hang, and consider deeply how, for fear of your life, you did decline from God and bow to idolatry.* No wonder that Cecil complained that letters from such a source did "no good."

Nor was this all. If Knox was suspect to Elizabeth, to Cecil himself on the other hand, to Throckmorton in Paris and to Croft at Berwick, he was an invaluable faction leader, on whose irreconcilable honesty they could always rely. Yet he laboured to convince them of his moderation. *None that professeth Christ Jesus usurpeth anything against the authority*, he wrote to Cecil on June 28th. *We mean neither sedition, neither yet rebellion against any just and lawful authority*, he wrote to Percy on July 1st. It was in much the same tone that on July 19th he induced the Lords to reply to Cecil's enquiries, when what Cecil hoped to hear from them was recognition of the truth which Stewart and his friends had in fact recognized long ago: that a Queen of France could never rule Scotland. Not till subtler heads took control of the Congregation's diplomacy would an understanding with England be reached.

4

From the moment of their entry into Edinburgh, the Lords of the Congregation floundered. They seized the Mint stamps, clearly a technical invasion of sovereignty. The Regent issued a manifesto accusing them of rebellion and intrigues with England. They replied disclaiming any intention to "usurp our sovereign's authority and to invade your person." In the same tone they engaged in negotiations, first with the Regent herself at Dunbar, then with Chatelheraut, Huntly and Erskine at Preston, then with the Regent again. They offered obedience in return for religious freedom, the removal of "unable ministers from ecclesiastical administration" and the withdrawal of the French troops. The Regent accepted religious freedom in principle, but raised the obvious objection: where her Court went in the itinerant life of Scottish government, there the Mass must be celebrated, and two incompatible forms of worship could not co-exist in the same churches at the same time. There the negotiations stuck; the Lords decided to settle down in Edinburgh for the winter, *for establishing of the Church there*; they took measures to establish the Church in Kelso too, to counteract the Hepburn influence among "the gentlemen of the East Borders." On July 19th they wrote their letters to Elizabeth and Cecil, proposing "a perpetual amity to stand betwixt the two realms" and praying for "your faithful counsel and furtherance." A week later they were in full retreat to Stirling.

Their bluff had been called. Only 1,500 men remained with them; at Dunbar, d'Oysel, with Chatelheraut, Huntly, Bothwell, Livingstone and Home, had at least twice that number. Suddenly, on Sunday, July 23rd, the Regent's troops marched on Leith, and Leith opened its gates. On Monday the 24th the opposing forces manœuvred and watched each other: the Congregation on the "Craigs," the slopes of Calton Hill, the loyalists along the road from Leith. Erskine in the castle declared for the Regent. The Congregation's position was untenable; a truce was agreed that evening. They were to evacuate Edinburgh and surrender the Mint stamps; they would recognize the Regent's authority, except in religion; they would not disturb the clergy nor attack Church property nor withhold Church rents and dues. The Regent, on her side, would leave the town of Edinburgh free to choose its religion; she would guarantee preachers from molestation; she would (some say) put no garrison in the capital. This arrangement was to last till 10th January 1560, and meanwhile a Parliament would be called to consider a settlement.

The preachers were aghast at these terms; the Lords dared not announce them publicly. Instead they proclaimed "by voice of trumpet at the Market Cross of Edinburgh" only the Regent's promises, adding apparently two promises she had never made: "that no idolatry should be erected where it is already suppressed," and (according to one copy of the proclamation) that the French troops should be withdrawn from Scotland "at a reasonable date." Nor did they dare to tell Croft or Cecil the truth; Kirkcaldy had written to Croft on July 23rd that "with all diligent speed the Frenchmen here present shall be sent away, and shall no others come in this realm without consent of the whole nobility"; and they did at least nothing to correct this misstatement.

They might well be afraid to tell London the truth, for Cecil was no less aghast than the preachers. This was just what he had feared: half-measures and capitulation. On July 8th he had warned Croft that the Protestants must act "with all speed, for it will be too late when the French power cometh"; and now here was postponement of the whole issue until a Parliament should meet, as it had met outside Haddington eleven years before, under the culverins of a French army! On July 1st, Kirkcaldy, frankly describing the destruction of religious houses, had made a virtue of declaring (probably with truth) that the Congregation "have never as yet meddled with a pennyworth of that which pertains to the Church." If the Regent would assent to a "general reformation" they would "annex the whole revenues of the abbeys to the Crown"; if not, the fruits of the abbeys and other churches shall be kept and bestowed upon the faithful ministers." Cecil was merely irritated by this virtuous abstinence: half-measures again. Why, he wrote to the Lords on the 28th, did not they seize the wealth of the prelates to finance their rising? Why ask help from England before they had drawn on such resources? And now, four days before these words were written, these Lords had tamely agreed to respect all their enemies' possessions for six vital months! On July 19th they had proudly asserted that, while they did not contemplate "any change in authority except that extreme necessity compel us thereto," they were "fully purposed to seek the next remedy: to withstand the tyranny" of the Regent "together with her priests and Frenchmen." Two days earlier Kirkcaldy had written even more proudly to Henry Percy of the approaching alliance between England and Scotland: "all Europe shall know that a league made in the name of God hath another foundation and assurance than pactions made by man for worldly commodity." And here was this proud confederacy in ignominious retreat, pledged to obey the Regent in return for a mere promise of temporary toleration! To cap all, these blundering Protestants had no idea of secrecy; all their goings and comings with Berwick were common talk. The Regent was protesting to Elizabeth; she was complaining to the Earl of Northumberland; she had sent a message by Bothwell to Henry Percy at Norham. The burden of all these communications was the same; Elizabeth's officials, and especially Percy himself, were intriguing with her rebellious subjects.

The Lords, arrived at Stirling, only made matters worse by deputing Knox to plead their cause in person with Croft and Percy.

He had quitted Edinburgh with them, leaving Willock in charge of St. Giles. He had reason to think that Percy would meet him at Alnwick. He travelled from Stirling to Pittenweem in Fife, and took boat for Holy Island, landing there on August 2nd. He could hardly have arrived at a more inopportune moment. The Government in London had just decided that a more reliable agent than Percy was needed on the Border; they had appointed Sir Ralph Sadler, a well-tried official, who had been ambassador to Scotland in 1543 and treasurer of the English army on the Border in 1548–49. Sadler had not yet arrived; Percy was lying low; and Béthencourt, the French envoy, was on his way through Alnwick and Berwick to Edinburgh. Just as Elizabeth's disclaimers were being despatched to the Regent, here was the best-known man in Scotland plumping down out of the blue, without precautions or concealment of any kind, under Béthencourt's nose. Croft sent for him to Berwick, kept him as quiet as possible, noted his instructions which prayed for ships to protect Dundee and Perth and for money and men to enable the Lords to make their good hold on Stirling and fortify Broughty, heard him urge the use of English influence with the Homes and Kers on the Border, listened to his (quite baseless) report that the Regent had pledged herself to evacuate her French troops by August 10th, and sent him back to Stirling with vague but comfortable words. Knox got back safely, though the Regent's men were on the look-out for him. His brother William and White-law, a Scots Protestant from Paris who was bringing Cecil's letter of June 28th to the Lords, started with him, but, travelling by another route, were mistaken for him and roughly handled by Lord Seton.

That was the end of Knox's brief career as a diplomatist. Cecil had played with the idea of meeting him himself, if it could be arranged secretly; he appears even to have suggested a rendezvous at his house of Burleigh, an invitation which for some reason Knox did not receive till too late. But after this indiscretion at Berwick, secrecy was obviously impossible; Knox himself recognized that he was not "meet to treat of so great matters," and spoke of his old friend Balnaves as the best substitute.

5

Knox and Whitelaw returned to Stirling on August 5th as messengers of discouragement. They reported that Croft thought the Congregation "slow, negligent and cold"; they brought Cecil's letter of June 28th pointing out how difficult it was for England 'to enter into war either not provoked or not foreseen," and adjuring the Lords to be more energetic in helping themselves. Only Stewart and Argyll were at Stirling; the other leaders, having signed a new Band on the 1st, had gone home, arranging to meet in Glasgow in ten days' time. On the 6th the brothers-in-law wrote a preliminary reply to Croft protesting against these suspicions; Knox added an emphatic warning that, in the absence of some promise of help, the Congregation was likely to disintegrate. On the 10th the Lords met at Glasgow and to Glasgow came also Béthencourt, bearing minatory letters from the King and Queen of France to Stewart and vowing that the King *would spend the Crown of France* to enforce his authority in Scotland.

But two days before Béthencourt's intervention something else had happened. Argyll had been summoned by his uncle Chatelheraut to Hamilton. The duke had heard from his son on his way home; would Argyll and Stewart write to assure him of a welcome? The duke was obviously weakening, though he would not commit himself beyond "a general promise that he will not be our enemy when the matter shall come to the uttermost." With that knowledge Stewart, on the 12th, answered the royal letters haughtily enough; and next day the Lords drew up their reply to Cecil, rebutting his criticisms and asking for more "plainness and simplicity" in his dealings.

By that time, Knox had had enough of politics. He handed over his half-secretaryship of the Congregation to Balnaves and left for St. Andrews. Thence on the 5th he wrote the best of his letters to Cecil, warning him plainly that his temporizing was *like to lose hearts of those that be here. Unless without delay money be furnished to pay their soldiers (who in number are now but 500) for their service bypast and to retain another thousand footmen with three hundred horsemen for a time, they will be compelled every man to seek the next way to his own safety. In the bowels of Christ Jesus I require you, Sir, to make plain answer what they may lippen to.* Knox might be a bad politician, but, unlike the circumlocutory diplomatists of the day, he knew exactly what he wanted and exactly how to say it.

Then for two months he dropped out of the English intrigue. His business was propaganda, religious and political. He was ill of an ague, desperately anxious for his wife's presence, but full of preaching work. Besides Edinburgh and Ayr, there were congregations to be organized in St. Andrews, Dundee, Perth, Brechin, Montrose and Stirling. Preaching had begun, too, in Jedburgh and Kelso; as he had hoped, the Kers, both of Cesford and Ferniehurst, were coming over to the Congregation. *We do nothing but go about Jericho, blowing with trumpets as God giveth strength.* But there were few to blow; Goodman had come as far as the Border but, finding no one to direct him, had turned back; only later did Knox hear that he had arrived in Ayrshire. At last, on September 20th, his wife arrived, having taken three months to get from Paris to Fife, in spite of Throckmorton's efforts to facilitate her journey.

It would have been well for Knox's reputation if in these weeks he had confined himself to preaching. But he had other propagandist work on hand. The Lords had asked him to write a reasoned history of the rebellion, proving their loyalty to the Crown and the Regent's bad faith. So began his *History of the Reformation*: what is now the second Book of that chronicle. It was a party pamphlet and the best that can be said of it is that for accuracy and honesty, it compares favourably with the party pamphlets of our own enlightened days. Knox himself was so little proud of it that, having written it in the heat of the moment as a manifesto for publication, he refused to let it see the light so long as he lived.

He was on sounder ground in another political activity of these weeks. A few days after his arrival at St. Andrews four companies of French mercenaries under an Italian captain arrived at Leith, and d'Oysel set himself to fortify the town. Immediately, Regent and Congregation plunged into a war of propaganda, and in the chief popular broadsheet of that war Knox's pen is evident.

His task was not easy. In the controversy the Regent had an almost cast-iron case. She had kept the agreement of July 24th; the Lords, meditating new treason, had tried to falsify its terms. They were forced to abandon the attempt; the falsification was too obvious; the English Government might find it convenient to believe that the Regent had made promises "both for restoring religion and sending away the Frenchmen," but Scotsmen knew the contrary. Characteristically, Knox changed the ground of battle to the main issue. The bringing in of French troops might not violate the agreement of July 24th, but it did violate the *ancient laws and liberties of Scotland*. More, it was socially and economically intolerable. It meant billeting and requisitions. On both sides of the Forth, in Lothian and Fife, *our dearest brethren are most cruelly oppressed by strangers; some are banished their own houses, some robbed and spoiled of their substance. The fertility of this realm has never been so plenteous that it was able of any continuance to sustain itself, far less able to sustain thousands of strangers. If ye will not be slaves, to have your lives, your wives, your bairns, your substance, cast at their feet, to be used and abused at the pleasure of strange soldiers—then, brethren, let us join our forces and both with wit and manhood resist these beginnings, or else our liberties hereafter shall be dearer bought.* We have seen in an earlier chapter how well based were these apprehensions; they are confirmed by d'Oysel's own correspondence at this time.

This was the popular shape in which Knox raised the constitutional issue against the Regent. Meanwhile, the Lords were formulating the same issue in more official terms. While Knox was at his preaching and writing work beyond Forth, the English-Arran intrigue had been coming to a head.

6

Sir Ralph Sadler reached Berwick about August 19th, to find the Lords' and Knox's letters awaiting him. He reported immediately to Cecil, confirming their arguments for immediate action, and especially Knox's estimate of the forces required. Croft wrote to Knox the same day, asking that "Mr. Henry Balnaves or some other discreet and trusty man" should be sent by sea to Holy Island. Sadler had £3,000; by the end of the month he had been given discretion to use the money as he saw fit. Knox passed on Croft's letter to Glasgow. On September 2nd, Balnaves was at Berwick. He reached a new agreement with Sadler: England would give a subsidy and the Congregation would burn their boats. They could no longer stop at half-measures; there must be a "change of authority." With the subsidy in his pocket he returned to Stirling, where the Lords had convened a meeting for September 10th.

Unknown to Balnaves, the torch for the boat-burning was being sent west from Berwick at this very moment by another road. A few days before, Arran, newly landed in England, had been smuggled into Elizabeth's presence; he had posted north with a young English agent for guide, one Thomas Randolph; he had been under the same roof with Balnaves during the talks with Sadler; now he was on his way to his father's house in Lanarkshire. Thence he went to the convention at Stirling, and that convention immediately took on a new character. It became something more than a Congregation; if Arran and his father would join it, it would be almost a constitutional body, the Council of the secular nobility. As such, the Lords adjourned to Hamilton on the 17th and on the 19th they issued a summons to the Regent, signed by both Chatelherault and Arran. The fortification of Leith portended a breach of the agreement of July 24th; in any case it had been undertaken "without any manner consent of the nobility and Council of this realm"; the Regent was therefore required "to cause the same work to be stayed." On the same day another letter was despatched to Erskine in Edinburgh Castle, adjuring him to join them. Finally, it was decided to occupy Edinburgh, and for that purpose the Lords agreed to assemble their forces at Stirling on Sunday, October 15th.

There followed an interlude of mutual defiance and futile negotiation. To Knox's disgust, one of the best-tried members of the westland Congregation—Lockhart of Bar, Wishart's host of former days—turned peacemaker and visited him, among others, with messages from the Regent. His importunities wrung from him a queer letter to Mary, protesting that no one who had lectured her so consistently for her soul's good could be justly charged with *hatred or enmity* against her. These interchanges naturally produced no result; on October 15th the musters met, Knox among them; the next day, Monday, they marched into Edinburgh. This time they came with still more imposing power. They were some 7,000 strong and, besides the Hamiltons, three more earls had joined them: Eglinton, Marischall and Sutherland. With them also were two significant clerics: Chatelherault's cousin, Gavin Hamilton, Abbot of Kilwinning, and Huntly's brother, Alexander Gordon, titular Bishop of Athens. Erskine now was friendly; Morton had promised his support, though he *did never plainly join*. Even Bothwell seemed to be wavering. As against this imposing façade, the Regent at Dunbar could boast hardly any open support from Scotsmen, save the prelates of St. Andrews, Glasgow and Dunkeld.

But Knox went with no light heart on this new cavalcade. A month before, returning from a flying visit to Stirling and from the enthusiasms of Arran's arrival, he had warned Croft again. The leaders of the Congregation were heavily in debt; they could not maintain their following; even if *money could not corrupt them, yet should extreme poverty compel them to remain at home*. It was an ominous plea for a revival of the English pensions system. And even as he wrote, even as the Lords' ultimatum to the Regent was being despatched from Hamilton, another small detachment of troops had arrived from France, and with them the Bishop of Amiens, charged with the reform of the Scottish Church. Again, as when the Castle of St. Andrews was besieged twelve years before, there was more will to action in France than in England; there was more determination at Dunbar and behind the new ramparts of Leith than among the mixed bands that clanked about the streets of Edinburgh.

Still, if English support was to be won, the game must be played out; the boats must be burnt, the "authority" must be "changed." A final ultimatum was sent to the Regent: "we most humbly require your Grace to cause your strangers and soldiers whatsoever to depart of the said town of Leith." All that week the Lords awaited her reply; on Thursday Chatelherault issued a proclamation at the Market Cross, denying that he or his son had designs upon the crown. On Saturday the 21st, Lyon King at Arms appeared, bringing the Regent's answer; it contained the fatal reminder that she had no need to conquer Scotland for France, "considering that it was already conquered by marriage." That same day the Lords met in the Tolbooth and asked the preachers whether it were lawful to depose the Regent. Willock replied like a theorist, with the full doctrine that the divine right of magistrates "is bounded and limited by God in His Word." Knox, intent as usual on the main issue, confined himself to the particular case: the Regent might be deposed provided that the authority of her daughter and son-in-law were preserved, and provided, further, that the act of deposition were not final. If the Regent should yield, it must be revoked. The advice heard, the deposition act was drawn up; old grievances and new, real and flimsy, were raked into one long-drawn indictment; the Regent had refused "to consult upon the affairs of the common weal" with those who were "born counsellors of the same by the ancient laws of the realm"; therefore "we, so many of the nobility, barons and provosts of burghs as are touched with the care of the common weal, in name and authority of our Sovereign Lord and Lady, suspend the said commission granted by our said sovereigns to the said Queen Dowager." The point was put even more clearly in the covering letter to Mary: "as your Grace will not acknowledge us, our Sovereign Lord and Lady's lieges, for your subjects and Council, no more will we acknowledge you for any Regent or lawful magistrate unto us."

Bold words, and ones that were to have many echoes in Scotland and elsewhere in the coming years. But young Randolph, now English agent with the Congregation, warned Cecil how weak was the challenge. Seldom were such words to be uttered again with less real force behind them; seldom did rebels venture a more perilous gamble.

CHAPTER XX

DISASTER AND VICTORY

OCTOBER 1559–JULY 1560

I

So CLOSED the Congregation's first week in Edinburgh. The next opened badly. It was decided to assault Leith, but how? While the rank and file made amateurish attempts to construct scaling ladders in St. Giles, to the annoyance of the preachers, the leaders debated. They needed 3,000 more men for an assault; they made *proclamation by the drum* for recruits, with little result; and, in any case, they had no money for pay. "The Scots," a Venetian agent had reported eight years before, "are incapable either of erecting fortresses or of defending them"; they were still less able to besiege them. Messengers from the Regent were offering terms; Knox had a *bitter battle* to prevent compromise; Morton sheered off, the Kers dropped away.

In this confusion Knox took up his pen once more. On Monday the 23rd a letter reached him from an old acquaintance, Railton, a Berwick official, asking for confirmation of a rumour which Cecil just then was chasing busily, for Elizabeth's benefit. Was it true that the quartering of English with Scottish arms had been adopted by the Court of France, not only on dinner plate and jousting scutcheons, but on official seals? Throckmorton thought not, in France itself; but heard that a new seal of this kind had been sent for use in Scotland. Knox, writing on Monday at midnight, confirmed this; the seal had come in the same ship that brought him to Scotland. Then he passed to more important issues. The position was desperate. *If ye frustrate my expectation and the promise that I have made in your name, I regard not how few my dolorous days shall be.* Two days later, on Wednesday the 23rd, he wrote again, this time to Croft; if England could not send open aid without breaking her treaty with

France, why should she not encourage volunteers to cross the Border, and if necessary, *declare them rebels when ye shall be assured that they be in our company?* Croft was annoyed; here was this blunderer blurting out the very idea that was in Cecil's mind and that he was to act on a few weeks later. On Sunday the 29th, Knox received a snub; he took it with good temper but he stuck to his argument. *Whether it may stand with wisdom to have such respect to that which some men do call honour, that in the meantime I shall see my friend perish, both to his destruction and mine, I refer to the judgment of the most honourable.*

By that Sunday, however, men *of better judgment and greater experience* than Knox had appeared in Edinburgh. Young Maitland of Lethington, the Regent's secretary, had long been playing fast and loose with his mistress, in correspondence both with the Congregation and with Cecil; now, that game up, he "steals out of Leith thifteously and quietly" and surrendered to Kirkcaldy. At the same time word came from Croft. He had received another instalment of cash from London; Cockburn of Ormiston was sent to get it. Knox probably did not hear of this; Maitland's arrival had *delivered* him *from the most part of these civil affairs.* He could henceforth devote himself to restoring *moral* by daily sermons, and he began an exposition of the Eightieth Psalm. How long would God be angry against the prayer of His people?—Let them take heart, *justly were they punished for idolatry committed,* but God would *assure them of deliverance.*

They needed encouragement, for on Tuesday the 31st came deadly news. Bothwell had pounced on Cockburn near his house of Crichton; he had seized the Berwick money-bags. That night, Stewart, Arran and Maxwell dashed out to Crichton, but the bird was flown. Next morning, in their absence, and while Chatelherault and the other nobles were at sermon, the men of Dundee, with some 500 soldiers, hauled two pieces of artillery up "the east part of the Craigs," and proceeded to shoot at random into Leith. Sermon was hardly over when a tumult was heard in the Canongate. The soldiers were crowding back pell-mell into the town, followed by the Dundee town bands and mixed with Frenchmen in hot pursuit. They had been surprised by a sortie from Leith; there had been panic; the artillery had been abandoned. Argyll rallied the fugitives and the French drew off, taking the captured ordnance with them, but it had been a day of "great shame and lack"; in the Canongate the Frenchmen "both reft, spoiled and slew both man and wife that they could apprehend"; and "the hearts of many of the Congregation began to faint."

The end came next Monday, November 6th. A food convoy was expected; the French marched to intercept it; Stewart and Arran led out the cavalry to ride them off. Pushing too far, they were caught near Restalrig between the pincers of two strong columns, converging on Holyrood in their rear. Retreating precipitately by the neck of ground between the Restalrig marsh and the park ditch of Holyrood, they became entangled with their own infantry supports and suffered heavily; again "the Frenchmen pursued the chase even to the ports of Edinburgh." That evening there was desperate debate; Lethington, Arran and Stewart were for holding out at all costs, *but men did so steal away that the wit of man could not stay them.* Erskine, though he had fired a warning shot or two from the Castle against the French, would promise nothing. Evacuation was decided; at midnight the Congregation straggled off along the road to Stirling, amid the jeers of the mob.

2

That dark and dolorous night was the worst of Knox's memories, a memory of *fear and shame.* But he met the crisis characteristically. He would preach at Stirling; there he would finish those sermons on the Eightieth Psalm. He did so on Wednesday, mincing no words to the dispirited Lords who listened to him. They had *put flesh to be their arm*; ever since the Hamiltons had joined them, there had been a new spirit, a *bragging of multitude*, calculations of this lord's armed strength, of that earl's local influence. Let them repent; and let the Hamiltons repent, too; had Chatelherault himself yet wept for his past, for the blood of the martyrs, for his support of the Regent at Perth and Cupar Muir and Edinburgh Craigs? Queer language to an already half-disrupted confederacy! But then Knox soared to the climax of his text in the eighth verse of the Psalm: "Thou hast brought a vine out of Egypt. Thou has cast out the heathen and planted it." The vine had been planted in Scotland; *whatsoever shall become of us and of our mortal carcasses, I doubt not but that this cause, in despite of Satan, shall prevail in the realm; for, as it is the eternal truth of the Eternal God, so shall it once prevail, howsoever for a time it be impugned.*

That sermon opened a new phase of the revolt. Romantic methods had failed; cavalcade and intrigue were over; it was now a question of war and open alliance. The gentry went home, pledged to gather again at Stirling on December 16th; Knox went back to his wife at St. Andrews. But a little later one of Noailles's spies in London reported that he had seen two Scotsmen taking boat at Westminster stairs, and identified one of them as Lethington. On December 20th, Noailles sent a secretary to Paris with a budget of news about English preparations both by land and sea. The Duke of Norfolk had been despatched to Berwick; Admiral Winter had been appointed to command "seventeen great ships, well armed and equipped for war"; six more ships were loading artillery and munitions in the Thames. In fact Lethington, with instructions from the Lords, was working out with Cecil the terms of an open alliance. The Lords, meeting at Stirling on the 16th, had to consider despatches from him, containing the draft of an agreement. Elizabeth still waited to choose her moment for open action, but her Council were solid for a Scottish expedition. There was no time to lose; the French had already completed their preparations; a full-dress expeditionary force under d'Elbeuf, the youngest of the Guise brothers, had been due to sail at the end of November. So Winter was given underhand instructions; let him sail and put what spokes he could in d'Elbeuf's wheel; if he fought he would be disavowed but approved.

Yet the English would have been once more too late if they had not had better fortune than they deserved. On Christmas Eve d'Oysel sent five companies of infantry from Edinburgh to catch the Lords at Stirling, following himself next day with eight companies more and all his cavalry. He found the birds flown; Chatelherault had galloped off at midnight on Christmas Day to Glasgow with Glencairn and Argyll; Arran and Stewart rode to St. Andrews;

word went round that each leader must fend for himself *till that God should send farther support.* Knox had left Stirling a day or so earlier, charged with the duty of despatching by sea from St. Andrews a last cry for help to Croft. D'Oysel, established astride the Forth, chose Fife as his first objective. But bad weather forced him to halt some days at Stirling and, while he halted, the same storm wrecked d'Elbeuf's fleet and drove it back to Dieppe.

Of this, however, no word reached Scotland. Word came, on the contrary, that d'Elbeuf's fleet had been seen running north before the storm; they might appear in the Forth at any moment. And in the first days of January 1560, d'Oysel was advancing by way of Culross and Dunfermline. Stewart and Arran concentrated their small forces at Cupar. On the 7th, d'Oysel lay at Burntisland and a detachment of some four hundred Frenchmen, crossing from Leith, landed at Kinghorn. The local levies of the Congregation incautiously attacked this detachment on the shore and, taken in the rear by d'Oysel's cavalry, were barely extricated, with heavy loss, by Ruthven and the Earl of Sutherland, hurrying up from Cupar. This reverse took the heart out of the main body of the Congregation. All seemed lost; Knox, preaching at Cupar, accused Arran of discouraging his men by his moodiness. The French were everywhere, looting and killing; on the 11th a small squadron of d'Elbeuf's fleet, under his lieutenant Martigues, limped into Forth with reinforcements and stores. D'Oysel's plan was to advance on St. Andrews by the coast, keeping in touch with his supply-boats from Leith. Stewart and Arran, marching from Cupar to intercept them, lay at Dysart, but they had only two hundred horse and their paid infantry was useless—*ciphers,* says Knox, cowards (according to another account) whom "the Lords could not retain for boasting nor praying, and durst scarcely show themselves, for every man that could had provided themselves for the last remedy, which was to flee from the apparent danger." Only the *gentlemen of Fife,* under the leadership of Kirkcaldy and the Master of Lindsay, waged a Homeric war of hand to hand combats with French raiding parties; for three weeks, *they came never in bed neither yet did they ever sleep but in their jacks and armour.* Knox watched the hopeless scene from St. Andrews *with sorrowful heart.*

But d'Oysel was slow; not till the 23rd did he begin to move on Dysart. Next day, as his men marched unopposed along the coast, they saw sails—not d'Elbeuf's, but Winter's. The English fleet seized two guard ships and an ammunition boat. It was enough; their communications cut, the French turned back within six miles of St. Andrews and retired by forced marches to Stirling in "great hunger and penury of victual." By the end of the month they were back at Leith.

3

That retreat marked Knox's final release from *civil affairs*. Since Lethington's departure for London and the division of the Congregation's forces between Fife and Glasgow, he had taken them up again as secretary of the Fife headquarters, while Balnaves acted for the westland Lords. He hated the business. He and his wife together could not keep abreast of his correspondence; in Edinburgh, at the end of October, *in twenty-four hours I have not had four free to natural rest*; at St. Andrews, the last of December, *the rest of my wife hath been so unrestful that scarcely could she tell upon the morrow what she wrote at night.* His nerves could never stand worry; *one day of troubles since my arrival in Scotland hath more pierced my heart than all the torments of the galleys.* By comparison, he cared little that *great watch is laid for my apprehension and large money promised to any that shall kill me*; that only made him beg his brother-in-law at Berwick for *a good and assured horse.*

Now, at the end of January, he dropped out of all this. He wrote to Railton that *I am judged among ourselves too extreme and by reason thereof I have extracted myself from all public assemblies to my private study.* But, by way of farewell, he urged once more that English pensions should be given to some of the leaders; Stewart alone had spent 1,300 crowns since May. And on February 6th, he fired a parting shot at the Congregation in the west. Several times in the past month he had protested to Balnaves at their *slow proceedings*; they had left the men of Fife to face defeat alone; they had done nothing to threaten the French base at Stirling. And now Chatelherault and the rest were boggling over an invitation to send delegates to Berwick. The Duke of Norfolk wished to confer with them, but Chatelheraut thought Carlisle would be more convenient. Knox blew up; *to speak the matter plainly, wise men do wonder what my Lord Duke's friends do mean.*

The explosion was effective; seven English ships were sent to Pittenweem; on the 23rd, Stewart and Ruthven, with Pitarrow, Balnaves and Lethington, just back from London, sailed thence for Berwick, while Maxwell made his way thither overland. Four days later they signed a treaty alliance with England in the name of "James Duke of Chatelheraut, second person of the realm of Scotland and apparent heir to the Crown, the Council, Nobility and principal Estates of the same." There was no word of religion in it; it was an alliance, not against the lawful sovereigns of Scotland, but against the Frenchmen who "intend to conquer the realm of Scotland and unite the same unto the Crown of France perpetually." For that purpose Elizabeth agreed to "accept the realm of Scotland unto her Majesty's protection and maintenance during the time that the marriage shall continue betwixt the Queen of Scots and the French King, and one year after."

From that moment the wheels of politics and war rolled forwards, needing no help from Knox. Early in March the French raided Glasgow; on the 15th, in full retreat to Linlithgow, "they spoiled all the country where their passage lay"; two days later they were driving into Leith all the cattle within reach. Between March 30th and April 2nd the English army, 5,000 foot and 1,800 horse, advanced from Berwick and met Chatelheraut and the Lords of the Congregation at Preston. On April 1st the Regent, sick to death, begged asylum from Erskine and entered Edinburgh Castle; in Leith, besides the French troops, only Seton and Bothwell, with the Archbishop of Glasgow, remained faithful to her failing fortunes.

Leith was invested, but the besiegers had no easy task. On Easter Monday, April 15th, Bothwell successfully raided the English trenches; on May 7th the first English assault was beaten back with heavy loss. By then Huntly had joined the Congregation; a new Band, with his signature, was concluded on April 27th. But this aid was worth little as against the ever present danger of French reinforcements. Francis and Mary might have won even now if they had been prepared really to stake their crown upon success. Bothwell was despatched to Europe to seek aid from Denmark and Germany. Knox, back in the pulpit of St. Giles since about April 23rd, watched the hazard and was uncertain of the end,

But this spring there had been panic in France. Henry II dead, the Guises had continued his religious policy. In December du Bourg had been executed; already, three months earlier, Calvin was finding it difficult to hold back the Huguenots from armed resistance. What Calvin discouraged, Throckmorton did his best to prick on. In March, while d'Oysel's troops were falling back on Leith, came the so-called Tumult of Amboise, an abortive attempt to arrest the Guises, which the Guises punished with all the savagery of fright. In April and May, Dauphiné and Provence were in almost open revolt. Nor was trouble at home the only check to a French reconquest of Scotland. Spain had now intervened to restrain French imperialism; Philip II was playing the balance of power game with Elizabeth.

The end of French policy in Scotland came a month later. On June 10th the Regent died. For a month she had sought peace; the Bishop of Valence had arrived as commissioner from her daughter and son-in-law, but his negotiations had broken down. Her death changed everything; on the 17th a truce was arranged; on July 6th, Cecil, arriving from London, concluded peace. Both French and English were to evacuate Scotland; a Convention of the Estates would meet in August and would pass an act of oblivion for all things done since March 6th 1558; deputies would be sent to the King and Queen in France to submit for their approval the transactions of this Convention. The government of Scotland was placed in the hands of a Council of Twenty-four, seventeen to be chosen by the Estates and seven by the King and Queen. There was no word of religion, save that all such questions were remitted for consultation between their Majesties and the representatives of the lords and nobility. On the other hand, the old Church was given protection against spoliation. Complaints by "bishops, abbots or other churchmen" of injury to person or property could be heard by the Estates, and in the meantime they should enjoy full possession of their goods. Elizabeth, for her part, secured a renunciation by Francis and Mary of the right to use the title or arms of England.

The Treaty was proclaimed on the 8th; Parliament met on the 10th and was adjourned for three weeks; on the 19th, Knox held a thanksgiving service in St. Giles. His prayer ended with a pledge to keep the promise of *mutual faith* with *our confederates of England: confound Thou the counsels of them that go about to break that most godly league contracted in Thy name and retain Thou us so firmly together by the power of Thy Holy Spirit that Satan have never power to set us again at variance nor discord.*

Chapter XXI

RECONSTRUCTION
1560–1561

I

THE TUMULT died. Four thousand French troops set sail, said the Bishop of Valence in rueful self-justification, from "a realm that could never have been reconquered but by the ruin and desolation of the realm of France." The English marched back to Berwick. The Lords of the Congregation and the preachers were left to marvel over their own success. Six years later, Knox was still marvelling. *For what was our force? What was our number? Yea, what wisdom or worldly policy was in us, to have brought to a good end so great an enterprise?*

What indeed? The Lords had muddled through to victory, like other men before and since. Now, like all men before and since, they were to find how easy it is to win a war and lose a peace. With the possible exception of Stewart, there was not a statesman among them. Morton, as time would show, had administrative genius of the rougher sort, but no instinct for policy. Lethington was talker and wit, unstable as water, without scruple and without purpose, a diplomatist of the negative school whose brilliant combinations could block an opponent's moves, but could never win a game, because he had no game to win. The Treaty of Berwick was the one positive achievement of his life. A few of the rest, Glencairn perhaps and some of the lairds, had honesty of purpose; but most of them were of the old mercenary breed. They and their fathers for a hundred years had been "the inventors, nourishers and simoniacal merchants" of ecclesiastical corruption; when they could no longer be pensioners of the Church, they would take care to be its legatees.

This lost peace was to be the nightmare of Knox's declining years.

It became his obsession, souring his nature, roughening his tongue and warping his judgment. He had known the politicians of old, in England; yet in Scotland he had put his trust in politics as the instrument of *a godly reformation*, and he paid the price. We who have lost a peace ourselves know just what that price is; disillusionment does not make a pretty picture, but to us it is an uncomfortably familiar one. In this July of 1559, however, the peace was not yet lost. It had already been fatally compromised, but it might still be saved. The patch of glory was not quite over. For a few more months Knox was to know the exaltations and exasperations of leadership. Poor politician as he was, he saw clearly that there was a political problem to be solved and, almost alone, he tried honestly to solve it. Law had to be changed, government remodelled, a social system reconstructed.

It is not only Knox's contemporaries who have ignored this. More than one historian, if one may venture the criticism, has shared their weakness, writing as if the Scottish scene in these crucial years had been a mere romantic riot of personalities. To write thus is to miss even romance. Thus written, the tragedy of Mary Queen of Scots itself becomes meaningless, for it is a tragedy without a plot. The plot was nothing less than a country's need for settled government, and the inability of its leaders to satisfy that need.

2

The Treaty of Edinburgh had left Scotland in an extraordinary position. The rising had been partly a revolt against absentee French government, partly a religious revolution. Yet the Treaty confirmed the sovereignty of the King and Queen of France and the property rights of the Scottish Church. Scotsmen, it is true, were under the protection of the Queen of England, but "only for preservation of the same in their old freedoms and liberties and from conquest." In the sixteenth century the first essential condition of order was a religious settlement, yet now all questions of religion in Scotland must be settled with the sovereigns at Paris. At this moment those same sovereigns were receiving from their ambassador at Rome, "sent to offer obedience" to the new Pope Pius IV on his accession, the Pope's gift to Mary of the Golden Rose and an exhortation that, "in the affair of Scotland," they would "support the decrees and ordinance of the Church and not suffer such a realm to go to perdition."

The position was the more extraordinary because, two months before, the Lords of the Congregation had taken steps towards a complete reorganization of Scottish religion. On April 29th, two days after the signature of their new Band, some of them had referred the question of future Church government to a committee of ministers: Knox and Willock, with Spottiswoode, the Vicar of Calder, Winram, the converted Sub-Prior of St. Andrews, and Row, for eight years the agent of the old Scottish Church in Rome. The result was the *Book of Discipline*, dated May 20th, but probably not put into final form until some months later. It was a comprehensive scheme for a new Church and for a complete system of universal education. The Church was to be a loose federation of self-governing congregations, electing their own elders and deacons, and choosing their own presiding ministers, subject to approval by *learned ministers appointed for their examination.* Federal unity was to be preserved by ten Superintendents, itinerant ministers with districts roughly corresponding to the existing dioceses and administrative headquarters in some central town. The Kirk Sessions were to be responsible for parish schools and for the relief of the poor; for these purposes and for the sustentation of the minister *at the discretion of the congregation,* each was to be endowed with the Church tithes on the parish lands and with all property in the locality *pertaining to priests, chantries, colleges, chaplainries, to friars of all Orders* and to nunneries. Tithes were to be reduced to so *reasonable* a level that *the brethren may feel some benefit of Christ Jesus now preached to them;* on the other hand the manses and glebes were to be restored to the ministers. The revenues of bishoprics, deaneries, archdeaconries and cathedral churches were to be allocated mainly to the universities, after meeting any necessary charges *at the discretion of the Prince and Council of the Realm* for the sustentation of the Superintendents.

Here was reconstruction with a vengeance, involving legislation wholly inconsistent with the Treaty. For the Church thus contemplated did not yet exist; the preachers, meeting in July, could appoint only five Superintendents (for Lothian, Fife, Angus and Mearns, Glasgow, and Argyll) and eight ministers (for Edinburgh, Leith, Dunfermline, St. Andrews, Perth, Aberdeen, Dundee and Jedburgh). If the scheme were to be carried out, ecclesiastical revenues must be appropriated by the Crown and allocated as the Church grew. There could clearly be no question of Parliament taking any such action this August, in face of the Treaty. But delay meant opportunity for every kind of encroachment by victorious lords on ecclesiastical property.

3

Was there any alternative? There was one, apparently advocated by the Primate who sent a message recommending it to Knox himself. Doctrinally, he saw that the battle was lost; Scotland must abolish the Mass with all it implied. But let the reformers, while changing the faith of the Church, keep its "policy" unaltered. Let them retain its hierarchy, its institutions recognized by law, and therefore its property rights. Such advice must be repugnant to Knox, to his honesty no less than to his fanaticism; but it had great attractions for a large number of Scottish Protestants. Their ultimate aim was union with England; the marriage between Elizabeth and Arran was, in fact, the official policy of the Congregation and Parliament. There could be no stronger basis for such a union than a union between the English and Scottish Churches; let the new Scottish Church, therefore, be evolved out of the old as the new Anglican Church had been evolved out of the Roman Church in England. Randolph, now English ambassador at Edinburgh, was urging this policy; his business was to get the Berwick "contract" with England confirmed by Parliament and to discourage any such divergence of Scottish from English Protestantism as might weaken that contract.

These were specious arguments, and Knox has often been blamed for rejecting them. But in fact the policy was absurd, for one simple reason. If the new Scottish Church had not yet been born, the old was almost dead. Of the thirteen Scottish dioceses, four were vacant and a fifth, Caithness, had only a lay postulant for its bishop: Lord Robert Stewart, Commendator of Holyrood, bastard of James V, who had joined his half-brother James the October before when the Congregation entered Edinburgh. A sixth was vacant for all practical purposes, for Beaton of Glasgow, the best of the episcopate, had left for Paris with the French troops, never to return. Of the remaining seven bishops, two had, indeed, turned Protestant: Hamilton of Argyll and Adam Bothwell, recently appointed to Orkney. A third Hepburn of Moray, might turn too. The four others were Hamilton of St. Andrews, whom we know; Chisholm of Dunblane, a gouty cripple of sixty-seven with a family for whom he had provided not too badly; Gordon of Aberdeen, Huntly's uncle, a still more scandalous figure; and finally, the only respectable figure of the four, Crichton of Dunkeld. Out of such materials, how could the old Church be perpetuated as the vehicle of a reformed faith and reformed manners? There were enough Protestant bishops to ordain new colleagues, but there was no authority who could appoint them.

Was the Congregation to petition the Pope to fill the sees, and then try to convert his nominees? That was precisely what Rome feared. Pius IV had become Pope the previous Christmas. His predecessor, Caraffa, had continued to muddle Scottish affairs to the end, refusing legatine powers to the Bishop of Amiens on suspicion of heresy, and giving the bishopric of Orkney to the heretic Bothwell. Pius had reversed the first mistake on January 25th, issuing a belated brief to the legate, and he was desperately afraid of repeating the second. That same January, the Regent's agent at Rome had been begging him to fill the vacant sees and the vacant abbacies of Cambuskenneth, Glenluce and Beauly, but the Cardinal of Lorraine had advised against his sister's request. No nomination should be made unless the candidate was "declared to be free from all suspicion of heresy by express letters" from the Regent herself. When Pius summoned the Scottish bishops to the re-convened Council of Trent in March 1561, there were still eight to whom no letter could be addressed.

No, in this direction the deadlock was complete. Clearly, the perpetuation of the old Church involved a fundamental change in the law: the establishment of the royal supremacy and the royal power of ecclesiastical patronage, as in England. But the royal supremacy in Scotland would be in the hands of Catholic sovereigns, who would refuse to accept or exercise it. Even if Parliament were to pass such an Act, even if Knox could accommodate himself to a doctrine so repugnant as the supremacy of secular authority over the Church of Christ, the Act would never receive the royal assent in Paris. Parliament, for diplomatic reasons, might recognize Huntly's brother Alexander as bishop of Galloway, but the recognition had no force of law.

The only remaining course appeared to be to leave the religious question entirely open. That would suit the diplomatists well enough, but it was intolerable to anyone who cared for coherent government. Knox set himself to force action. It must be revolutionary action; the law must be changed without the concurrence of the sovereigns; the Treaty must be violated. But all this was better than anarchy and haphazard spoliation. Revolutions cannot stop half-way; the Christian who has used his Master's name to justify violence can hardly boggle over a mere breach of constitutional order or of pledged word. *Our religion from God has full power and needeth not the suffrage of man.*

4

So, as Parliament met, Knox launched into a course of sermons on the prophet Haggai, summoning all men to help in the rebuilding of God's Temple. *In application whereof* he was not only *vehement* but *special*, with no lack of personal references to the nobility who were *unjust possessors of the patrimony of the Church*. Lethington sneered, others were angry, but the sermons fulfilled their purpose of gathering a party.

That party gathered—a group of *nobles, gentlemen, burgesses and others*—he fired in his programme of immediate action. Three things must be done. First, *such doctrine and idolatry as by God's word is condemned* must *be abolished by Act of this present Parliament*. Secondly, Parliament must *find remedy against* the abuse of the sacraments and the decay of *the true discipline of the ancient Church*. Thirdly, the

Pope's authority over *the patrimony of the Church* must be abolished. In support of these three points the petitioners claimed that *in all the clergy there is not one lawful minister,* that all must be *decreed unworthy of honour, authority, charge or cure within the Church of God and so from henceforth never to joy vote in Parliament.*

Historians have been shocked at the language of this manifesto, but have perhaps hardly done justice to its statesmanship. The first and third points were negative, but the second raised the whole positive issue of the *Book of Discipline.* It was characteristic of Parliament that it accepted the negatives and ignored the positive. Acts were passed repealing in general terms all statutes in favour of the old Church, forbidding the celebration of the sacraments "conform to the Pope's Church," and abolishing the jurisdiction of the Pope. Penalty for unlawful celebration of the sacraments was confiscation for the first offence, banishment for the second, death for the third, for recourse to Rome, "proscription, banishment and never to brook honour, office nor dignity within this realm." Such penalties were common form in the Scottish legislation of the day; death, for instance, was the punishment prescribed by an Act of 1551 for ferrymen on the Forth overcharging their passengers. They were the lawyers' version of popular hyperbole, threats half meant and never executed. With such repeals, prohibitions and threats, Parliament was content; constructive action was not even discussed.

Parliament did, however, take one positive step, though it was hardly a legislative act. The Lords requested Knox and his fellow-petitioners *to draw in plain and several heads the sum of that doctrine which they would maintain and would desire that present Parliament to establish.* Four days later the *Confession of Faith* was presented to them. Randolph, intent on keeping all doors open, advised against its discussion, but was amazed at the unanimity with which it was received. The Primate, with his colleagues of Dunkeld and Dunblane were silent, or almost so, and abstained from voting; of the laymen, only one earl, Athol, and two lords, Somerville and Borthwick, voted nay (but one account adds the Earls of Cassilis and Caithness). The *Confession* was passed on August 17th. Few, if any, can have foreseen its enormous effect upon the future of Scotland; at its passing it was rather an apology than an Act of Parliament—*issued partly for satisfaction of our brethren whose hearts have been and, yet are, wounded* by accusations of heresy, *partly for stopping of the mouths of impudent blasphemers.*

With that, and with the passing of the Act of Oblivion prescribed in the Treaty, Parliament adjourned. It had no illusions about its own work, or even about its constitutional status. It had met as provided in the Treaty, but it had met without royal authority. It had gone through the motions necessary to quiet the preachers and the faithful, but it did not take those motions seriously. It sent no imposing delegation to France, as contemplated in the Treaty; it merely appointed old Sandiland's son, known by the title of Lord St. John, to obtain from Francis and Mary their ratification of the Treaty, and their nominations to the Council of Twenty-four. It seems doubtful whether St. John was even instructed, or thought it worth while, to ask ratification of the anti-Church Acts. In any case, he started back empty handed in November from the Court at Orleans, with an intimation that Francis and Mary would "send two worthy and distinguished persons to convoke a lawful Parliament."

Meanwhile, the Lords devoted themselves to their real policy: the marriage of Arran and Elizabeth. They deputed very different representatives to London: Morton, Glencairn and Lethington. They wrote to Francis coolly recommending the project, in a letter signed, among others, by the Primate and the Bishop of Dunblane. In other words, they would have neither revolution nor loyalty; their policy was to balance between the two, leaving Scotland without a government or a settled system of law, until diplomacy could turn the English alliance into a constitutional union.

This dickering with England was to cripple Scottish government for years to come. Only as clever a policy-monger as Lethington could have miscalculated so consistently. His diplomacy was always based on the lucky turn of some card. At this moment it was based on the assumption that Francis would live and Mary would die. Her ill health, her fainting fits, were the talk of the French Court. The crown would pass to Chatelheraut, whose son would be King of England. But politicians who trust to luck cannot complain if luck is against them. At this moment Elizabeth was not thinking of Arran, but of Lord Robert Dudley. Tongues were busy with her infatuation for this married nobleman. Hardly had Parliament adjourned when scandal exploded in her Court. On September 8th, Lord Robert's wife was found dead at Cumnor; yet Elizabeth seemed to continue her favours; Cecil was on the brink of resignation. In face of such a situation few embassies have set out on a more futile errand than Lethington and his two earls, when they left Edinburgh on October 12th "to move Queen Elizabeth of England to take the Earl of Arran to her husband." In fact they accomplished nothing; they were back by the end of the year with fair words, but with a clear indication that Arran's suit had no chance.

5

Knox was deep in Arran's counsels; he no doubt encouraged the marriage project. But he had no intention of letting domestic reconstruction wait on a foreign alliance. Time, which was nothing to Lethington, was for him the essence of the contract. Religion was not only a chaos in Scotland, it was at bay in Europe. He was in close correspondence with the Huguenots, *both with the Churches and some of the Court of France*. Europe was full of rumours that the Peace of Câteau Cambrésis had included a secret league of Catholic princes against Protestantism. There was no such league, but the domestic policy of the princes seemed to confirm the report. The first of the two great *autos-da-fé* which crushed Protestantism in Spain had taken place at Valladolid within seven weeks of the Peace—on that Trinity Sunday, 1559, when Knox at Perth was drafting the manifestoes of the Congregation. The second had followed at Seville on October 8th. We have seen how events were moving in France, and now, this August of 1560, they were coming to a head.

While Parliament had been sitting in Edinburgh, an Assembly of Notables had met at Fontainebleau. Protests had been made by Coligny against the Edict of Romorantin, the somewhat milder decree which had been substituted in May for the Edict of Compiègne. On September 5th there was a Huguenot rising at Lyons; de Bèze had come from Geneva to Nérac to urge Antoine of Navarre to action. Then, on October 30th, the Guises struck; Antoine's brother Condé was arrested. When St. John left Orleans in November, the nobility were assembling in the city; *there was not a hangman in all France which was not there.* On November 26th, Condé was condemned for treason; his execution fixed for December 10th.

Certain knowledge of all these things came to our ears whereat many were effrayed. The Huguenots once crushed, men said, the Guises would send another expedition to Scotland; preparations for it were already in full swing. In Scotland itself, the Catholic earls in the north met to consult at Perth—Huntly and Eglinton, with the waverer Sutherland. Home had visited them there and, returning, called his Border friends to meet him in Dunbar on December 10th. *The Papists were proud for they looked for a new army from France at the next spring.* Under these shadows, Knox laboured to make good the ground already gained in Scotland. The *Book of Discipline* was elaborated into its final form. Knox put all his eloquence into the appeal to the nobility, which prefaced the sixth section of the *Book: Of the Rents and Patrimony of the Church.* Tithes and church dues must be lightened; finance must be provided for the ministers, for parish poor relief and for a national system of education, *We must crave your Honours, in the name of the Eternal God and of his Son Jesus Christ, that ye have respect to your poor brethren the labourers and manurers of the ground. With the grief of our hearts we hear that some gentlemen are now as cruel over their tenants as ever were the Papists, requiring them of whatsoever before they paid to the Church, so that the Papistical tyranny shall only be changed into the tyranny of the lord or of the laird. The gentlemen, barons, earls, lords and others must be content to live on their just rents and suffer the Church to be restored to her liberty, that, in her restitution, the poor, who heretofore by the cruel Papists have been spoiled and oppressed, may now receive some comfort and relaxation.*

Pending this comprehensive redistribution of the national wealth, the *Book* insisted on the most effective form of disendowment immediately available. All ecclesiastical corporations must be dissolved; *idolatry with all monuments and places of the same, as abbeys, monasteries* (and so on down a long list of institutions) *must be utterly suppressed.* And as there was at the moment no machinery of law to effect the suppression, the corporations must be dissolved by the dismantlement of their homes. From the beginning, the gutting of religious houses was much more than an act of fanaticism; it was sober policy.

Controversy raged over the *Book*, but meanwhile the organization of the Church went on. The Forms of Worship in the Church of Geneva were expanded and prepared for adoption by the congregations; forms for the election of superintendents, elders and deacons were drawn up; above all, arrangements were made for the summoning of a first General Assembly of the new Church. It met at Edinburgh on December 20th: a little body of forty-one, only six ministers. Thirty-five new ministers were appointed and a few readers. Then the faithful turned their attention to their policy of violent disendowment. The churches of Edinburgh and Leith, might at least be provided for out of an old pious foundation of James II, which uselessly supported a dean, nine prebendaries and two singing boys. The Assembly resolved that "the parishioners of Restalrig repair to Leith church and the church of Restalrig be razed and utterly destroyed, being a monument of idolatry."

On the eve of this Assembly, Knox's wife died. *He was in no small heaviness*, that is all we know of his bereavement. And just at this moment of private loss and public conference, a letter arrived from a correspondent in France which sent him hurrying out to find Chatelheraut and James Stewart at the former's house in the Kirk of Field. The King of France *was mortally sick and could not well escape death*. While the three were talking, confirmation came from Berwick: Francis was dead. He had died in the night of December 5th–6th, just in time to save Condé's life. Chatelheraut acted at once; a convention of the Estates was summoned for January 15th.

6

The first effect of the news was a feeling of relief. The fear of invasion passed; traditional loyalties revived; Scotland might have her own queen back again. But many had cause to fear Mary's return; Chatelheraut felt sure she could mean no good to him or his; Lethington, who had betrayed the mother, could hope little from the daughter. Her return to Scotland was, indeed, urgently desirable; already she was being sought by all and sundry in the marriage market of Europe, by Denmark, Sweden, Austria, Spain.

Till she was safely in Scotland, Scotsmen would be in continual doubt to what new foreign master they might be subjected. But at least it would be well to present her with a *fait accompli* in matters of religion. For the moment Knox's policy looked like winning. Even Lethington was for action; he disliked "vehemence," but "marry, as things are turned out now, there is need for some vehemence."

So the Lords examined the *Book of Discipline* and, though no final action was taken upon it by the Convention, an impressive array of earls and gentlemen signed acceptance of it on January 27th, subject to a few reservations. The signatories included Chatelheraut and Arran; the Earls of Argyll, Glencairn and Rothes; James Stewart; the Ayrshire group of lords and lairds; the provost of Dundee; St. John for Lothian; Maxwell, Crichton, Lochinvar and Drumlanrig for the West Marches; and a Scott and a Ker for Selkirkshire. Three more earls, though not signing, seem to have promised support: Marischall, Menteith and Morton, with the Lindsays, father and son.

Such approval was a great point gained, but practical action could not be expected on any national scale in the next six doubtful and crowded months. All eyes were fixed on Paris. Thither James Stewart was despatched by the Estates to invite Mary home; the Catholics were agog to get their messenger there before him, John Lesley, chief administrator of the diocese of Aberdeen, a Gordon stronghold; Arran wrote, and excited the wildest suspicions by doing so; Morton sent a kinsman, praying for a grant of Angus lands. From Paris arrived Scottish commissioners, of no great weight but as good as Mary could collect, to summon a Parliament; they were closely followed by a French envoy, Noailles, lately retired from the London embassy, to treat for a renewal of the old alliance; Elizabeth wrote insisting that Mary should be advised to ratify the Treaty of Edinburgh before her return. Diplomacy held the field once more; again reconstruction must wait.

But in one field Knox could make good his ground: in Edinburgh itself. Even Lethington approved his warnings from the pulpit of St. Giles that Francis's death had created as many dangers as it had averted. And as the months passed the "provost, baillies and council" of the City bestirred themselves to some purpose.

In one direction, unfortunately, they bestirred themselves after the fashion of new brooms with deplorable results. It was not only that they passed a stringent Sunday Trading Act, and closed all taverns during sermon time. That was a sober enough enforcement of the principle enunciated in the *Book of Discipline* that *the Sunday must straitly be kept*. It would have been well if their action had stopped there.

On the previous June 10th they had issued a proclamation against "idolaters, whore-masters and harlots daily resorting within this burgh." In November, acting on these threats and on a pre-Reformation Act of 1551 against adulterers, they had ordered the deacon of the fleshers' gild "to be carted through the town and banished from the town for manifest adultery." There had been open conflict with the craft gilds, a riot of "certain young fellows, craftsmen's servants"; Knox had had to intercede and make peace. Now on March 24th another proclamation was issued against "priests, monks, friars and others of that ungodly sort and that opinion" who, taking advantage of a relaxation of previous prohibitions, were "sowing their ungodly opinions and detestable works" among the "simple people." On April 23rd, acting again on an old law of 1555, the city fathers prohibited a "Robin Hood" procession organized by the craft prentices for Sunday, May 11th. The prohibition was disregarded; a number of the prentices were arrested; this time Knox refused to intervene in favour of the offenders. On June 21st a riot broke out; the burgh council was besieged in the Tolbooth. In the interval they had imprisoned an advocate "for taking and receiving of the diabolical idol called the priests' sacrament at Easter last" and had expelled a priest. For two months, almost up to the moment of Mary's arrival in her capital, the city was in almost open insurrection. On July 11th the prentices were "at the horn"; the provost and baillies were mobilizing "twenty-four hagbutters" to help in their apprehension; a fortnight later they were begging Arran to lend them "his guard of men at arms" to keep order.

But the city fathers were engaged in more constructive work than offending gild traditions and censoring metropolitan morals. They had to lodge and pay their minister; in the twelve months ending May 1561 they had disbursed between £450 and £500 for these purposes; Knox's salary had been fixed at £300 a year, payable every two months. They had to repair and refit St. Giles; they were also disbursing "great sums of money for their school" and were much concerned over the problem of poor relief. They were hard put to it to meet these liabilities. They had abolished all the old "pensions or duties" to churchmen; they were collecting the "vestments and kirk gear" and selling them, "the money thereof to be applied to the works of the kirk"; they were diverting the wine duty of a quart in every tun from the old "fraternity of St. Anthony" to the "misterful and faillit brethren" of the city. On March 24th they ordained a compulsory levy for poor relief to be administered by the elders and deacons of the Church; on April 2nd they appointed city collectors for the purpose. Three weeks later they had a comprehensive scheme before them for (among other things) the conversion of the wine duty into a tax of 12d. on the tun, for the assumption by the city of responsibility for probate of wills, for a succession duty of 4d. in the pound to be applied to poor relief, and for the diversion of all ecclesiastical rents and annuals to public purposes, "such as for sustaining of the true ministers of God's word, founding and building of hospitals for the poor and colleges for learning and upbringing of the youth, and such other godly works."

It is not fanciful to connect this access of reforming zeal, wise and unwise, with the celebration of Knox's first Sacrament at St. Giles on March 2nd. Like so many such celebrations to come, it was a demonstration as well as an act of worship. Arran came to the city for it and, in the suspense of the times, his appearance was a political gesture. Two meetings had been fixed for the end of May, a Convention of the Estates and the second General Assembly of the Church. The months between were a time for the mobilization of opposing factions.

7

Indeed, in these months civil war seemed ready to break out again. James Stewart was away in London and Paris; Bothwell, who had been at the French Court since the Regent's death had interrupted his recruiting mission in Denmark and Germany, had returned to Scotland in February. The Catholic earls had suggested to Mary, through Lesley, that she should land in the north with French troops, and march to Edinburgh, with the Gordons behind her. Their men were beginning to swagger in the Edinburgh streets. Later, in June, an ominous deputation was to leave Scotland to bring Mary home: Bothwell himself, with the still ambiguous Bishop of Orkney and the Catholic Eglinton.

It was amid these doubts that, on May 28th, the General Assembly, meeting at the Tolbooth, tried to translate the municipal experiments of Edinburgh into a national scheme of reform. They petitioned the Lords of the Council once more to suppress idolatry and abuse of the sacraments; they demanded also that the support of the ministry should be made a first charge on tithe, that all actions at law for recovery should be stayed until this charge was met, and that ministers should be given legal title, against existing owners, to all alienated manses and glebes. The petition was presented by the Master of Lindsay and three lairds from Kirkcudbrightshire, Roxburghshire and East Lothian.

Again Knox's policy looked like winning. Within a week after the presentation of the petition, James Stewart returned. He had been well received by Mary and had established his influence with her, but it was evident from her conversations with him, with Throckmorton and with Elizabeth's special envoy to Paris, the Earl of Bedford, that she would neither change her faith nor ratify the Treaty with England. In the light of that knowledge, and of the attitude of the Catholic party, the arguments for a *fait accompli* gained new weight. The Assembly was assured that favourable action had been ordered on every point of the petition. In fact, however, any constructive measures which may have been taken (the records are lost) apparently remained a dead letter. Again, the only effective action was destruction. James Stewart *was appointed to the north, where he made such reformation as nothing contented the Earl of Huntly*; Arran Glencairn and Argyll went to purge the great abbeys of the west, Paisley, Failfurd, Kilwinning and Crossraguel.

With this peitition, Knox's patch of glory ended. His second Sacrament Sunday was held at St. Giles on June 8th. The next two months were full of rumour and diplomacy. Noailles was sent back empty-handed; Elizabeth was assured that, if Mary refused to ratify the Treaty, it would not be the fault of the Estates; Knox, hearing that Mary was meditating a confutation of the *First Blast*, was moved, on August 6th, to write to Elizabeth a new exculpatory letter. A fortnight later, on the 19th, a morning of thick mist, he heard cannon from Leith and hurrying crowds in the High Street. The Queen of Scots had come back to her kingdom.

VI. Scotland
The Barren Years

CHAPTER XXII

THE HOUSE IN TRUNK CLOSE
AUGUST 1561–AUGUST 1562

I

WE NOW approach the best-known story in all history, the six years of Mary's reign in Scotland. We cannot, and need not, tell that story again. Our story is of a man who during the first four years of the six, watched the Queen and her ministers from his "ludgeing" in Trunk Close, on the north side of the Edinburgh High Street. He had moved in there, thanks to the good offices of the city council, at the beginning of September 1560, after four months in various dwellings. There he had set up house, with his wife and children, and perhaps his mother-in-law, who had come to visit them earlier that year. There, three months later, Marjorie had died. In August 1561 he was probably alone, looking after the two little boys as best he could; a year later he was anxious for Mrs. Bowes's return, that she might be "a relief unto him in the burden of household and bringing up of his children."

It was a fair-sized house, with its own garden and space of open ground, some way down the face of the hill towards the North Loch. Above it the crowded tenements rose to the castle on the west; to the east lay the Netherbow Port and, beyond it, outside the walls, the Canongate suburb with its noblemen's mansions and the palace of Holyrood. Preacher and Queen were near neighbours, too near for this ageing little man, with his one fixed idea, and the tall girl of eighteen, *brought up in joyousitie*, in love with colour and movement, eager for friendship, who had set her heart on wearing two crowns, and to whom policy meant little but the winning of personal loyalties to that end.

It is as a little man that we may best think of him, as he sits in the "warm study of daillis above the hall," constructed for him by the

Dean of Gild at the beginning of his second winter in the house. Outside the pulpit, there was little of the prophet about him, either in appearance or in manner. We have no succession of portraits of him, as we have of Calvin, showing the premature shrinking of the compact figure, the stoop of the shoulders, the cramping of the sensitive fingers. But we have hints of growing frailty. Age, indeed, was probably kinder to him than to Calvin. A little taller, of heavier build and coarser featured, suffering and nervous strain could refine before they began to waste him. To use Randolph's phrase, he became "precise" in more than doctrine, neat in figure, careful in his dress—so careful that a Catholic lampoon could represent him later, in one breath, as "an old decrepit creature" and as something of a *petit maître*. The general effect of neatness was perhaps spoiled only by the beard. Exaggerated in posthumous portraits, it was long but not overthick—much fuller than Calvin's thin wisp, but still the sort that must be allowed to grow because it cannot be trimmed. There was, too, the same neatness in his manner; his inclination to the pompous gave him a formal courtesy of speech, however uncompromising his words might be. Only, there was still thunder in the jutting brow and grey-blue eyes; to the end, he remained blackavised, the hair and beard no more than touched with grey; the dark flush of the cheeks gave warning of high temper. "He ruleth the roost, and of him all men stand in fear," wrote Randolph, a week after Mary's arrival. Little, dapper, and, on occasion, formidable, with an almost legendary reputation; old men of that kind have not been so very rare, especially perhaps among Scotsmen.

2

For the first twelve months after Mary's arrival, Knox was little away from Edinburgh. His only recorded absence was in January 1562, when, after the third meeting of the General Assembly in December, he went to Dundee for Erskine of Dun's election as Superintendent of Angus and Mearns. Until April 1562, his only assistant at St. Giles was a "reader of the common prayers," John Cairns; he must bear all "the tedious and heavy burden" of preaching in St. Giles "thrice in the week and twice on Sundays." After sermon he would go straight to his desk, *occupied in directing of writings*. His correspondence was large. Though declining any higher office than that of parish minister, he regarded himself as the Church's political intelligence officer, charged by the General Assembly *to advertise the brethren from time to time of dangers appearing*. He always had plenty of such advertisements to give. Then there were his foreign letters, for he wrote occasionally to Geneva and was in constant touch with the Church in France. For some time, too, he kept up his correspondence with Mrs. Locke in London. There were other more official letters to England besides, but he does not seem to have written to Cecil between October 1561 and December 1562, preferring to confide his forebodings to Randolph.

Pulpit and desk were his weekly routine; the milestones of the year were the quarterly Sacrament Sundays and the meetings of the Assembly in December and in May or June. Each Assembly meeting was marked by the usual recurring protests against the Government's failure to repress idolatry and immorality or to provide for the needs of the new Church, but meanwhile the work of Church organization went steadily on. In the six years of Mary's reign, its strength grew to 269 ministers, 508 readers and 151 exhorters—little enough among 1,080 parishes, especially since twelve of the ministers' posts and fifty-three of the readers' were then vacant, but still a substantial achievement when compared with the original eight ministers of seven years before.

But in these months Knox's routine was often interrupted. He had many visitors from the Canongate. They were months of attempted reconciliation and abortive negotiation: reconciliation between James Stewart and Bothwell, between Bothwell and the Hamiltons, between Knox himself and the Queen; negotiation for some temporary *modus vivendi* whereby the Queen might "keep her Mass," the old churchmen and their lay parasites might keep most of their wealth, and the new Church might be provided with enough to keep its ministers. The centre of these conferences was sometimes the house in Trunk Close; sometimes the house of James Macgill, husband of Knox's old friend and, since his conversion to his wife's views, himself a friend; sometimes the "abbot's lodging" at Holyrood, when the Lords wished to confer more officially with the ministers.

To the house in Trunk Close came Mary's messenger, within a fortnight of her landing, summoning Knox to the palace. On her first Sunday at Holyrood, August 24th, Mass had been said in her chapel; a crowd had protested; James Stewart had kept the door against them. Next day Mary had issued a two-clause proclamation, commanding her subjects, on pain of death, that none should "make alteration or innovation of the state of religion, or attempt anything against the form" which she had "found publicly and universally standing" on her arrival; and that none should "molest or trouble" her servants or retinue. That ambiguous ordinance was, for all practical purposes, the only religious settlement that Scotland was to know for the next six years. Next Sunday, the 31st, Knox had protested vehemently from his pulpit; better that Mary had come, as Huntly had suggested, with French troops than with a French chaplain; *one Mass was more fearful than if ten thousand armed enemies were landed in any part of the realm.* Mary's summons followed that sermon; the interview took place on Tuesday, September 2nd. Of that interview we shall have more to say; the two did not meet again for fifteen months.

The same question of the Queen's Mass was debated again in early November, at Macgill's house. A solemn All Saints' Mass at Holyrood had roused the pulpits again; Knox and three colleagues met James Stewart, Morton, Marischall and Lethington. The Lords *urged that the Queen should have her religion free in her own chapel;* the ministers retorted *that her liberty should be their thraldom or it was long.* Lethington said he would write to Calvin, but did not do so; Knox had already written on October 24th, but we know nothing of Calvin's reply. The debate ended inconclusively, but the Queen's Mass went on.

A month later, in December, the abbot's lodging at Holyrood witnessed a more serious tussle. *The rulers of the Court* did not come to the General Assembly; this budding counter-parliament was growing dangerous. So representatives of the Assembly met them at the abbey. The debate was chiefly between Knox and Lethington. There was a preliminary argument: should the Assembly meet without the Queen's sanction? Knox met that suggestion with a flat defiance: *take from us the freedom of assemblies and take from us the evangel.* Then debate passed to the *Book of Discipline.* Lethington sneered at it as a dead letter; Ochiltree dared its signatories to go back on their promise; Knox called on God to require at their hands the injury done to *this poor commonwealth.* That debate did produce results. On December 22nd the Queen's Council approved an Act, appropriating one-fourth—or, if that were not sufficient, one-third— "of the fruits of the whole benefices ecclesiastical within this realm" to the Crown. This income was to be used "for entertaining and setting forward the common affairs of the country," and, at the discretion of the Queen and Council, as much of it was to be applied "unto the ministers and sustentation of the ministry, as may reasonably sustain the same." On that uncertain endowment the new Church was to subsist for many years to come.

Through all this, Knox seems to have retained his affection for the Queen's chief adviser, James Stewart. He might seem cold to old enthusiasms, but it was his way to keep his own counsel; in the end he had always proved staunch. So when James, newly created Earl of Mar, announced at the year's end his betrothal to Agnes Keith, Marischall's sister, Knox was no doubt glad to do a friend's office for a friend. He married the two in St. Giles on February 8th, paying tribute in his sermon to the bridegroom's labours for the Church of God, and warning him, in a tone between pawkiness and earnest, that *if hereafter ye shall be found fainter, it will be said that your wife hath changed your nature.*

3

A few days later the scene shifts to the house in Trunk Close. Thither came the Earl of Bothwell on his best behaviour, honestly seeking a way out of his feuds. Besides his two-year-old quarrel with James Stewart and Cockburn, which Mary had done her best to smooth over, there were old family hatreds between the Hepburns and the Hamiltons, and these some recent follies had fanned to a blaze. As if Edinburgh were not troubled enough by political dissensions, municipal and national, the gallants must needs use the city as their playground.

They were, as the Queen pleaded in excuse, a "young company." She had brought with her from France, besides Bothwell, her three youngest Guise uncles and the son of the Constable Montmorency; she had found at Holyrood her two half-brothers, Robert and John. Of the seven, only one was over thirty. No worse entourage could have been found to inaugurate a reign. Edinburgh had heard shocking stories of French court morals, and the citizens found their prejudice confirmed. On October 2nd they thought fit to proclaim once more the ejection from the city of "monks, friars, priests, nuns, adulterers, fornicators and all such filthy persons." The Queen was furious at the insult and forced the city to choose a new provost and baillies. Then Arran came to town, the youngest of them all, talking wildly in the first stages of dementia. All the Hamiltons came too, Duke and Primate, with Abbot Gavin and a troop of horse. In mid-November, when James Stewart and Bothwell were on the Border, hanging thieves, there was a palace scare; Arran would kidnap the Queen; the Lords Robert and John made a great business of nightly guard mounting. When Bothwell came back, the three, with d'Elbeuf, the youngest of the Guises (the rest had gone home), set about disturbing Arran's amours in the city. There was uproar, breaking down of doors and public scandal. The Church Assembly, just met, protested against this "heinous and horrible impiety." On Christmas Eve Hamiltons and Court gallants were out in force, armed for a pitched battle; the combatants were separated only just in time by James Stewart and Huntly, It was characteristic that Lords Robert and John, who enjoyed the ecclesiastical revenues of Holyrood and Coldingham Abbeys, were at this moment engaged in getting married: Robert to Cassilis's sister, John to Bothwell's.

Bothwell certainly had enough on his hands. Knox met him courteously, and bestirred himself with Arran. On Tuesday, March 24th, the reconciliation took place at the Hamilton house in the Kirk of Field, outside the south wall of the city. But on Friday, after sermon, the house in Trunk Close had another visitor. Arran burst in, distraught and weeping; Bothwell had trapped him into a plot to kidnap the Queen, kill James Stewart and Lethington, "and so shall he and I rule all." There followed the whole miserable business of Arran's madness. Knox was deeply ashamed: *God hath further humbled me than ever I have been in my life, in my business that God put in my hands.* Edinburgh had laughed at the reconciliation itself:

when the two chief roysterers were agreed, it would be Knox that would be carted out of the town. And now, against Knox's plain advice, James Stewart had thought fit to take Arran's ravings seriously; the Hamiltons were disgraced, Arran shut up, Bothwell imprisoned and exiled. What must the world think of the man who had played the peacemaker between such suspects?

Struggling to find his feet in this morass of feuds and makeshifts, Knox caught his pen once more, to reformulate his programme of reconstruction. The General Assembly met for its fourth session on June 29th and drew up a Supplication to the Queen and Council, *having in mind that fearful sentence pronounced by the Eternal God against the watchmen that see the sword of God's punishment approach, and do not in plain words forwarn the people.* They regretted that the Queen had not been willing even to hear the reformed doctrines, and urged that she should delay no longer in enforcing her own proclamation against mass-mongers. They saw the *horrible vices* of immorality and blasphemy run riot *for lack of punishment.* They protested against the neglect of *the poor who be of three sorts: the poor labourers of the ground,* whose dues were being raised to pay the Thirds to the Crown; the *indigent,* who got no benefit from the tithes; the ministers whose *livings are so appointed that the most part shall live but a beggar's life,* and whose manses and glebes were still withheld. They complained of the rising insubordination of Catholics against the ministers and superintendents. They asked that church fabrics should be repaired; secular judges appointed to hear divorce suits; Papal nominees excluded from benefices (at least two of the vacant sees had been filled by Rome the summer before). They drew attention to remissions from the payment of Thirds granted to powerful lords, lay and ecclesiastical, and demanded that such should *be compelled to sustain the ministry within their bounds.*

And, as usual, nothing happened. Lethington protested against the language of the Supplication and insisted on watering it down. Knox held hot debate with him and Bellenden, the Justice Clerk, an ambiguous lawyer who, like other lawyers, got the name of a time-server because he followed his brief. Lethington's amended draft was presented to Mary who could make nothing of it and did nothing about it.

4

So ended for Knox these first twelve months of Mary's reign. Two years after a revolution, Scotland had made no single step towards settled government. Knox knew the reason well enough. London was the centre of Mary's policy, not Edinburgh; diplomacy, not administration, was the order of the day. When Lethington had argued for the Queen's mass in Macgill's house, again when he had criticized the drafting of the Supplication, he had just returned from diplomatic visits to Westminster. Elizabeth must be induced to recognize Mary as heir presumptive to the English crown; to that end the two queens must meet, and until that meeting Mary's hands must be kept free of commitments to her own subjects—free, for instance, to establish Anglicanism in Scotland, if need be.

This scheming only added to Knox's alarm. His policy, no less than the Queen's, was "amity and hearty love with England"; his eyes, no less than Lethington's were turned abroad. But his policy was not union with England on the basis of the Book of Common Prayer, and his eyes were on Paris rather than on London. Was God's Church in Scotland, established in so *great purity*, to be used as a bargaining counter with English bishops, that another Catholic Mary might rule both realms? Were the ministers of such a Church to copy Elizabeth in parading altar cross and candles, that the Catholic princes of Europe might think them no worse than Lutherans? And all this at a moment when their Calvinist brethren in France were in desperate danger? Those brethren, like Scotsmen, had been living under interim settlements since Francis's death; Catherine de Medici believed, no less than the daughter-in-law she so disliked, in government by personal tactics. And now her provisional edicts were wearing thin. The King of Navarre had gone over to the Guises—that was known in Scotland in February; a few weeks later came news of the massacre at Vassy on March 1st, when the Guise retainers had fired on a Huguenot congregation. What a warning to Scotland of the danger of interims; what a reminder to Lethington that popular movements meant more than palace conversations! For the firing at Vassy blew the English negotiations away in smoke; Elizabeth's ear was now for Condé and Coligny; the meeting of the queens was postponed. Must this postponement mean a prolongation of uncertainty in Scotland; must Scotsmen live without settled law for yet another year?

We have told the story of these months in terms of conferences, but we must imagine these negotiations punctuated by the minute-guns of Knox's sermons. Their burden was ever the same: the Mass and the *Book of Discipline*. The Mass was *the fountain of all impiety*; the device of the Thirds was a mockery—*two parts freely given to the devil and the third divided betwixt God and the devil*. There were variations: in February he denounced Elizabeth's cross and candles; in May (not before it would seem) he began to take notice of the dancing at the palace; in July, hearing that a Papal nuncio had been in the neighbourhood of Edinburgh since June 19th, "he raged wonderfully against the Pope as Antichrist" and (so wrote the nuncio) "against me whom he called an emissary of Satan." But, in all this time, there is no evidence that his sermons attacked the Queen personally; when they did so later, Mary was quick to summon the preacher to her presence, and she sent no summons in these months. He would "sometimes utter such sentences as cannot easily be digested by a weak stomach"; the Queen's Protestant friends "would wish he should deal with her more gently"; but their complaint was not that he insulted her, but rather that he was going the wrong way to convert "a young princess unpersuaded."

Nor was there, one thinks, in his pulpit voice during these months, any gusto of denunciation. About the time of Mary's arrival his thoughts were running on more intimate themes. In October he was completing a long course of sermons on the Gospel of St. John; and he would have been willing that this labour of love should be his last. *Oft have I craved the miseries of my days to end with the same, for now I seek rest.* It was with little of the old delight that he turned back to controversy.

Indeed, he has been strongly criticized for his reluctance to engage in controversy. Benoist, Mary's French chaplain, challenged him in November; from February onwards he was persistently challenged by Ninian Winzet, ex-schoolmaster of Linlithgow, able and honest forerunner of a new generation of Scottish Catholics.

But beyond some replies from the pulpit, Knox refused to be drawn. By political standards he was wise; an elder statesman does not advertise his young opponents by sharing his platform with them. Moreover, doctrinal debates, as he knew, had no effect but to confirm the disputants in their opinions; he had held one such debate with two diocesan dignitaries from Aberdeen in January 1560, with just that result. He preferred to leave the city magistrates to seize Winzet's tracts at the printers', which they did on July 31st. Winzet fled; Benoist had already left. Knox's behaviour was not heroic; but, again, the Christian who draws the sword for religion cannot be expected to baulk at repressing freedom of speech, And the law under which the magistrates acted was, after all, Mary's own interim proclamation of 25th August 1561. She did not want controversy; nor, for different reasons, did Knox.

In short, there is small foundation for the common belief that Knox hectored a lonely girl in her first days of homesickness among strangers. He was utterly opposed to Mary's policy, and he declared his opposition with all his old distrust of *lenitie and dulceness*; but his concern was not with persons but with principles, and he kept the battle to that honourable ground. If we are to judge him it must be by an estimate of his and Mary's rival policies. It may be well, at this point, to attempt such an estimate, for without it the rest of our story, now drawing to a close, will have little meaning.

Chapter XXIII

POLICIES AND TACTICS

I

THERE ARE three possible views of the issue between Knox and Mary. No doubt there are more than three: Mary can be depicted as a wanton, or as a murderess, or simply as a gay butterfly, thoughtless and innocent, crushed by the wheels of a workaday world. But we can dismiss such romantic fancies and consider only three serious interpretations, putting each in its extreme form, for sake of contrast.

One is that Mary was in an impossible position, a convinced Catholic, trying to rule a country where the Catholic Church was almost dead and a heretic Church almost triumphant. The heretic Church was a budding tyranny, inhuman where the old Church had been easy-going, but rigidly respectable where the old Church had been scandalously lax. Mary had to fight the new tyranny and she had to fight Knox as its blundering apostle; but she had not the materials for a counter-reformation, even if she had had the political ability to use them. Not for ten years at least could Rome be ready with missionaries of the new Catholic spirit; meanwhile she had to work with treacherous politicians like James Stewart and Lethington, and ruffians like Morton, Ruthven and Lindsay. She must marry, if only because, in her rough kingdom, marriage was an essential protection; yet the ruinous spoilt boy she married was almost the best of her seven suitors; of the other six, three (Arran, Eric of Sweden, and Carlos of Spain) were mental defectives, Charles IX of France was little better, Robert Dudley was a sister-queen's discarded favourite, only the Archduke of Austria was reasonably eligible. On this view Mary was half a Catholic martyr, half the heroine-victim of a Greek tragedy.

Another view is that Mary was a bigot, the agent of the Pope for the extirpation of heresy both in Scotland and England. To that end she played for the English crown; to that end she opposed, in Scotland, by every shift at her command, the reformation of a corrupt Church and the reconstruction of an intolerable social system. Her designs on England came to nothing; by her policy in Scotland she succeeded only in making way for a new social system even more intolerable than the old. Her reign inaugurated an era of aristocratic greed, a lay scramble for Church property, a tradition of economic selfishness which persisted for three hundred and fifty years. She could not arrest the victorious advance of Church reform but she did make the new Church poor, with all the vices as well as the virtues of poverty; she did confirm and perpetuate the depression of Scottish peasant agriculture.

The third view is that Mary was the only statesman in Scotland, playing a difficult game with high courage and considerable ability. She was no bigot, but a sort of High Church Somerset, using toleration and her claim to the English crown as means to religious compromise in a united Britain. She could not accept a Knoxian reformation, because Knox's church was a counter-government; but she was prepared to accept Anglicanism, with its royal supremacy, its Book of Common Prayer and its apostolic succession. To reach that position, however, she must break Knox and his co-fanatics, and to do that she must have Elizabeth's support. Unfortunately, Elizabeth's ministers, in collusion with her own, set themselves to prevent any meeting between the queens or the adoption of any common policy. Knox and Cecil together broke her in the end, and with her went Scotland's last chance, for two hundred years, of social freedom and religious moderation.

In order to judge Mary's policy, it is not really necessary to decide between these three views. All that is necessary is to reject the despairing plea that her position was impossible. In government there are no impossibilities; the most impregnable Jerichos have a way of falling flat before courage and singleness of purpose. Only, he who attacks such a citadel must learn the secret of political courage: that a given course of action is to be judged, not by its own inherent dangers, but by the dangers inherent in any alternative course. The commonest spectacle in history is the cautious politician, visited in the end by all the calamities which he had pleaded in defence of inaction and half-measures.

2

On any of the three assumptions we have advanced, Mary had to make a provisional religious settlement, and that settlement had to include the legalization of some form or forms of Church worship and some transfer of property from the old Church to the new. She professed to make such a settlement, but it was one that settled nothing, even temporarily.

She proceeded by royal proclamation and Act of Council, documents whose validity was open to at least as much doubt as the unratified acts passed by the Reformation Convention of 1560. And the content of these ordinances was as ambiguous as their form. One legalized the religious practices "universally existing" on 19th August 1561; but there were no practices which, by any stretch of imagination, could satisfy that definition. It exempted the Queen's household, without confining the exemption to private worship and without facing the old difficulty that the Queen's household might be anywhere, and, for a good part of the year, was certain to be in at least two places at once. The other ordinance taxed the old Church without endowing the new; it neither lightened the burden of tithe nor applied any part of tithe to poor relief or education. It offended the ecclesiastics, commendators and mortgagees of the old Church, and yet left them free to transfer the tax to their tenants. With its supplementary regulations, it put assessment and collection of the tax in the hands of a Protestant committee, but Mary and her Council reserved to themselves, not only sole control over the expenditure of the proceeds, but in practice also the right to grant exemptions from liability to pay the tax. Worst of all, it forced Queen and Kirk to live out of the same pocket, so that every masque and dance at Holyrood, every royal progress, every gift to a favourite, every sign of ostentation in the celebration of Mass in the chapels of Holyrood or Stirling, seemed a direct robbery of the poor. *It is a wonder*, said the Supplication of July 1562, that *the sun*

301

giveth light and heat to the earth, where God's name is so frequently called upon and no mercy shown to his creatures.

And Mary, whatever her virtues, was no economist. Her mother had ended by barely balancing the royal budget; she ran heavily into debt. That was the background of all the pulpit denunciation of court frivolity.

It would be futile to speculate on what Mary might have been able to accomplish by wiser methods, but at least one thing is clear: the key to any real settlement was a frank nationalization of Church property with compensation (as contemplated by the *Book of Discipline* itself) for lay assignees, and pensions for the dispossessed ecclesiastics (as originally opposed by Knox, but advocated by many of his colleagues and approved by Calvin). Mary would, no doubt, have had to allow many exemptions and bribe many nobles by grants of Church lands, but she did give exemptions from the Thirds and she did later, after her marriage, make numerous land grants to her supporters without Papal sanction. Knox and his friends would not have objected to the retention by the Crown of much Church property, so long as definite grants had been made to each congregation as it was organized—that had been, indeed, Kirkcaldy's account of their programme two years before. Mary could have diverted discontent from herself by placing an initial grant in the hands of a committee composed of signatories of the *Book of Discipline*, and leaving Glencairn (for instance) to fight out with the ministers his contention that six acres of glebe was too much "where manses are of great quantity."

It is no answer to this suggestion that it would have meant a breach between Mary and Rome. If she was aiming at an Anglican settlement, she had little to fear from such a breach. If, on the other hand, she was a faithful daughter of Rome, she had ways of appeasing the Vatican. Rome swallowed without protest her proclamation of August 25th, which, if it meant anything, at least threatened death (a heavier penalty, be it noted, than that provided for a first or second offence in the Convention Act of 1560) to any Catholic who, like Winzet, impugned the lawfulness of Knox's ordination. The Pope was always ready to listen to Mary's plea, advanced in her secret interview with his nuncio De Gouda on 24th July 1562, that she was labouring "to save a spark of the old faith and the germs of of future Catholicism." She could have as easily represented that to nationalize the Church's wealth was the only way to preserve some part of it for the Catholic Church of the future. And if, in addition, she had been able to represent nationalization as the price paid for some definite measure of legal toleration, her task would have been easier still.

Whether she could have concluded such a bargain must, of course, be doubtful. She would have had to fight Knox, but, as we shall see, she had to fight him in the end, and she beat him. If all she wanted was toleration, Knox's milder colleagues like Winram, who doubted whether she ought to be deprived of her Mass by force, might well have seen that restricted legal toleration would be less dangerous than the uncertainties of the proclamation of August 25th. Steadily, from 1563 onwards, her chapel became the open centre of a Catholic revival; in March 1565 it had as many worshippers at Holyrood "as sometimes come to the common churches to the sermon"; that Easter "greater triumph there was never in any time of most popery" than at the Queen's Mass in Stirling Castle; in the last Lent of her reign, February and March 1567, 12,600 people, it is said, communicated at Holyrood. This insidious spreading of reaction from a single centre of infection was precisely what the reformers feared, what the General Assembly repeatedly protested against; it would have been worth their while to pay a considerable price in order to confine it within legal limits.

Mary's policy can, in fact, be defended only on one ground: that her assurances to the Pope were genuine, that her aim was not toleration or Anglicanism, but a Catholic revival. On that assumption the ambiguities of the proclamation of August 25th may well have served her purpose better than any legal settlement. But she had to pay a price for that success which ruined her in the end. That price was lonely personal responsibility. It was to her, to her household, to her chaplains, that exemption from conformity had been allowed; it was she who had played a double game and won it; it was on her personally that all the fire of all the pulpits was concentrated.

This, indeed, was Mary's fundamental weakness. Like her grandson, Charles I, she could think of policy only in terms of personal rights and personal authority. And she could not conceal that attitude. With all her real shrewdness, she was on this point naïvely indiscreet. The first person singular was always in her mouth; her personal arrangements were announced to the world as if they must be above criticism. "My uncle, the Cardinal of Lorraine, hath the ordering of all my affairs,' she had told the English ambassador in February 1561—as if that were not exactly what all England and Scotland suspected and feared. "Ye think that I have no just authority," she insisted to Knox seven months later—as if that theoretical point were not the one, of all others, on which it was impolitic at that moment to press for an answer.

This first interview with Knox was, indeed, a blunder throughout. It has been said that she had the best of the argument, but that is a sort of victory that no statesman can afford, let alone a monarch. Knox did not want to argue; he was tactless as usual, but conciliatory. He would not retract his *First Blast* or his judgment of the *Roman Antichrist*; but, whatever his private opinions might be, he would *be as well content to live under your Grace as Paul was to live under Nero*. But Mary would not take that answer; had he not "taught the people to receive another religion than their princes can allow"? So she pressed him until she got his theory of rebellion. Subjects might treat *princes that would murder the children of God* as sons might treat a mad father: they might shut them up. But, even so, it was not for him to set the people against their rulers; he would pray that Mary might *be as blessed in the commonwealth of Scotland as ever Deborah was in the commonwealth of Israel*; only let her be a *nurse unto His people*. The retort came at once: "ye are not the Church that I will nourish." So she dragged him into religious argument and got a sermon on the *Roman harlot*, with the frank reminder that *conscience requires knowledge and I fear that right knowledge ye have none*. If Knox went away with the impression that Mary had *a proud mind, a crafty wit and an indurate heart against God and His truth*, had she not done her best to make him think so?

The same self-centredness marked her whole diplomacy with England. As Scotland was bidden to trust her good intentions without asking for ratification of the Convention Acts, so Elizabeth was expected to trust her personal desire for friendship without insisting on ratification of the Treaty of Edinburgh. On this basis of personal confidence, she claimed recognition as Elizabeth's heir presumptive, and to that claim she devoted all her energies. Never was miscalculation more profound. Even if Elizabeth could have pledged her Parliament to a Catholic queen, the pledge would have been valueless. Mary's succession must depend on events; her chances were good, but they could not be improved by promises. They could be improved only by the spectacle of a strong and settled Scotland, with a religious life not too unlike that of England. That, in these years, meant a Protestant establishment, with practical toleration for private Catholic worship.

The truth is that Mary relied throughout her reign on the formation of a personal party to support a personal policy; the tragedy is that she had just enough personality to form such a party, but not enough to maintain it. If it is true that she had poor material to handle, it is equally true that the best material in Scotland was not susceptible to a purely personal appeal. She could never "go to the country," for Knox had given the country a policy, good or bad, and she had not counter-policy to offer. When she lost James Stewart, the one man who represented the country in the court, she had to make shift with court romantics like Bothwell, court ruffians like Ruthven, and court servants like Riccio, and the sorry combination fell to pieces in her hands.

All this is not necessarily a condemnation of Mary. There remain all sorts of unresolved doubts: the real intentions of James Stewart and Lethington; the real policy of Elizabeth's ministers; above all, the almost insoluble problem of Mary's marriage. But a description of Mary's tactics, however we may judge them, is the essential background to a consideration of Knox's policy. If those tactics ended in inevitable failure, did that policy deserve to succeed? Was it one to which a great public agitator might worthily devote his failing powers, to which he was justified in sacrificing personal friendships, the forbearances of public life, and the charities of Christian conduct—or was it indeed a social tyranny which was to warp the natural genius of a great people for centuries to come?

4

There is no doubt about the central tragedy of Knox's last years. Old and tired, he wanted peace, and he found himself the slave of the sword he had invoked. He had thought himself into the doctrine of the "covenanted people," to whom God had revealed His will and who were pledged to make His will the law of the land. That doctrine wrenched out of shape every perception he had ever had of God's truth, every ordinance he might devise for Church government. If the Church was anything, it was the teacher of God's will, but, by the standard of Knox's doctrine, every truth it taught must become a political manifesto and an appeal to force.

It is this that makes any fair judgment of Knox's policy so difficult. The *Book of Discipline* is partly a programme of national reconstruction, partly a sketch-plan of a "separated" Church. And the two parts do not fit. As rules for a separated Church, Knox's most criticized ideas are perfectly sound. Such a Church must have the power of excommunication; it ought to confine baptism to children presented by its faithful members. These very rigours contradict the intolerant fancy that there is no salvation outside the Church, *the gross error that children be damned if they die without baptism*. Such a Church, too, in a lax society, whether at Corinth or St. Andrews, must have its discipline, lest it become a scandal to the world. And in such a Church, the relation between clergy and laity is properly expressed in the high doctrine: that the admission of ministers is subject to the consent of the congregation, but that, once admitted, the congregation must *obey the commandments which they pronounce out of God's mouth and book*. If, however, the Church is, not a separated company, but a State institution, the one lawful form of public worship, the only agent of public benevolence, the norm of public law, then these provisions take on a very different complexion: excommunication of an offender from *any kind of conversation* with the faithful, *be it in eating and drinking, buying or selling, yea, in saluting or talking with him*, becomes a gross tyranny; obedience to ministers may at any moment result in the erection of a counter-government within the State. Such a Church can be allowed to exercise such powers only within limits prescribed by State law and subject to appeal to State courts.

But that, after all, was just Knox's contention. He was pressing for a legal settlement. The worst rigours of the *Book of Discipline* were justified by its authors on the very ground that State law was too weak to punish public offences, even murder. If, in the process of legal settlement, the *Book* had been watered down, Knox would no doubt have fought its modifiers, as Calvin fought the city fathers of Geneva, but he might not have fought very hard. He had a high doctrine of the State as well as of the Church, and his heart was with the ideal of the separated company. This is the worst aspect of Mary's delaying tactics; in these years the new Church was weak and malleable; public sentiment was against the establishment of a new clericalism.

Viewed in that light, as a draft programme, the *Book of Discipline* at least deserves this commendation: that it dealt not unworthily with real issues. It prescribed, for the most culturally backward nation in western Europe, the first programme of universal compulsory education; it provided, for an over-centralized yet laxly administered country, a whole machinery of local self-government. The last point is the most interesting and is rarely understood. Knox's whole scheme rested on the individual kirk session; in the end, it broke down because, except in the burghs, the kirk session remained unrepresentative. It failed, in most "landward" congregations, to enlist the real co-operation of the gentry; it became a peasants' or, at best, a small farmers' committee, dominated (in the absence of Knox's parish schools) by its only educated member, the minister. The result was the usual experience of premature attempts at democracy: the rise of the caucus. In the early years of uncertainty, the central General Assembly, which did, in some sort, include the nobles and the lairds, assumed an authority not contemplated in the original scheme; after Knox's death, the district presbytery, which formed no part of the scheme, became what the kirk session was intended to be.

This failure can be as little laid to Knox's charge as the uncontrolled censorship of morals exercised by strong kirk sessions like St. Andrews. Both were largely the result of the politicians' failure to deal in any way with the real issues he had raised—to give the kirk sessions real administrative work to do or to set legal limits to their interferences with individual liberty. And is it fanciful to say that the breakdown of this scheme of local democracy was, in some measure, due to the very union of the English and Scottish crowns to which Mary had sacrificed every other consideration of policy? Those who condemn Knox for hindering Anglo-Scottish union by his prejudices against the English Prayer Book ignore the question whether, even thirty years after his death, the union of the crowns did not come too soon for the health of Scotland. By attracting her natural leaders, especially her local leaders, to Westminster, it delivered their tenants, not only to the caprices of absentee landlordism, but to the vagaries of district caucuses. Of all the queer misjudgments of history, one of the queerest is the modern Scottish Nationalist's admiration for Mary and dislike of Knox.

The same sort of misjudgment appears in the allegation that the Scottish Renaissance was blighted by "the cold wind blowing from Geneva." If there is one thing clear in the history of Europe during the sixteenth and seventeenth centuries, it is that the First, the International, Renaissance died in the horrors of the Hapsburg-Valois feud, and that the Second, the National, Renaissance dawned only in each nation as that nation achieved unity and settled government. If Calvinist Scotland produced less art and learning than Calvinist Holland, her loss lies mainly at the door of those who neglected the work of legal and administrative reconstruction entailed by revolution.

As for Knox's obsession about the Anglican settlement, his talk of the *mingle-mangle now commanded in your churches* and so on, that, like his invectives against the *spiritual fornication* of the Roman Church, must be judged by religious standards rather than political. There are few today who will not approve the criticism made on him by his contemporaries, of which he was well aware, that *such preciseness appears to proceed from curiosity*. On the other hand, there are few who will not sympathize with his dislike of measuring questions of faith and worship by the standard of political utility. In fact, there are few, perhaps, even among Anglicans, who do not sympathize with his reluctance to exchange the *Confession of Faith* for the Thirty-nine Articles. For if we are sometimes tempted to dismiss Knox as a pettifogging schismatic, that *Confession* is enough to correct our judgment; it will always rank, with Cranmer's Litany, among the great documents of the Christian Church.

5

But, by religious standards, there remains one charge against Knox to which there is no reply. No man has ever preached so forcibly, so baldly, so blasphemously, the Christian duty of persecution. It matters nothing that he was not by nature a persecutor, that in fact there was little persecution of Catholics in his day: "few exiled on the score of religion, fewer imprisoned, none put to death." The disseminator of an idea is not to be excused because neither he nor his contemporaries acted upon it in practice. The idea remained, passing from mouth to mouth for generations; among a people less prone to religious persecution than perhaps any other on earth, Knox's perpetual quotation, *the idolater shall die the death*, became the charter of sporadic violence.

The truth is that Knox suffered profoundly from the fact that he spent almost his whole life in opposition. For a few months in 1560 he knew power and public responsibility, for the first and only time. In those months he ceased, for a moment, to be a critic; he showed a capacity for the positive formulation of policy, a grasp of real issues, which deserve our respect. If he had continued longer in that position, he might have handed down a very different tradition to posterity. Hitherto the idolaters against whom he had thundered had been rulers; he had evolved a doctrine of rebellion, not of repression. But events forced him back into opposition, and it was in these years of pulpit war against a negligent government that he became identified with the advocacy of persecution as a normal principle of law. For a year after Mary's arrival he remained, so to speak, a glooming figure on the back benches, but the opposition temper was rising in him. Then, at the end of 1562, he launched out into open hostility.

And in active opposition, confined perforce to criticism and negation, all his worst qualities came out, as of old. He was shrewd, where more skilful politicians were blind; he took a European view, where they thought only of parochial tactics. He was right in foreseeing the effect of the Queen's Mass; he might well fear a Catholic revival. He might well fear it, not only in Scotland, but in Europe. In the remaining five years of Mary's reign, 1562–67, the forces of religious war were being finally ranged in France and the Netherlands. They were the years between the outbreak of the first and second Huguenot wars, the years when William of Orange was being gradually forced into the leadership of a rebellion. In the end, the summer that saw Carbery Hill and Mary's fall, saw also Alva's march across Europe to Brussels and Condé's attempt to kidnap the King of France at Meaux. But shrewdness and a broad view of the European scene could not save Knox from the creeping taint of perpetual opposition. He lost all sense of proportion; his Scriptural arguments grew wilder; hatred laid hold of him; he broke with old friends and made new enemies. And, ageing as he was, he had lost the power of recuperation; he slid, gloomier and more despairing, from one outburst to another. At last, as self-control failed with the failing body, he lost even dignity; a latent streak of vulgarity came out, at least in his writings. The cloud of constant failure lay on him to the end. When it seemed to lift for a moment with Mary's fall, it closed down again with James Stewart's assassination. Then the failing body took its final revenge and Kirkcaldy's rebellion drove a dying cripple from the pulpit of St. Giles.

That is the story we now have to tell; it is unfortunately the aspect of him which the world chiefly remembers. But if the story is one of decay, it is the decay of a leader who deserved better things of his countrymen than to be jostled into barren opposition.

CHAPTER XXIV

THE LAST CAMPAIGN
(AUGUST 1562–AUGUST 1565)

I

KNOX DID not go into opposition at once after the Supplication controversy, but he became an active organizer. By this summer of 1562 he had been freed from some of his burdens at Edinburgh. In April John Craig had assumed "the half charges of the preaching" at St. Giles. The first use Knox made of his freedom was to accept a mission from the General Assembly to preach in Kyle and Galloway, while George Hay, minister of Eddilston, was despatched to Carrick, and Goodman, with Erskine of Dun, to the north. He left Edinburgh on August 12th, but on no mere preaching tour.

It was time for the faithful to bestir themselves. Knox was full of information about "practisers" on "the West Borders"; he bombarded Randolph with "warnings": English agents were hatching trouble with Quintin Kennedy, Abbot of Crossraguel. By his treatment of the Hamiltons and Bothwell, James Stewart had established his power but had made enemies. And Pope Pius IV had determined to restore communications with Scotland. The Jesuit De Gouda had been in Scotland since June 19th; he did not leave till September 3rd. He had brought Mary a Papal brief, assuring her that the "assistance of this Holy See, both spiritual and temporal, shall be ready, and also the assistance of all princes who remain devout and obedient to the See Apostolic." Though only one bishop, Crichton of Dunkeld, had dared to see him, he had despatched Papal briefs to Huntly and two other lords. And Huntly's son was married to Chatelherault's daughter. Tales were about of his communications with the Hamiltons, of his boast to James Stewart that he could restore the Mass in three shires, of conferences held by the Primate at Paisley. Gordons and Ogilvys had been at blows in the streets of Edinburgh; on August 28th Bothwell escaped from Edinburgh Castle, and, after pausing at Crichton, rode for Liddesdale. Meanwhile from overseas came news of Condé and the Guises gathering their opposing forces, of manœuvres for the possession of the King and Queen Mother, of the capture of towns, of iconoclasm and the first atrocities of a war of reprisals.

Knox's reply to these threats of counter-reformation was another Band, signed at Ayr on September 4th by Glencairn and seventy-seven gentlemen of the west. Two days later Quintin Kennedy challenged him to a disputation. After nearly a month of correspondence the two met at Maybole on the 28th and argued inconclusively for three days. It was not a trial of reasoning between two creeds, but a parade of strength by two parties. Then Knox passed to Nithsdale and held conference with Maxwell. Meanwhile Mary and James Stewart were in the north, on the expedition that ended with the battle of Corrichie, the death of Huntly and the breaking of the Gordons. By that affray Stewart won almost sole power and the earldom of Moray; Mary lost the one great Catholic magnate in Scotland. "Excuse me to his Holiness," wrote Mary to her uncle, the Cardinal, "if I have failed in my duty to religion." This autumn, for the moment, Knox and Stewart, seemed to be working on the same lines, but it was to be their last co-operation for at least five years.

Back in Edinburgh in November for the General Assembly, Knox gave a Sunday supper-party at the house in Trunk Close. The guests were Randolph, the English agent, and no less a person than Chatelherault himself. The duke gave assurances; he would be staunch to religion and the English alliance, he would be loyal to the Queen. He had just given proof of loyalty by delivering his Gordon son-in-law to Mary. Knox on the back benches was still acting as an independent supporter of the Government.

2

It was a fortnight or so later that Knox's real breach with the Government began. Imagine the situation. A victorious court returns to the capital. The north has been subdued; Huntly's unburied body lies in the Tolbooth awaiting sentence of treason on him and his blood. England, at war with the Guises in Normandy, is full of fair words for their niece in Scotland. Holyrood may well celebrate this prosperous weather with masque and music and dancing.

But Knox is in a very different mood. Everywhere Calvin's reformation hangs on the edge of defeat. All is wrong in Scotland, churches without ministers, ministers without stipends, *avarice, oppression of the poor, excess, riotous cheer*. In France, public feeling is turning against the Huguenots; they have bought English help with the promise of French territory. English troops have been in Havre since October 4th; the main Huguenot army is at Orleans waiting for German mercenary reinforcements from the east; Guise, to prevent a junction, has laid siege to Rouen; on October 26th he has taken and sacked it. In the Netherlands, an increased staff of bishops is pushing on the work of the Inquisition; Orange, Egmont and Horne have just concluded their league of notables against persecution; a French cardinal, governing for Philip of Spain, has wrung from a reluctant nobility a subsidy for the French Catholic cause.

It is no wonder that such a conflict of temper should have broken out in controversy. Knox waxed *wondrous vehement in reprehension of all manner of vice*, the court complained that all his *preaching was turned to railing*, he retorted with a reminder of God's judgment on Huntly—*have ye not seen one greater than any of you, sitting where presently ye sit, pick his nails and pull down his bonnet over his eyes, when idolatry, witchcraft, murder, oppression and such vices were rebuked?* Then, on December 13th, came a smashing sermon on the text; *Understand, O ye kings, and be warned, ye that judge the earth.* Who were these princes of Europe who, in days of blood and persecution, exercised themselves in *fiddling and flinging? What shall we say but that the devil hath taken possession in the throne of God?* Dancing itself was not sin, but if for that they neglected their vocation—still more, if they danced *for the pleasure they take in the displeasure of God's people—they shall receive the reward of dancers and that will be drink in hell.*

This was too much. Knox's suspicions were quite unjust. Civil war in France had grieved Mary as much as him; war between France and England had wrecked her diplomacy. Knox's old pupil,

Alexander Cockburn, appeared in Trunk Close with a summons to the palace. This second interview with Mary began like a public arraignment; the new Earl of Moray was there, with Morton and Lethington; the room was full of the Queen's ladies and servants. But Knox convinced Mary that his sermon, though "sharp enough," was not what had been reported to her. She then made a bid for a better understanding; let Knox come to her personally if he had any complaint against her. Knox rejected the overture, ungraciously but, from his point of view, inevitably; there is no surer way of crippling a public opponent than the offer of private confidence. Let Mary come to sermon, as the Supplication of last summer had urged her. The interview ended amicably enough, but war had been declared.

And, if Knox was going to turn irreconcilable, it was the right moment to declare war. Mary's diplomacy was running into a blind alley; she could not much longer temporize with her subjects, or allow Elizabeth to temporize with her. For her the next few months brought a succession of troubles and disappointments; for Knox they seemed likely to bring a succession of triumphs.

3

Within a fortnight all Europe was agog with news from France, news of the Battle of Dreux on the 20th. Rome heard of it as a victory and expressed "infinite joy," hoping that now God "will show us the mercy also of seeing the Queen of Scotland delivered from her troubles." To Geneva came exasperated reports of Huguenot leaders unreasonably discouraged by a drawn fight. The news reached Scotland in a form that stopped most of the merry-making at Holyrood. When the ministers rode into Edinburgh for the fifth General Assembly on Christmas Day, full of the old complaints, they found a more conciliatory court. No action had been taken on the Supplication, but Parliament was summoned for May, and then *such order should be taken as all men should have occasion to stand content.*

The ministers relied on that promise and, pending its fulfilment, set themselves to put their own house in order. Knox received two commissions: to visit Jedburgh at once, where Paul Methuen had involved himself in serious scandal, and to go to Galloway at the end of April for the election of a Superintendent. The first commission he discharged with vigour; he was in Jedburgh early in January 1563; Methuen was removed from his charge and excommunicated. The sentence was probably justified by the facts; for Knox it was even more justified as a declaration of the new Church's moral standards on the eve of a fresh struggle with the old.

Mary, meanwhile, made a last effort to win her diplomatic game. Lethington left for London on February 12th; he was to attempt mediation between England and France, he was to press again for Mary's recognition as Elizabeth's successor, he was to press also for Elizabeth's advice as to Mary's marriage. That very night, on the eve of her own departure for Fife, began Mary's run of pure bad luck; Chastelard was found in her bedroom; ten days later, after a new piece of folly, he was summarily executed at St. Andrews. After that scandal, the court could not point the finger of scorn at Methuen, or complain too loudly about Knox's sermons against dancing.

In March, Mary, holding court at St. Andrews, suffered a fresh blow: news of the assassination of the Duke of Guise before Orleans on February 18th. She also had to despatch a delicate piece of business: her reply to the Pope's invitation to send representatives to the Council of Trent. Her reply, on March 18th, was an assurance of "her constant mind and will to revere and submit to the Holy See" and a request that the Council would listen to the explanations of her uncle the Cardinal of Lorraine. And in the same month a storm began to gather which threatened to put these professions to a practical test. With the Queen and her Mass at St. Andrews, the Primate saw the chance of an Easter demonstration; there should be public Mass then in his diocese. So, too, thought the Prior of Whithorn in Galloway; if the choice of the heretics for Superintendent there was going to fall, as men said, on Alexander Gordon, who called himself Bishop of Galloway, he should be given a demonstration of the strength of the old Church he had forsaken. Kennedy of Crossraguel followed suit, with others. The retort was immediate; the western lairds arrested some priests and threatened, if others persisted, to take the Queen's law into their own hands. Mary, hunting at Lochleven, was faced with a double challenge.

As usual, she tried to temporize. She summoned Knox from Edinburgh on Easter Tuesday and implored him to calm the lairds. Knox's reply was obvious: let her enforce her own law; if she would not, she must expect disorder. Again she raised just the theoretical point on which she would have been wise to be silent: "Will ye allow that they shall my sword take in their hand?" She got the old Knoxian reply; Samuel, Elijah and Phineas were all produced for her admonition, and there was an ominous reference to the *mutual contract* between sovereign and people. Mary slept on her rebuff and it is difficult not to suspect her decision: she would give way, but she would drive a wedge between Knox and his old associates, especially Argyll who, as hereditary Justice-General, would preside at any trial of the bishops. Before sunrise, she sent for Knox to the hunting field, and began to talk personalities. She did not like Ruthven; she blamed Lethington; she warned Knox against Alexander Gordon; finally, she asked him, in confidence "for her sake" to make peace between Argyll and his wife, her half-sister. She then dismissed him with the assurance that she would summon the bishops and do justice.

Knox went off to Dumfries and, on his way home via Glasgow, wrote to Argyll on May 7th. It was not the first time he had intervened in the earl's matrimonial troubles; this time he burnt his fingers. At any rate he thought that Argyll bore him a grudge for his interference, and he added this to his score against Mary's *craft*.

4

Nine days later the roads to Edinburgh began to fill up with riding parties. On May 16th the Queen left St. Andrews for the capital; the Primate and the cited priests rode in; the judges were assembling for the trial, lords and provosts for the Parliament, ministers for the General Assembly. There was *styncken pride of women*, with the "targetted tails" that had annoyed old Sir David Lindsay years before,

> *Whilk through the dust and puddles trails*
> *Three quarters long behind their heels*
> *Express against all commonweals.*

It was a great occasion. The priests' trial was soon over; begun on the 19th, sentences of imprisonment were given on the 24th and next day the Primate was lodged in the Castle. Then, on the 26th, Parliament was opened by the Queen in great state, with *a painted oration.*

But beneath the pomp, all nerves were on edge. *All things misliked the preachers;* court display was a queer commentary on the Church's desperate need of money and on the almost famine conditions that had followed a tempestuous winter. Abroad in France peace between royalits and Huguenots had been proclaimed at Amboise on March 18th and both parties had turned their swords against the English invader. Havre, where Knox's old friend Whittingham was army chaplain, was besieged and plague-stricken. In such bad times Mary's chance of an interview with Elizabeth had gone again for another year. And her diplomatic chickens in other quarters were coming home to roost. Lethington, still away, had gone on from London to Paris; as a goad for Elizabeth, he had revived the idea of Mary's marriage to Carlos of Spain; as a goad to Carlos's father, he mooted the idea of a marriage to Charles IX. Mary's uncle the cardinal had used her commission to make an oration on her behalf on May 10th, in open session of the Council of Trent; the Council had replied expressing their satisfaction at "her great filial devotion to the Apostolic See" and their hope that the Almighty would "give her force both to extend the boundaries of her kingdom and to carry afar the name of the Catholic religion." Meanwhile the cardinal was pressing another suitor on her, the Archduke Charles of Austria; just before she left St. Andrews a French envoy had arrived there with this proposal. Such diplomacy could not be concealed; rumours of the Carlos match had been going round Scotland already six months before; now it was common talk that the Queen's hand was being competed for by *dukes, brethren to emperors, and kings,* all Catholics.

And frayed nerves went to pieces when it appeared that Parliament would, after all promises, do next to nothing for a religious settlement. Final sentence of forfeiture had to be pronounced over Huntly's unburied corpse; James Stewart had to be confirmed in the earldom of Moray; an act of oblivion must be passed. That business was enough; the Queen, having submitted to the imprisonment of the priests of her religion, must not be pressed further at the moment; the time for that would be when Parliament had to be summoned again to give consent to her marriage with one or other of her suitors. Knox lost his temper; there were high words between him and Moray; recalling their long acquaintance since their first meeting in London eleven years before, he solemnly broke off the friendship: *Seeing that I perceive myself frustrate of my expectation, I commit you to your own wit, and to the conducting of those who better can please you.*

But if Parliament failed, Knox had another resource; he would fall back on the validity of the Convention Acts of 1560; he would assert, with a pointedness which historians have rather missed, that if that Convention were not a lawful Parliament, Mary was not lawful Queen. That assertion he made in a sermon *before the most part of the nobility*, prefacing it with an appeal to the memory of past dangers shared and adding an ultimatum on the marriage issue— almost the same ultimatum as he had delivered to Mary Tudor at Amersham just ten years before. *Whensoever the nobility of Scotland professing the Lord Jesus consents that an infidel (and all papists are infidels) shall be head to your sovereign, ye do so far as in ye lyeth to banish Christ Jesus from this realm, ye bring God's vengeance upon the country, a plague upon yourselves and perchance ye shall do small comfort to your sovereign.* Was this just fanaticism, embroidered after the event into prophecy; or was it shrewd prediction, based, after all, on fairly obvious data?

Whichever it was, it caused almost universal offence. Mary lost her temper too, sent for Erskine of Dun, the only new churchman who had won her confidence, and then, Erskine still with her, summoned Knox to her presence. She was in tears; genuinely hurt, naturally resentful, but as usual fatally indiscreet. "What have ye to do with my marriage?" Knox evaded that question, reminded her simply that it was his duty to convince all men of sin. Again she cornered him. "What have ye to do with my marriage, or what are ye within this commonwealth?" The retort has become famous: *a subject born within the same, madam.* And then he repeated his ultimatum: it would be apostasy, it would be treason, for the nobility to *consent that ye be subject to an unfaithful husband*. The interview ended in a storm of tears and, by way of postscript, a half-playful sermon by Knox to the *fair ladies* in the antechamber on the vanity of their *gay gear*. Knox heard that Mary would have liked to prosecute him, but was dissuaded. He had outfaced her with impunity and he would continue the campaign.

5

He had no doubt now that there must be a second revolution. He could only hope, he would only pray, for *quietness and concord for a season*. Soon after their interview the Queen left for the west, for Ayrshire, Galloway and Argyll. Her Mass went with her, *through those quarters which longest have been best reformed*. And Mass went on at Holyrood. That was felt to be intolerable; on Sunday, August 15th, while Mary was at Dumfries, a messenger from the palace hurried into St. Giles during sermon with news for the laird of Pitarrow, Comptroller to the Queen. A crowd had forced their way into the chapel; the priest's life was in danger. The news was probably exaggerated, but there was ground enough for a prosecution, and two Edinburgh burgesses were cited for trial on October 24th.

Knox seized the opportunity to make a demonstration in force. On October 8th he despatched letters to *the brethren in all quarters*, summoning them to Edinburgh on the 24th, *even as ye tender the advancement of God's glory, the safety of your brethren and your own assurance, together with the preservation of the Church in these appearing dangers*. The summons seems to have achieved its immediate purpose; the trial was postponed and apparently petered out. And if Knox also intended a trial of strength, that purpose was achieved too. Mary took up his challenge; Knox should be put on trial in December before an assembly of the nobility.

The interval was occupied in private remonstrances. Maxwell came to see Knox, found him obdurate and broke off their friendship. Moray and Lethington met him at Macgill's house but could make no impression. Moray did his best in friendly fashion, but Knox rebuffed him coldly. On the day appointed, shortly before Christmas, he appeared at Holyrood with an escort of brethren, *in such number that the inner close was full and all the stairs, even to the chamber door where the Queen and Council sat.* It was between six and seven of a winter evening. Mary, at the head of the Council table, counted on a quick conviction; Knox was hopelessly in the wrong; she would be quit of him at last. But, on the contrary, Knox had the chance he wanted. Yes, he had convoked the Queen's lieges, but not for the first time; *what convocation of the brethren has ever been to this day, in which my pen served not?* Would the Lords of the Congregation sitting round that table—Chatelherault, Argyll, Glencairn and the rest—deny their own past? Lethington might retort "then was then, and now is now"; but were they so sure that they would never need again to resist *the insatiable cruelty of the Papists?*

The challenge was pointed enough, with a Catholic husband for Mary in the offing; it would have been more pointed still if the challenger and his hearers had known that, since the previous June, the Pope and the Council of Trent had been linking Mary's marriage with the idea of excommunicating Elizabeth and recognizing Mary as rightful Queen of England. But, even without that knowledge, the Council could not risk giving Knox the opportunity of repeating his challenge publicly at a State trial. The arraignment petered out; Knox was dismissed to his house "for this night," and heard no more of the charge. Again he had outfaced the Queen, and this time in the presence of all her advisers.

But he was determined to press his advantage. Not content with a mere dropping of the charge, he delivered an ultimatum to the General Assembly, when it met on Christmas Day. The Assembly must judge his action by positive vote; *otherwise never shall I in public or in private, as a public minister, open my mouth in doctrine or in reasoning.* He had his way; his action was approved. Even without that, the proceedings of this Assembly sounded very like the prelude to revolution. Five years before, Knox had told the commonalty that they might lawfully withhold tithe from the old Church; now, in *quick speeches betwixt courtiers, barons and ministers,* there was more than a hint of the same threat against Crown, ecclesiastics and lay impropriators, if the financial demands of the Church were not met.

And in the next few months tempers rose still further; *the threatenings of the preachers were fearful*; the breach between Church and courtiers widened. The width of the breach was revealed when the eighth General Assembly met on 25th June 1564. The court party refused to sit with the brethren. Protests were exchanged; at last a deputation from the Assembly met the Lords. The meeting degenerated into a long wrangle between Knox and Lethington; *and so did that Assembly in long reasoning break up.*

6

This wrangle marked the end of Knox's two-year campaign, and it showed his weakness—or his strength. He had done what he set out to do. He had mobilized the lairds and the rank and file of the congregations; he had vitalized the issue on which they might fight the Queen. He had not only kept alive the demand for religious settlement and social reconstruction; he had suggested that Mary's refusal to meet that demand was a breach of her obligations to her people; he had suggested further that if her motive for refusal was a design for a Catholic husband, that design was nothing less than treason.

And this mobilization had been achieved at just the crucial moment. On 4th December 1563, the Council of Trent had held its closing session and approved its final decrees. Those decrees might be disagreeable to the Parlement at Paris and to the Emperor, but they gave Catholic Europe a fighting programme and Philip of Spain took it up at once. Protestant Europe seemed in no case to fight back. English prestige had been almost fatally damaged by the surrender of Havre on 28th July 1563; on 13th April 1564, Elizabeth had to accept defeat in the Peace of Troyes. Knox's correspondents on the Continent sent him ominous warnings: anti-Protestant feeling was rising in France, there was mustering of soldiers throughout Germany. His chief fear was a French invasion; his eye was on Inchkeith, the Gibraltar of the Forth. *The Inch*, he wrote to Cecil in October 1563, *is left void; what strange fowls shall first light there, God knoweth.* Next May he wrote to Randolph that strange craft had been seen circling the island; *our solan-geese use to visit the Bass before the great company take possession.*

These particular fears might be well based or not; the point was that in the existing state of Europe anything might happen, and anything that happened might mean death to Protestantism. But there was still a chance of victory. That May of 1564, Knox had letters from Flanders; they must have included news that the Prince of Orange and his friends had won the first round of their fight; they had driven out Cardinal Granvelle. They had retired ostentatiously from the Council of State at Brussels in the previous June, while Moray had been encouraging the Parliament at Edinburgh to shirk issues; in December, while Moray was trying to wring from Knox an apology to the Queen, Egmont's servants had donned their famous anti-cardinal livery; now, this March of 1564, Granvelle had left Flanders. What had been done in the Netherlands might be done in Scotland, if only Scottish nobles would show the same determination.

Yet at this point Knox dropped out of the fight. For nearly fourteen months we hear no more of him. Apparently he did not stir while Mary, changing her policy, drove steadily towards the Darnley marriage. All that summer of 1564 from July to September she was in the north, taking her Mass through Athol, Ross, Aberdeen, Dundee, and so back to St. Andrews; since Huntly's fall, the Earl of Athol had inherited the Catholic leadership. In September, Lennox, appearing once more in Scotland from his long exile, met her at Holyrood; in the following months he and Athol were "seldom asunder"; in December Parliament restored him to his title and lands; in February 1565 Darnley arrived and waited on Mary at Wemyss Castle. English diplomacy seemed bankrupt; Moray and Lethington were in "great agonies and passions." But Knox held aloof: he held aloof when Bothwell returned from exile, when Moray summoned Argyll and 5,000 men to Edinburgh on May 1st to outface that old enemy and drive him abroad once more; he held aloof even while Moray mobilized his old friends of the Congregation in the two following months. He took at least no prominent part in the General Assembly at the end of June when, to the accompaniment of warlike meetings of the Edinburgh citizens, Glencairn was despatched to the Queen at Perth with a final petition for the establishment of religion, the suppression of the Mass and relief of the poor—to receive the old reply that an answer to such proposals must await a meeting of the Estates. He was silent when Mary married Darnley on July 29th in Holyrood chapel. He was not implicated with Glencairn, Boyd and the rest of his old friends in Moray's insurrection; the Chase-About Raid came to its ignominious end at the beginning of October, when Moray crossed the Border into England, without help from him. His only contribution to the history of the times was one sermon on 19th August 1565, of which more anon.

There are three possible explanations of this abdication; all of them probably contain an element of truth. One is simply that Knox was old and a little discredited. Early in 1564 he had astonished everyone by taking a second wife: Margaret Stewart, Ochiltree's daughter, a girl of seventeen. For a man of fifty, it was the sort of marriage which no one has any right to condemn, but must always be damaging to prestige. Another explanation is that Knox had won his victories at too great a price. He had quarrelled both with Moray and with Maxwell, and he had never been a man who could lead alone; he could play Abiathar to a David, but he was no Samuel to judge Israel himself. But there is a third explanation: shrewd as usual in choosing the right moment, he knew that the right moment had passed. He had presented Moray with the only issue on which popular support against Mary could be won, and it was essential that this issue should be forced on its own merits, uncomplicated by suspicion of personal motives or foreign intrigues. But Moray waited until his own position was in question and until Mary had chosen a marriage to which the only obvious objection was that Elizabeth opposed it. Lennox had attended sermon at St. Giles; Darnley was at least not a certain Catholic. Moray's attempt to raise Knox's old issue with these complications could not carry conviction; Elizabeth's money, which might have been invaluable to an armed demonstration eighteen months before, was useless now. And this is to put Knox's motives at their lowest; it would also be true to say that, prone as he was to take God's name in vain, he never did so in a cause which his conscience could not clearly approve.

The missed opportunity was not Moray's last, but it was Knox's.

He had worked himself out; at least, he had not the energy to begin again. For seven and a half years more he preached; he did Church business; he even, during Moray's regency, acted again as liaison officer between Church and State; but he never again played a political part. The story of those years will be soon told.

CHAPTER XXV

THE LONG LEAVE-TAKING

AUGUST 1565–NOVEMBER 1572

I

Lord, in Thy hands I commend my spirit; for the terrible roaring of guns and the noise of armour do so pierce my heart that my soul thirsteth to depart. So Knox wrote in the study in Trunk Close on the afternoon of 31st August 1565, as Moray's horsemen clattered up the Canongate and the Castle cannon warned them that the Governor held to the Queen and King. The writer was a half-inhibited preacher, silenced partly by the royal Council, partly by himself.

On the 19th, the fourth anniversary of Mary's arrival in Scotland, Knox had preached almost a farewell sermon. The new King was there, seated in a raised chair opposite the pulpit, anxious to show at least his open-mindedness. But Knox preached over his head, as one whose eyes are set on a scene beyond. Beyond lay a Scotland on the eve of *more vehement battle*, and a Europe where *he that seeth not a fire begun that shall burn more than we look for, unless God of His mercy quench it, is more than blind.* Amid *the rage and fury of* this distracted world, he called on *the poor church of Jesus Christ* to be guided by two examples: by *the cunning mariner, compelled oft to traverse lest, by too much resisting to the violence of the waves, his vessel might be overwhelmed;* and by the prophet Isaiah, content sometimes *to be carried away with the violence of the tempest, without further resistance than by pouring forth dolorous complaint before the Majesty of God.* The time for action had passed; the night was coming in which no man could work. In that *day of our temptation, which in my judgment approacheth fast,* let the Church *call to mind the wondrous works of our God from the beginning.* The preacher's voice poured on through its long involved periods, exalting those works, the sure vengeance of God on *all*

325

cruel persecutors, the sure hope of resurrection for the faithful. Then it rose to its climax: *Come, my people, enter thou into thy chambers and shut thy doors after thee; hide thyself for a very little while, until the indignation pass over. Grant unto us, O Lord, to repose ourselves in the sanctuary of Thy promise till that Thou Thyself appear to the comfort of Thy afflicted and to the terror of Thy enemies.*

Of all this eloquence, the lank boy in the royal chair understood nothing. He caught only passing allusions that made him frown. *Babes shall rule over them*—perhaps the preacher glanced at the chubby face below him. *Did Ahab correct his idolatrous wife Jezebel?*— in the context the question comes naturally, but surely the voice must have hardened? Anyhow, King Henry marched out in the sulks; the Council summoned Knox and prohibited him from preaching while the court was in Edinburgh.

The burgh council protested; the court left on the 25th; but Knox had given his testimony and he seems to have acted on his own injunctions. During the next months he entered his pulpit only to brood and lament. In October and November he was praying God to comfort the banished Lords of the Congregation, calling them *the best part of the nobility.* That caused some offence to the court, but Lethington thought the sermons harmless. In December, the eleventh General Assembly used his pen to bring the needs of the ministers and the poor to the attention of the congregations. Since the Government would not help, let *the faithful in every parish* contribute more generously to their support. That month, too, the Assembly decided to summon the faithful everywhere to a General Fast and Knox was commissioned to draft the summons.

He seized the opportunity to spread the whole European issue before Scottish eyes. How little had Scotsmen known of the agony of Europe! *The body of this realm hath long enjoyed quietness, while that other nations about us have been severely plagued.* That quietness could not long continue; had not the Queen now openly declared her intention to *maintain and defend* the old Church? But whatever Scotsmen might think of their internal politics, let them remember their *afflicted brethren in France, Flanders and other parts.* War against them had been declared at Trent; a Catholic league had been formed for the conquest of Geneva; the Calvinists of France, already the victims of wholesale massacre three years ago, would be the next object of attack, then the Lutherans of Germany.

This was almost the last of Knox's public manifestoes. We must think of him as writing it in a new house in Trunk Close, to which he moved about this time. There, towards the end of the year, his first daughter was born; there he sat brooding over his news from abroad. History shows us the background of his warnings—the events he knew and misinterpreted, those he did not know which would have confirmed his fears, those he knew and judged only too accurately. That spring of 1565 Philip of Spain had taken his vow to enforce, at all costs, the decrees of Trent in his own dominions. That summer the King and Queen Mother of France had met the Queen of Spain and Alva at Bayonne; no anti-Protestant league had been concluded, but France would soon take fire again from Flanders. That September, Mary's envoy in Rome, the new Bishop of Dunblane, had asked for a Papal subsidy sufficient to raise an army of ten or twelve thousand men, that she might "remove all the enemies of the holy faith, free herself from those who disturb religious peace, and restore the Church to its pristine obedience and tranquillity." That November, Philip's final orders for persecution had been received at Brussels; the "fine tragedy" which Orange foresaw had already begun. That December, Rome had changed Popes; to Pius IV had succeeded Pius V, inquisitor and militant saint.

2

To deplore the miseries of these our most wicked days can neither greatly profit us, neither yet relieve us of our present calamities; and yet utterly to keep silence cannot lack the suspicion of apostasy. That was Knox's attitude at this time. In January and February 1566 he may have been away from Edinburgh, for he had been commissioned by the General Assembly to preach in the south; but at the beginning of March he was home again. A few days later he was more effectually silenced than by his own feeling of helplessness.

On Saturday night, March 9th, the citizens of Edinburgh were roused by the tocsin; "there was murder committed within the King's Palace"; Riccio was dead. On March 18th came Mary's counterstroke; her troops occupied the city in force, "in most awful manner"; Knox fled to his wife's country. He remained in Kyle for some five months; he was at St. Andrews in September but did not return to Trunk Close till towards th end of that month.

And he did not stay long. He was at the General Assembly in December. He wrote for his colleagues a circular to the congregations, protesting against the re-establishment of the Primate's consistorial court, not suspecting Lethington's plans for a royal divorce and seeing in it only the beginning of persecution. He joined also in a plea to the bishops of the Church of England for "Christian charity" towards ministers who scrupled to wear vestments. Then, with formal leave from the Assembly, he left for England, where his sons were now living under their grandmother's care. There he stayed till Mary's fall, returning only for the fourteenth meeting of the Assembly on 25th June 1567.

Nine days before that, Mary had been imprisoned at Lochleven. Through all this last act of her tragedy Knox had hardly moved or spoken; he had been not actor, but spectator; for the final five months he had even turned his back on the stage. *Lord Jesus receive my spirit and put an end, at thy good pleasure, to this my miserable life, for justice and truth are not to be found amongst the sons of men.—John Knox, with deliberate mind, to his God.* So he had written three days after Riccio's murder; in that deliberate mind, *with half dead tongue*, he lived through the next fifteen crucial months.

But public silence is not good for a public man. He cannot forget the principles or drop the policies in which he passionately believes, even though, like Knox, he knows that such cares are but *pride and ambition, covetousness and malice*, even though he confesses to his God that these *affections of the flesh do almost suppress the operation of Thy Spirit*. A slave to speech and pen, he must relieve himself in words, privately if not publicly; and in private self-expression he loses the instinctive self-restraint which publicity imposes even on the plainest-spoken controversialist. It was in these spring and summer months of 1566 that Knox wrote most of the passages in his *History of the Reformation* by which his character has been commonly judged. In public, even in his most violent moments, he had always shown at least a sense of style; indeed, compared with the pamphleteers of his day, of all parties, he can claim to have kept a distinctly high level of good taste. But in these private note-books taste was too often lost in coarseness; even the style broadened into vulgarity.

3

Knox had probably taken with him to Kyle the completed drafts of the Second and Third Books of the *History*: the party pamphlet of 1559 and a chronicle of subsequent events up to Mary's arrival in Scotland, including a frank account of the English negotiations of 1559, the truth about which he had prudently but dishonestly suppressed in the pamphlet. These documents he now, one thinks, retouched. He had always distrusted Mary of Guise, now he hated her as her daughter's forerunner. He poured his hatred into such brutal passages as the description of her death and pointed the moral with an unforgivable insinuation: *God for His great mercy's sake rid us from the rest of the Guisian blood. Amen, Amen. For of the tyranny of the Guisian blood in her that now reigns above us we have had sufficient experience; but of any virtue that ever was espied in King James V (whose daughter she is called) to this hour we have never seen any sparkle appear.*

He brought also with him full notes, and probably a completed draft, of the Fourth Book, recording events from August 1561 to June 1564, the end of his last campaign. He may have written most of this in the silent months before the Darnley marriage, but he now prefaced it with a deliberate statement of its purpose: to show *from whence cometh this miserable dispersion of God's people this day, anno 1566, in May.* It is the best of the Books, written ruthlessly from one prejudiced point of view, but on the whole with dignity. Save for one parenthetical lapse, its case against Mary is free from the slanders of later controversy; it shows that, until the Darnley murder, her bitterest enemies charged her private character with nothing worse than frivolity.

But Knox's main task in these months was the writing of a First Book, a record of the beginnings of the Scottish Reformation up to 1559. That Book contains much of his best writing and nearly all his worst taste. Apart from its autobiographical passages—in particular, Wishart's mission, the siege of St. Andrews Castle, his own mission of 1555–56—it is a brutal piece of work. Perhaps the most interesting thing about it is that one of Knox's closest colleagues refused afterwards to believe that it was his work at all. Archbishop Spottiswoode, son of the Superintendent of Lothian, no doubt reported his father's opinion when he denied that his father's friend could have been guilty of these "ridiculous toys and malicious detractions," this "spiteful malice against the queen regent," these "scurril discourses, more fitting a comedian on a stage than a divine or minister, such as Mr. Knox was."

As a matter of fact, modern taste is not much offended by Knox's comic relief, even when he *writes merrily* of Beaton's corpse *shown dead over the wall* of his castle to the townsmen below and then salted *in the bottom of the sea tower to await what exequies his brethren the bishops would prepare for him.* Worse than such savagery is the almost gloating exposure of Church scandals, the raking up of tales new and old about bishops' mistresses, the spiteful hints about d'Oysel's morals, the innuendoes about his relations with Mary of Guise. Worst of all are the more deliberate violences of the Book, all focused in hatred of one woman, *mischievous Mary, Mary that now does reign for a plague to this realm,* Mary of whose *abomination we have but seen only the buds, but we will after taste of the ripe fruit of her impiety, if God cut not her days short.* In the Fourth Book, though he was working on it at the same time, he would not impugn her moral character; in this First he bade *men patiently abide and turn unto their God, and then shall he either destroy that whore in her whoredom or else he shall put it in the hearts of a multitude to take the same vengeance upon her that has been taken of Jezebel and Athalia.* He had had no more part in Riccio's murder than in Beaton's; at most he knew that something was stirring; but now, as he wrote of Melville's *godly fact* upon Beaton, he went out of his way to approve Ruthven and his accomplices *for their just act and most worthy of all praise,* to exult over the destruction of *that great abuser of this commonwealth, that poltroon and vile knave Davie,* and to invoke God's vengeance also on Mary's new officials: *blasphemous Balfour; Sinclair, Bishop of Brechin, blind of one eye in the body, but of both in his soul; John Lesley, priest's get; Simon Preston of Craigmillar, a right epicurean.*

This is undoubtedly the worst moment of Knox's life. There is no more intolerable spectacle than the stewing hatreds of fallen states-men, of Bismarck at Varzin, for instance; and the spectacle is doubly intolerable when the object of hatred is not a self-assured emperor but a lonely woman, desperately unhappy, pleading for help from the Pope as her only possible friend, yet rejecting his ex-hortations to rid herself of Moray, Argyll and Lethington because "she could not stain her hands with her subjects' blood." Still, in palliation of Knox's furies, it must be remembered that those ex-hortations were in fact delivered; that the Pope's nuncio to Scotland, on his way to Paris in July, did urge the Duke of Savoy to attack Geneva; and that, whatever troubles Mary passed through in the twelve months from April 1566 to April 1567, a blacker tragedy was being played in Europe. On 8th April 1566, as Knox was settling down in Kyle, the party of the Gueux had held their inaugural dinner at Brussels; all that summer Flanders was full of preaching and armed musters, till between August 14th and 17th the blaze of insurrection and iconoclasm ran from St. Omer to Antwerp; next spring, on 13th March 1567, when Knox was with his sons in England and the Council at Edinburgh was making a perfunctory search for Darnley's murderers, this first brief flash of revolt was extinguished in the rout of Austroweel; on April 22nd, when Mary at Stirling was saying goodbye to the baby son she was never to see again, William of Orange took refuge at Dillenburg from the premature violence of his friends and the threatened retaliation of his enemies. It was hard to keep enforced silence at such a time, to watch against the dark background of Europe the *great pomp* of a royal christening at Stirling on December 17th, *the excessive expenses and superfluous apparel*, the *gorgeous company* of an English ambassa-dor, the font of gold that was Elizabeth's christening gift, the diamond pendant that was Charles IX's, the whole scene which delighted Catholic Europe: the solemn reception of the heir to the Scottish throne into the bosom of the Roman church, with the full rites of Roman baptism.

4

At the end of June 1567 the silence was broken at last. Knox was back in Edinburgh on the 21st; he appeared at the General Assembly on the 25th to find a broken and divided Church. The Assembly adjourned for a month and sent Knox, with three other ministers, to the dissident lords in the west. It was in vain; the breach between Moray's party and Argyll's could not be healed, even by Knox who had friends in both camps.

The causes of that split are no part of our story; they were political, not religious. Indeed, there was but one cause, and that was Mary herself. Equally, there was only one way to union: if Mary were out of the way, all Protestants at least might rally round her son. The Hamiltons might continue their old game of faction, but they would be isolated. On July 17th, Knox was back in Edinburgh; Throckmorton, now Elizabeth's ambassador, urged him "to preach and persuade lenity," but found him adamant. On the 19th he began a course of daily sermons, thundering against Mary, "threatening the great plague of God to this whole country and nation if she be spared from condign punishment." On the 29th he preached at the baby King's coronation "in the great church of Stirling"; on August 22nd he saw Moray, once more his friend, take oath as Regent. But Mary was spared, in deference to Elizabeth, in deference to decent feeling—out of *foolish pity*, said Knox; *foolish Scotland would not obey the voice of God when he had delivered that vile adulteress, and cruel murderer of her own husband, in their own hands.*

This short whirlwind campaign of vengeance has stained Knox's memory even more than the record of his private broodings. The campaign itself was brief. By the end of this year 1567, with the Convention Acts of 1560 formally ratified in full Parliament, he could regard his work as done, *above all men's expectation*; his prayer was that his *days should not be long* and that he might finish his course as *a painful preacher of the blessed evangel*. Only when Mary escaped from Lochleven on 2nd May 1568 did he flare out once more in a letter to the faithful. But in this campaign he had not spoken merely in the heat of the moment. He never changed his opinion. Mary's sovereignty did not exempt her from the law of the land, and by that law her life was forfeit. He died in the belief that to spare *that wretched woman, the mother of all mischief*, had been a grievous sin. *If ye strike not at the root*, so ran his famous letter to Cecil of 2nd January 1570, *the branches that appear to be broken will bud again. Yours to command in God, John Knox, with his one foot in the grave.*

An old man clamouring for a girl's death, for Mary was only twenty-four when the key turned on her in Lochleven—can anything be more hateful? Yet this ruthlessness is in an altogether different category from his libels of 1566. If we think his moral judgment unjust, it was shared at the time by the Pope and in vary ing degrees by Mary's own friends; if we think his Christianity weak, his political judgment was sound. We know what Mary's existence meant to England during all the years of her imprisonment; it was certainly a curse to Scotland for the rest of Knox's life. He never saw peace again. In January 1569, the leading Scottish Jesuit in Paris was writing to Rome of the new prospects opening for the discredited Queen: "it may be that some day all things will work together for that sinner's good and that she may hereafter become the doer of great deeds." All that year Catholic hopes rose, as Alva's Council of Blood did its work in Flanders and the French civil war ran its course from Protestant disaster to Protestant disaster, from Jarnac in March to Moncontour in October, while Knox *meditated upon death and upon the troubles I have long feared and foresee.* Then, in November, came the first of Mary's "great deeds"; the northern earls rose against Elizabeth; Yorkshire was boiling round the home of Knox's sons; his brother-in-law, George Bowes, was fighting desperately to save Barnard Castle from the rebels. It was after the collapse of that revolt that he wrote his letter to Cecil; three weeks later the Regent Moray was assassinated at Linlithgow. True, his Hamilton murderer bore him a private grudge, but had not Knox been warning his correspondents, sixteen months before, of Hamilton designs on the Regent's life, and anticipating a French invasion with old Chatelherault at its head? And, whatever the immediate motive of the murder, there was no doubt of its result. The Kirkcaldy-Lethington-Hamilton rebellion broke out; Edinburgh Castle, held by Kirkcaldy in Mary's name, cast a black shadow over Knox's evening days. Better, of course, for his gospel ministry if he had never meddled in politics; but, condemned by his past to meddle, was he not, after all, politically right?

But his meddling was over now. He said goodbye to Moray in a despairing cry for God's mercy on a desolate Church, and in a foreboding funeral sermon: *Blessed are the dead that die in the Lord.* More than ever, after that, he wrapped himself in his melancholy. The two miserable regencies of Lennox and Mar dragged over him like a bad dream. Civil war sputtered or blazed about him: "fathers against their sons, sons against their fathers, brother fighting against brother." Old friends failed, old enemies passed: Kirkcaldy, entangled in the last of Lethington's futile webs, captain of a rebel castle dominating a distracted town; John Hamilton the Primate, hanged as a traitor at the market cross of Stirling. But he had already left all this behind him; God must look after the world, *for I have taken my good night of it.*

Yet the curse of political slavery was on him still. He would no longer play politics, but he must still preach politics. He must "do according to his accustomed manner, publicly reproving the murder of King Harry Stewart, invented by the Queen." So long as there was a Marian party in Scotland, he must still take sides; there could be no more distinction between Church and realm, between civil government and divine purpose, than in Israel of old. And at last the strain of that slavery was too much for the failing body. This autumn of 1570 he had a slight stroke. It left him hardly able to write, or to walk without support, but after the first few days his speech was not impaired. That Christmas his speech drove him into his last quarrel.

On 21st December 1570, the Castle garrison sallied into the town, broke into the burgh gaol and released a comrade. It was an organized expedition; Kirkcaldy and Home were there in person. On Christmas Eve, Knox denounced the outrage: *if the committee had been a man without God, a throat-cutter—but to see stars fall from heaven!* Kirkcaldy did not appreciate the antithesis; he complained that Knox had called him a cut-throat. For four months they wrangled miserably; libels and sermons flew about; Glencairn and the westland congregations were dragged in to warn Kirkcaldy that he lay no finger on "the first planter and chief waterer of the Church amongst us"; the General Assembly itself was dragged in at its March meeting. At last the pace grew too hot. In April 1571, tempers rose; Dumbarton had been taken by the King's party and John Hamilton hanged. By the beginning of May Lennox and Morton were holding Leith for the King; Kirkcaldy and Lethington in Edinburgh had been joined by Ker of Ferniehurst, the Maxwells and Chatelherault himself, with, sure enough, money and munitions from France. Knox's position in Edinburgh was untenable; on May 5th he left, not to return for sixteen months. Before leaving, however, he, with Winram and Craig, had (strange to say) a farewell interview at the Castle, which resolved itself into an almost good-humoured fencing match with Lethington. Perhaps we forget that in those days mere public vituperation may have broken as few bones as pre-war Parliamentary debates.

Knox betook himself to St. Andrews, lodging in the Priory with his wife and three little daughters, and a servant-secretary, Richard Bannatyne. Even here he did not find peace. The University was split between queen and king, two colleges against one. Donnish tongues wagged about his past, speculating on his complicity in Riccio's murder, gossiping about his affection for Mrs. Bowes, who had died some little time before. Catholic libels were beginning to circulate on the same themes. He did not make matters easier by refusing to join in the consecration of a new bishop, when the Church reverted to episcopacy in 1572. He took some notice of these attacks; he suggested precautions against old corruptions in the new episcopate; he warned the General Assembly to *preserve the Church from the bondage of the universities*. But, more and more, all this was shadow-work, less real than his books and his talks with students in the "college yard," far less real than the weekly sermons to which he tottered on Bannatyne's arm.

6

Most real of all was one determination; he would go back to St. Giles to die. In August 1572, when the factions had come to a short truce, he was recalled by his congregation. Journeying by easy stages, he reached Edinburgh at the end of the month, settling in a

new home hard by the Netherbow, the traditional "Knox's House."
He was "now so feeble as scarce can he stand alone." On the last
Sunday in August he was preaching again in the cathedral, but in a
corner of the nave, audible only to a few nearest to the pulpit. On
September 7th, he was writing to Lawson of Aberdeen, his chosen
successor: *haste lest ye come too late.* A few days after came news of
St. Bartholomew, of another massacre at Rouen, of new outrages
planned at Caen and Havre. In October, Knox's voice rose loud
enough in denunciation of Charles IX to evoke a protest from the
French ambassador; Elizabeth's envoy was propounding to him his
mistress's new plan for sending Mary back to Scotland for trial; the
General Assembly "abhorring the fact of France and fearing their
tyranny" was demanding counter-measures against Catholics. So
the swords of the world still rattled round the dying man; still,
weary of the world, he must go on whispering from his pulpit new
invocations to the sword of God.

But the slave of the sword was near his release. On November
9th, he inducted his successor at St. Giles and went home for the last
time. Two days later he "was stricken with a great hoast"; the
illness dragged on painfully for nearly a fortnight, while he held
court in his bedroom, bidding farewell to his elders and deacons, to
Morton, just taking over the regency, to Glencairn, Ruthven,
Boyd, Lindsay and many more. He sent a message of farewell to
Kirkcaldy too, recalling *his old courage and constancy in the cause of the
Lord. John Knox remains the same man*; let the laird for his part *consider what once he was and the estate wherein he now stands; go and tell
him in my name that unless he is yet brought to repentance he shall die
miserably.*

Controversy still pursued him. In a recent sermon he had called
Lethington an atheist; Lethington wrote a letter of protest to the
Kirk Session with a characteristic sting in its tail: the Session would
do well to "believe not every spirit, but try the spirits whether they
are of God or not." There were other voices, too, about him, murmuring "opprobrious things." He was revered by his disciples, he
was loved by not a few friends; but he was not over-popular, either
in the streets where the craftsmen, in their old feud with the merchants, had taken Kirkcaldy's side, or among the quieter sort of

educated men. He had been too much the stormy petrel; he was thought of, in the words of a contemporary chronicle, as the man "who had the most part of the wit of all the troubles in Scotland since the slaughter of umquhile the Cardinal." The aimless anarchies of a century seemed to Scotsmen less fearful in retrospect than the more deliberate violence of the last twenty-five years.

Perhaps they were right; we shall attempt no death-bed judgments. We have given, as best we could, the colour of Knox's tragedy; we have already told, at the outset of our story, the most significant incident of his last days. There we might well take leave of him, as he listens to "the 17 of John's Evangel"—to the language of intercession which, in all his life of vehement prayer and prodigal speech, he had never dared to use. That may be the core of his tragedy; the language of intercession, which he had thought unlawful for mere man to utter, may be the only alternative to the language of force. And perhaps, at the end, he understood; perhaps he found the door to that *sanctuary of Thy promise* on whose threshold he had stumbled all his life. So many of his words have been taken in evidence against him, that he has a right to be heard once more, for the last time. He died about eleven o'clock in the evening of Monday, November 24th. Some thirty hours before, he had spoken suddenly, "after that he had lain a good space very quiet." He would surely have wished those words to stand as the final expression of all that he had sought and, until now, failed to find.

I have been in meditation these last two nights of the troubled Church of God, the spouse of Jesus Christ, despised of the world but precious in His sight. I have called to God for it, and have committed it to her Head, Jesus Christ. I have been fighting against Satan, who is ever ready to assault; yea, I have fought against spiritual wickedness in heavenly things and have prevailed. I have been in heaven and have possession, and I have tasted of those heavenly joys where presently I am.

337

INDEX